city-pick

AMSTERDAM

Oxygen Books

Foundation for the
Production and
Translation of
Dutch Literature

Published by Oxygen Books Ltd. 2010

This selection and commentary copyright © Heather Reyes 2010

Illustrations © Eduardo Reyes

A CIP catalogue record for this book is available from the British Library.

ISBN 978–0–9559700–2–3

Typeset in Sabon by Bookcraft Limited, Stroud, Gloucestershire

Printed and bound in Great Britain by
Henry Ling Ltd, Dorset Press, Dorchester

Praise for the series

'Brilliant ... the best way to get under the skin of a city. The perfect read for travellers and book lovers of all ages' – **Kate Mosse, best-selling author of** *Labyrinth*

'An inviting new series of travel guides which collects some of the best writing on European cities to give a real flavour of the place ... Such an *idée formidable*, it seems amazing it hasn't been done before'
Editor's Pick, *The Bookseller*

'This impressive little series' – *Sunday Telegraph*

'An attractive-looking list of destination-based literature anthologies ... a great range of writers' – *The Independent*

' ... something for everyone – an ideal gift' – *Travel Bookseller*

'All of a sudden the traditional travel guide seems a little dull. *The Rough Guide* and *Lonely Planet* series have conditioned us to expect certain things: accommodation listings from budget to luxury, the lowdown on the best bars, restaurants and cafés, information on all the obvious sights, and the kind of prose which even makes civil war, poverty and dictatorial government seem as if they were established just to make our trip more interesting.
    city-pick offers a more soulful guide to the metropolises of the world in the company of journalists, musicians, playwrights, bloggers and novelists past and present. They are beautifully produced books and can be read from cover to cover or just dipped into. They not only fill you with an intense desire to pack bags and head away, but also to seek out the complete texts from which the extracts are taken.
    Oxygen Books is restoring intellectual discovery to travelling, inviting would-be adventurers to view cities as irrepressible compositions of wisdom, wit, conflict and culture, rather than excuses to get the digital camera out and tick off another sight from the list. A very hearty bravo indeed!' – **Garan Holcombe, The Good Web Guide**

'The perfect books for the armchair traveller as well as those of you visiting cities around the globe' – **Lovereading**

'A breath of fresh air ... each volume offers what it says on the tin: *perfect gems of city writing*' – *Mslexia*

Editor's Note

My first encounter with Amsterdam was through two inno-
cently banal but irritatingly memorable songs from early childhood, one about an unlikely 'little mouse with clogs on' who
lived in a windmill 'in old Amsterdam', the other a love-song,
'Tulips from Amsterdam'. Much later I heard Belgian singer
Jacques Brel's powerful tribute to a different, darker side of
the city in his equally unforgettable song beginning 'In old
Amsterdam ... '. More recently, I discovered 'the' Amsterdam
singer, the late Ramses Shaffy, whose haunting performance of
'It's so quiet in Amsterdam' added a deeper, more appreciative
dimension to how the city presented itself to me in song. If one
can talk about 'the truth of the city', it probably lies somewhere between these four songs – between the '*leuk*' (a Dutch
word perhaps best translated as 'cute'), the straightforwardly
romantic, the hauntingly dark, and the movingly lyrical.

One cannot help falling in love with Amsterdam, as I
certainly did on my very first visit – its watery light and the
modest beauty of the houses that line the canals, the exquisite Vondel Park, the wealth of art in the city's museums, and
even the bicycles. The length of the first section of this book
testifies to the deep affection in which the city is – and has
been – held by a wide range of people, both natives and foreign
visitors. And this, like the collection as a whole, is only the tip
of a possible ice-berg. In fact, the vast quantity of marvellous
writing about Amsterdam has made the process of selection
both a great mind-expanding joy and a source of frustration as
there simply wasn't room to include everything that we would
have liked.

For the wide and fascinating range of material from Dutch
writers translated into English for the first time here, I am
hugely indebted to my diligent and enthusiastic co-editor in

Amsterdam, Victor Schiferli. His vast knowledge of writing in Dutch, of a national literature that has yet to be more fully discovered and appreciated by an often translation-phobic Anglophone readership, has made the process of creating this book a personal education for me of the most satisfying and pleasurable kind. I am also grateful for additional extracts and editorial suggestions from translator Laura Vroomen. To move beyond Dutch authors already well-known in translation – such as Geert Mak and Cees Nooteboom – and discover the delights of writers such as Martin Bril, Stefan Hertmans, Maarten Asscher, Marcel Möring, Doeschka Meijsing, Abdelkadi Benali, and H. M. van den Brink, has been a delightful journey that I hope the reader will enjoy as much as I did. And it has been with an ever-growing sense of gratitude to the many excellent (and so often under-appreciated) translators that I have encountered these writers for the first time. The support of the Foundation for the Production and Translation of Dutch Literature for much of the translation cost has been greatly appreciated.

We hope that this collection will give a renewed sense of Amsterdam's beauties but also take you beyond these to the deeper realities of the people, culture, history and even the difficulties of a city that has played such a major part in the story of European civilization.

Heather Reyes

Contents

'Must see ... '

Art seen in Amsterdam

Contents

The Amsterdam-nation

Amsterdam the tolerant

Contents

In old Amsterdam

World War II – the occupied city

That was then ... this is now

Contents

* = already translated from Dutch

** = translated from Dutch for this anthology

Introducing Amsterdam …
by Sam Garrett

Nothing about Amsterdam is linear, nothing is black and white. Amsterdam is a kaleidoscope of earth, water and sky, of cloud, glass and brick. Many of the streets you see and down which you trundle by bike or tram were once water. Much of the water you see was once part of the city's system of low-friction roads. A topsy-turvy world.

Perhaps it is that unpredictability, running contrary to what one might expect of a city so endowed with tradition, history and culture that makes Amsterdam attractive to outsiders, to nonconformists and adventurers. Estimates have it that some 25% of the population of the high-rent ring of central canals consists of expats – the lost boys and girls of our age. At many medium-sized local elementary schools, the parents may easily represent more than three dozen nationalities: Amsterdam itself is official home to more than 170.

And within even a single nationality, these new Amster-dammers may range from the successful New York entrepre-neur and his chain of hip muffin-and-espresso shops to the toothless and musically blessed jazzman Chet Baker, who died here in 1988 after plummeting from his hotel window like a wayward angel: people are drawn to this city because it allows you – for better or for worse – to be yourself. Or, as Alain de Botton says elsewhere in this volume: 'What we find exotic abroad may be what we hunger for in vain at home.'

That magnetic attraction on outsiders is nothing new: one of Amsterdam's most famous citizens, philosopher Baruch Spinoza, was (as Ian Buruma notes here) the son of Sephardic refugees; Rembrandt van Rijn – in many ways the city's inter-national figurehead – was a provincial boy who found acclaim in the big city. More recently, director Quentin Tarantino lived and worked here for a time, as did rock star Dave Matthews, who busked for pennies not far from the house where René Descartes lived in the early 17th century. At the end of her life, the 'high priestess of soul', Nina Simone, took refuge along these same canals and performed in local clubs.

Amsterdam is, and has been for almost eight hundred years, a playground to the world. That wild and giddy place you and perhaps even your parents talked about running away to, the breathtaking labyrinth Geoff Dyer has portrayed so well in 'Hotel Oblivion', the city where, as gangster Vincent Vega in Tarantino's *Pulp Fiction* noted, people eat mayonnaise on their French fries and drink beer in movie theatres, where everything forbidden or outré at home has suddenly become legal and normal, the place John and Yoko chose to hold their first 'Bed-In', the home of the notorious and aptly named 'Banana Bar', the cradle of soft-drug liberalism, the place where anything goes …

Amsterdam is all of that and, in keeping with its non-linear nature, none of that as well. To set the record straight, for example, prostitution in the Netherlands is seen as just another variation on freelance work, and therefore taxable and regulated. The possession and sale of marijuana and its derivatives, on the other hand (hilariously portrayed in the excerpt from Tommy Wieringa's *Joe Speedboat*), are *not* legal here: they are 'allowed', within limits. Distinctions of little interest to the visitor, but all the more to politicians exercising a peculiarly Dutch brand of domestic Realpolitik.

For, paradoxically enough, if Amsterdam is wild and giddy, that wildness and giddiness are made possible by virtue of Dutch sobriety and pragmatism. Gambling, prostitution and the use of controlled substances, along with the official hours for beating the dust out of carpets in housing-association tracts and the location of official 'doggy toilets', are regulated here – if not always by law, then certainly by ordinance and decree. This playground to the world is padded against falls by an intricate safety net of regulations and social covenants. In Holland – the birthplace, after all, of Western *laissez-faire* – your right to do as you please is boundless … until it runs up against the sacred boundary of *my* right to do as *I* please. The Dutch often speak of themselves, with a hint of perverse pride, as 'Calvinists'. And they are right, in that they are staunchly tolerant as a rule, almost overbearingly so at times, and have little regard for anyone who is not. And they do, really, eat mayonnaise on their French Fries.

Beyond the romantic canals and bridges, the city itself has many faces. Amsterdam North, for example, on the far bank of the IJ, is only five minutes by water from downtown; in soul and being it is as antithetical to the nonchalant flair of Real Amsterdam as the Land of the Ants is to the Land of the Grasshoppers. Take the free ferry behind the central train station on a windy workaday morning with a tang of salt in the air and you may find yourself back in the staid Holland of the 1950s – with crowds of office workers clutching their bag lunches in one hand, the handlebars of their bike in the other, with madly wheeling gulls and some of the most beautifully melancholic urban scenery in all of northern Europe. Travel by tram to the 'Southern Axis' at the edge of town, however, and you will see some of the strangest of what post-modern architecture has to offer – including a bank building in the form of a shoe (the Dutch call it 'The Skate').

Hopefully, as you read on in this anthology and find out more about this multi-city, you will be struck as I was by two recurring motifs. The first is expressed in phrases like "I had a Dutch friend … " or " … a Dutch friend of mine, who … " The whole world, it seems, has a Dutch friend. For the Dutch may be Calvinists, but they are inquisitive, worldly-wise Calvinists at that, with a flair for languages and an admiration for travellers. And they have the tendency to recognize a good thing when they see it.

The second recurrent theme is what we might call the "Amsterdam epiphany": you are staring out the window, you are crossing a bridge, you are cycling through traffic, when the heavens open. Amsterdam suddenly feels as right as your favourite pair of old slippers, as heartbreakingly beautiful as that lover you once tossed aside during an eclipse of reason. You wonder whether you will ever have the heart to leave this place. As the writing in this volume proves, this same epiphany has dawned through the long years on the likes of Charles de Montesqieu, Dubravka Ugresic, Alain de Botton, Simona Luff, Chris Ewan and many, many more.

Fortunately, I am no exception. Thirty years ago, not long after I moved to Amsterdam, I was riding my bicycle one blustery February afternoon along the Singel canal, not far from the city's central train station. Suddenly, the sun broke through the towering cumulus clouds and the houses along the far side were bathed in a light that seemed to etch sharp lines around each brick, every notch in every gable, that threw fat black shadows between the crazily teetering house fronts. Dutch light, I realized, this was the famously oblique Dutch light. As a university student I had loved German Expressionist cinema, and here, in an instant, I remembered why, and saw where Robert Wiene could have gained his inspiration for the weirdly skewed architecture of *The Cabinet of Dr. Caligari*, why Werner Herzog had later chosen a Dutch mediaeval cityscape for his 1979 remake of *Nosferatu*. It was the unbending light made immortal by Ruysdael and his fellow Dutch masters, throwing into relief an old city going into its eighth century of sinking back, with raucous good grace, into the morass from whence it came.

As aboard all sinking ships, of course, gaiety in Amsterdam goes hand-in-hand with a remarkable, almost heroic empathy, as you will see in Simon Carmiggelt's matchless anecdote about the Nazi beer belly. It is that same dry-eyed, ironic bent that gave birth in Holland to the centuries-old tradition of the *stadskroniek*, which expresses itself in vignettes of city life so precise as to seem written on the head of a pin. In addition to Carmiggelt's musings on café encounters, the world of Dutch letters has been graced by other chroniclers, more recently among them the late Martin Bril, who wisely followed Admiral Michiel de Ruyter's maxim that 'in Amsterdam, a gentleman goes by foot'. Before his untimely death, Bril's pavement-pounding resulted in a series of columns, some of which are found here, that not only nail down the peculiarities of the Dutch capital, but at the same time underscore its universality and, therefore, its timeless humanity.

Giddy Amsterdam, staid Amsterdam. Empress, fishwife, lady of the night. Hero, artist, traitor, beggar. Visionary, Calvinist and clown. It is that timeless humanity of which this anthology sings.

SAM GARRETT, a prize-winning literary translator and writer, has been living in Amsterdam since the early 1980s. He is currently working on a book about his experiences as an American émigré in Holland.

'I ♥ Amsterdam'

We fly in with prize-winning Dutch writer Marcel Möring.

It was cold, that day, and I was tired, the way people are tired after a long trip: too little sleep, your mind both here, in your body, and there, somewhere else, it doesn't matter where. Around me, the silent company of men in white shirts, Business Class, the *Financial Times* or *Newsweek* or an airport thriller on their lap, head against the papery headrest, mouth open slightly. Outside, under the wing lights, where the clouds grew thin, so thin that the giant Dutch scale-model glimmered through, I could see the tiny houses with their tiny gardens, the straight grey stripes of road, the floodlit well of a soccer field, wisps of white steam above chimneys. And I felt myself slipping into the comfortable coat of my native land. Half my life I had spent in other countries; I had left, as a child, with my parents and Uncle

Herman, for America, returned and gone to secondary school here and then travelled the world like a man who was searching for something but didn't know what or where, yet despite all that travelling and roaming — I knew it the moment the asphalt spaghetti around Amsterdam came into view — despite all that, I was a Dutchman. Not a feeling of national pride, the Golden Age simply a curious fact in the history books, not the faintest notion of national grandeur. Cheese, order, care, coffee, sturdy dykes, hesitant forests, straight canals, square meadows, potato fields under the summer sun, slopes they called hills, hills called mountains, long rows of yellow brick houses on long red brick streets and rectangular gardens with pruned conifers.

Sunset swept over this land, while down below, toy cars went shooting along the motorways, the runway lights of Schiphol lay in the fields like a fallen Christmas tree. I thought: This is where I want to die.

Marcel Möring, *In Babylon* (1998)
translated from the Dutch by Stacey Knecht

✳ ✳ ✳

Australian Sean Condon made Amsterdam his home
for three years … and adores it!

No matter where I have been I am always very grateful to get back to Amsterdam, especially when I'm returning from large, polluted, crowded and ceaselessly noisy cities like London, Paris and New York, or just plain depressing joints like Düsseldorf and Hanover. Amsterdam feels like it's the perfect weight and density, and the city's quietness, the sedate calm of the canals, has an almost narcotic effect on my jangled nerves. There's even a comforting familiarity about hearing the Dutch language again (although this wears off after about one minute). And as I sit on a tram or in a cab, ticking off landmarks on my route home, I think about how I will soon be taking out my keys and unlocking the door to the flat, unpacking then putting the suitcase back up on top of the wardrobe, breathing

7

slowly and deeply. And even though I am not actually there yet —
I'm just anticipating it — I feel as though I have truly come home.

Sean Condon, *My 'Dam Life* (2003)

✳ ✳ ✳

Clive, in Ian McEwan's novel, Amsterdam, *tells us
why he loves the city so much.*

The flight was two hours late into Schiphol airport. Clive took
the train to the Central Station and from there set off on foot for
his hotel in the soft grey afternoon light. While he was crossing
the Bridge it came back to him, what a calm and civilised city
Amsterdam was. He took a wide detour westwards in order to
stroll along Brouwersgracht. His suitcase, after all, was very
light. So consoling, to have a body of water down the middle of
a street. Such a tolerant, open-minded, grown-up sort of place:
the beautiful brick and carved timber warehouses converted into
tasteful apartments, the modest Van Gogh bridges, the under-
stated street furniture, the intelligent, unstuffy-looking Dutch on
their bikes with their level-headed children sitting behind. Even
the shopkeepers looked like professors, the street sweepers like
jazz musicians. There was never a city more rationally ordered.

Ian McEwan, *Amsterdam* (1998)

✳ ✳ ✳

In The Art of Travel, *Alain de Botton uses his arrival at
Schiphol and a visit to Amsterdam to meditate on our
pleasures in 'the exotic' when we travel abroad: a tap, a
jam jar and even a sign at the airport can be an insight
into the different national character of the Dutch.*

On disembarking at Amsterdam's Schiphol Airport, only a few
steps inside the terminal, I am struck by a sign hanging from the
ceiling that announces the ways to the arrivals hall, the exit and the
transfer desks. It is a bright yellow sign, one metre high and two

across, simple in design, a plastic fascia in an illuminated aluminium box suspended on steel struts from a ceiling webbed with cables and air-conditioning ducts. Despite its simplicity, even mundanity, the sign delights me, a delight for which the adjective 'exotic', though unusual, seems apt. The exoticism is located in particular areas: in the double *a* of *Aankomst*, in the neighbourliness of a *u* and an *i* in *Uitgang*, in the use of English subtitles, in the word for desks, *balies*, and in the choice of practical modernist fonts, Frutiger or Univers.

If the sign provokes such pleasure, it is in part because it offers the first conclusive evidence of having arrived elsewhere. It is a symbol of abroad. Though it may not seem distinctive to the casual eye, such a sign would never exist in precisely this form in my own country. There it would be less yellow, the typeface would be softer and more nostalgic, there would — out of greater indifference to the confusion of foreigners — probably be no subtitles and the language would contain no double *a*s — a repetition in which I sensed, confusedly, the presence of another history and mindset.

A plug socket, a bathroom tap, a jam jar or an airport sign may tell us more than its designers intended, it may speak of the nation that made it. And the nation that had made the sign at Schiphol Airport seemed very far from my own. A bold archaeologist of national character might have traced the influence of the lettering back to the De Stijl movement of the early twentieth century, the prominence of the English subtitles to the Dutch openness towards foreign influences and the foundation of the East India Company in 1602 and the overall simplicity of the sign to the Calvinist aesthetic that became a part of Holland's identity during the war between the United Provinces and Spain in the sixteenth century.

That a sign could evolve so differently in two places was evidence of a simple but pleasing idea: that countries are diverse and practices variable across borders. Yet difference alone would not have been enough to elicit pleasure, or not for long. Difference had to seem like an improvement on what my own country was capable of. If I called the Schiphol sign exotic, it was because it succeeded in suggesting, vaguely but intensely, that the country which had made it and which lay beyond the *uitgang* might in critical ways prove more congenial than my own to my temperament and concerns. The sign was a promise of happiness. [...]

In Amsterdam, I took a room in a small hotel in the Jordaan district and, after lunch in a café (*roggebrood met haring en uitjes*), went for a walk in the western parts of the city. In Flaubert's Alexandria, the exotic had collected around camels, Arabs peacefully fishing and guttural cries. Modern-day Amsterdam provided different, but analogous examples: buildings with elongated pale pink bricks put together with curiously white mortar (far more regular than English or North American brickwork and exposed to view unlike the bricks on French or German buildings), long rows of narrow apartment buildings from the early twentieth century with large ground-floor windows; bicycles parked outside every house or block (recalling university towns); a democratic scruffiness to street furniture; an absence of ostentatious buildings; straight streets interspersed with small parks, suggesting the hand of planners with ideas of a socialist garden city. In one street lined with uniform apartment buildings, I stopped by a red front door and felt an intense longing to spend the rest of my life there. Above me on the second floor, I could see an apartment with three large windows and no curtains. The walls were painted white and decorated with a single large painting covered with small blue and red dots. There was an oak desk against a wall, a large bookshelf and an armchair. I wanted the life that this space implied. I wanted a bicycle. I wanted to put my key through the red front door every evening. I wanted to stand by the curtainless window at dusk looking out at an identical apartment opposite and snack my way through an *erwensoep met roggebroood en spek* before retiring to read in bed in a white room with white sheets. [...]

My love for the apartment building was based on what I perceived to be its modesty. The building was comfortable, but not grand. It suggested a society attracted to a financial mean. There was an honesty in the design. Whereas front doorways in London were prone to ape the look of classical temples, in Amsterdam they accepted their status, they avoided pillars and plaster, they settled on neat undecorated brick. The building was modern in the best sense, it spoke of order, cleanliness and light.

Alain de Botton, *The Art of Travel* (2002)

❊ ❊ ❊

Two eminent eighteenth-century Frenchmen were great admirers of Amsterdam: political philosopher Charles de Montesquieu (1689–1755), and the even more famous Enlightenment philosopher, dramatist and early 'human rights' campaigner Voltaire (1694–1778).

The streets of Amsterdam are beautiful, clean, wide. There are broad canals lined with trees. In the principal roads of the town, boats pass directly in front of the houses. I like Amsterdam more than Venice because, in Amsterdam, one has water without being deprived of land. The houses are clean inside and neatly built on the outside, all in a similar style; the roads are straight and wide; in a word, it's one of the most beautiful cities in the world.

Charles de Montesquieu, *Travels* [*Voyages*] (1719)
translated from the French by Erica King

❊ ❊ ❊

I looked with respect upon that city which is the warehouse of the world. There were more than a thousand vessels in the port. Of the five hundred thousand people who live in Amsterdam, there is not among them a single shirker, not one who is poor, arrogant or insolent. We met the governor going about on foot without lackeys in the midst of the general populace. One does not see there anyone who has to pay court; they don't line up to watch a prince go past; they know only work and modesty.

Voltaire, *Letters* [*Correspondance*] (1714–1743)
translated from the French by Erica King

* * *

A city of 'sky, glass and water' – Croatian writer
Dubravka Ugresic makes us feel the thrill of it all …

The heart of the town had the form of a partially bisected cobweb. First came Magere Brug, whose filigree made me think of a dragonfly, then the Chinese fish shop at Nieuwmarkt with its wriggling catch, then the Waterlooplein flea market. The scenes flashed by before me, fragile, lace-like, limpid like the caps on the girls' heads in the painting by Nicolaas van der Waay. I saw canals overhung with shady trees; I saw the façades of the houses along the canals – the Herengracht, the Keizersgracht, the Prinsengracht and Singel – in neat rows like pearls; I saw Munttoren, the flower market and Artis, and took in the heavy, warm, intoxicating sight of the Botanical Museum. The entire city lay before me, a city of sky, glass and water. And it was my home. […]

I suddenly realized that I lived in the largest doll's house in the world. I refused to look out of the window. What would I see? Only the giant pupil in the giant eye of a child.

Then I would alter my perspective and Amsterdam would again become 'one of the most beautiful cities in the world', a 'desert rose'. I thought of desert winds ingesting indifferent desert sand, grinding it with their teeth, burnishing it with their burning tongues and spitting out a stone flower. On rainy days, when the sky came down so low it seemed to rest on the roofs, the stone rose had a dirty, ghastly cast to it. But the moment the sky lifted, the 'rose' would fill with light and shine with a glow that left me breathless.

Dubravka Ugresic, *The Ministry of Pain* (2005)
translated from the Croatian by Michael Henry Heim

* * *

Set in the eighteenth century, Arthur Japin's novel,
In Lucia's Eyes, *reminds us that it isn't just physical
beauty that can make us love a city.*

I had set my heart on Amsterdam. The city's name was one of the
first that Monsieur de Pompignac had taught me. I saw it many
times in the books he gave me to read, the most important of which
had all been printed in Holland, the place, he told me, where both
Descartes and Spinoza had found refuge. Now and then, almost in
awe, he opened a title page, showed me the name of the printer and
praised the Dutch for their intellectual freedom. He told me that
the Hollanders were clean and tolerant, prosperous and Christian;
they were convinced of the equality of all people and would never
stop anyone from expressing an opinion. They traded all over the
world, importing not just pepper and coffee, but also the beliefs
of other nations. Men like Locke and Bayle had found sanctuary there and praised the climate that permitted them to move
and think freely. From Signora Manzolini's library in Bologna, I
knew the *Systema Naturae* and the *Genera Plantarum* with all
the flowers and species that Linnaeus had studied in Amsterdam's
Botanical Gardens. I only had to think of that city to see before me
a paradise where, amid all the flowers of the world, the liberated
human spirit and all the branches of science blossomed.

Arthur Japin, *In Lucia's Eyes* (2003)
translated from the Dutch by David Colmer

* * *

*Belgian writer, poet and essayist Geert van Istendael
loves Amsterdam and would visit the city even more
if the train from Brussels was quicker!*

My friends in Amsterdam look after my books. When my books
are orphaned my friends give them shelter. When my books are ill,
they receive care. My friends support my books when I callously

banish them to a hostile world. They do this with the books of several dozen writers. They are father and mother to a large book orphanage. It's a jolly orphanage, with food and drink in abundance, secret rooms everywhere, and tales of wisdom and folly from attic to cellar. That's why I call Amsterdam: my orphanage.

Or my village. I've never lived in a village. One of these erstwhile book parents – he no longer lives in Amsterdam, having retired to an island years ago – once took me for a stroll along the canals at dusk. A light was on behind a high window. I need to collect a book up there, he said, and we ascended the steep stairs. He went to three more houses after that, giving and taking books, exchanging news and nodding with approval. We ended up at the Athenaeum bookshop on the Spui. Again he popped in to see that the order of things had not been upset. He was greeted with polite obeisance. His local was only one street away. He hadn't even sat down when his usual tipple appeared in front of him. […]

If for whatever reason I was forced to move to Amsterdam I would look for a house on the Vondel Park, either in the Vondelstraat itself or in the Ruysdaelstraat or the Palestrinastraat, but I would be more than happy with the lesser masters of music, literature or painting. But not with Johannes Verhulst – the street named after him is too long and too straight for my liking. Needless to say I want a whole house, none of this fiddly business with three separate doorbells. A house should be a dowager or at least a girl of the well-to-do classes, with crinolines and a dowry. They never had three doorbells. In Brussels such houses were built by the thousands; I have lived in one for a quarter of a century (a single doorbell!). But I prefer the streets in South Amsterdam, with their overgrown gardens and neo-Gothic churches round the corner. If I ever receive the Nobel Prize for Literature I shall install unemployed organists in each one of these churches where, on blustery evenings, they will perform César Franck amid the falling leaves.

If South Amsterdam is distinctly autumnal, the ring of canals craves spring or snow. Amsterdam resembles Paris as much as a frog resembles a cockerel, but both cities demand the same seasons. I once saw the Notre Dame covered in snow, which is something I'll never forget. Snow turns Amsterdam's canals into etchings by a genius greater than Rembrandt.

In April everybody in Amsterdam is seventeen, everybody is in love and jealousy is forbidden by law. In Amsterdam and Paris April is *not* the cruellest month and the only reason the famous jazz song isn't called "April in Amsterdam" is because it doesn't exactly roll off the tongue, whereas April and Paris are practically anagrams. But the foliage! Every spring the tops of the trees on the boulevard Raspail and the Herengracht exchange April foliage, the softest quality, the greenest light, the down of innocent pride.

Of course the women in Paris are more … let's not go there. Amsterdam has changed for the better. The girls of Amsterdam, oh why didn't they start dressing more elegantly when I was still young and impetuous? […]

Amsterdam has one terrible drawback. It's too far. I'm a spoilt twenty-first century Western European, I know, but that the train still takes nearly three hours to get me from Brussels to Central Station is surely too much for a modern man to bear. […]

Not so Brussels-Paris! It takes less than ninety minutes. To add insult to injury I can never join my Amsterdam friends for a decent meal in the evening. It's always just a quick bite. The last train to Brussels leaves at the God-fearing hour of twenty-three past eight. The last train from Paris to Brussels leaves at five to ten. But you get home around the same time. The high-speed rail link to Amsterdam – will we live to see it?

> Geert van Istendael, *My Netherlands (Mijn Nederland)* (2005)
> translated from the Dutch by Laura Vroomen

✳ ✳ ✳

And a glimpse of the city's beauty on a winter night.

In the winter months in Amsterdam there were nights of such perfect stillness that, if you were out walking, you could hear the ticking of bicycle wheels in the next street, or a couple talking in their bedroom three floors up. This stillness had always reminded me of the fairy-tales I had read when I was young.

Rupert Thomson, *The Book of Revelation* (1999)

❊ ❊ ❊

The beauty of the city on a spring day strikes the narrator of H. M. van den Brink's novel, On the Water, *so power-fully that it forces from him 'a wild strange cry' and he relishes becoming part of such a wonderful place.*

There was a morning in spring when I woke at first light and left the house earlier than usual, just to be able to walk along the water's edge and see the rest of the world awaken. I stopped on the bridges as before, but I also walked along one of the wide access roads into town, between the tram rails, in the middle of the street. Everything around me was so unusually clear, etched with such razor-sharpness, the houses, the leaves on the trees, the cobbles in the street – as if the finest master of realism had painted his masterpiece. If it had not been so beautiful, it would have hurt my eyes. I stretched, full length, and let loose a wild, strange cry.

In the distance I heard a horse's hooves scraping between the houses and the rattle of milk churns that was echoed by the house fronts. The sound was like music. I felt like saying good morning to everyone. But there wasn't anyone, so I said good morning to animals and inanimate things. A bird, a wonderful red postbox, a cat crossing the road. I revelled in the morning and the city and at the same moment wanted it to be afternoon already so we could take to the water and again row away from town.

Another day found me in the early evening, with tired limbs after the training session, on the balcony of a tram that was brushing past the terraces of houses and throngs of people on the way to the station, which was gleaming in the late sunlight with its red-brick front and its decorations like those of a cathedral. I had wanted to shout something to the people, but didn't know what. They looked so beautiful and so pleased with themselves and with walking through the town.

A little later I saw the sun go down from the ferry that sails from behind the station across the great expanse of water to the docks and warehouses. I imagined I could smell the sea air. I'd never been here before and had no business here; I stood by the railing when the deck emptied and went back immediately. I threw my head back and sniffed again. Beneath me, I felt the deck moving up and down; behind me, the engine pounded, the funnel spewed white clouds. I felt at home. The city gradually became mine and I became part of the whole city.

H.M. van den Brink, *On the Water* (1998)
translated from the Dutch by Paul Vincent

✳ ✳ ✳

In Stefan Hertmans' Cities [Steden], a young Flemish author who has a romance with a Dutch woman finds himself falling in love with Amsterdam as well.

You don't get to know a city until you love one of its people – only then will every scrap of newspaper flying across the pavement take on meaning, will every face have something to say to you, will there be something behind every corner that can spell the life or death of the dream. Wandering through cities that unfurl through a new love: it carries a hint of perpetual danger. You're always on the alert, because any overlooked detail may throw you back on yourself, back to square one, hitching a ride beside the motorway or waiting on a platform with a newspaper featuring a date you'd rather forget.

I got to know Amsterdam nearly twenty years ago on a small Greek island because I was approached in the late afternoon sunshine by a young woman from Amsterdam. [...] When six weeks later I bumped into her again on a street in De Pijp she took my breath away. I was to share the next four years of my life with her. But long after these four years something endured which will

17

stay with me for life: when I'm having coffee at her place, when we're going for the occasional walk together, in the pub where, like brother and sister, we're being concerned or happy for each other just because the other is – all this has become inextricably linked with Amsterdam; it smells of canal water or evokes the Leidseplein at two-thirty in the morning, it sounds like the bottom step when you get off the tram – a sound which, the first few months after we parted, haunted my dreams like the symbol of everything I'd lost because I couldn't choose. Amsterdam had in fact become a home. Every time I drove into the city, caught a distant glimpse of the big building on Frederiksplein, parked on one of the streets named after seventeenth-century landscape painters, joined her later at the Albert Cuyp market, bought groceries and took the aromas of cinnamon, curry powder and olives up to her small attic room, I knew that this, more than anywhere in the world, was home and yet it was only a home as long as my other home, in faraway Belgium, was still there. I got to know the city from within, the way people who have lived there for a long time know it. I adopted customs, the things you do at certain times, the things you do on a Sunday (coffee at the Stedelijk Museum, or an out-of-town bike ride along the Amstel), as well as the ordinary things you only do during the week and all the things you do or experience simply by virtue of being there and living your life: cooking Indonesian food, talking to a squabbling couple in the Marnixstraat, meeting up with someone in Frascati, getting drunk in Café De Jaren, which wasn't there yet, but the metaphor of drinking to years gone by happens to suit my purpose here. I became familiar with the peculiar paradoxes of a city where I bought books without suspecting that one day I would publish here myself, got the broad and the narrow picture, visited lots of friends and acquaintances with my girlfriend, went round all the pubs with her, felt at times that anything was possible in this city, at others that everything was over-regulated. Figure out what's what with the latter relationship, I lectured, and you're beginning to get an idea of what Amsterdam is all about; but the code is never explicit. Nobody shares it with you; it's up to you to work it out and each signal has a specific meaning – meanings that were quite different in my old Flemish hometown. I began to translate gestures, a glance, a knowingly half-finished sentence, a waving hand into what felt like another language, in a city which, like most big cities, constantly and deliberately reflected itself in its residents, who combine a great sense of solidarity with a latent indifference to others and to the place where they live. The labyrinth gradually laid itself bare and when things began to make sense I realized how bare I myself had been to friends and acquaintances in the city. The body of the city became the body of the woman I loved, just as I discovered that the city became more and more of a mirror for my foreignness, the fact that I had grown up within a completely different environment. I hurried to learn the many elusive things that could be learned (the terms and expressions at the bakery, for example, not a single one of which was the same in Flemish), only to find that in this growing intimacy with the city I became more acutely aware of even the tiniest aspects of my outsider status. After a while I knew all the nuances of the seasons in an Amsterdam street, the nocturnal sound of fire-crackers in the run-up to New Year's Eve and the sense of emptiness after the bang in a street full of parked cars, the ambulance's series of three rising notes at night. How different a drizzly Wednesday there felt compared to a Wednesday in the town where I was from and where I always went back. I discovered the fixations of the average city-dweller and how best to deal with them, how to explain things that you initially thought were inexplicable. I got a sense of how migrants in my own town and perhaps also in this city often felt – just as I learned that Amsterdam is untypical and at the same time wholly representative of the rest of the Netherlands. All clichés, of course, but clichés come to life when you live somewhere and everything you thought you'd left behind taps you on the shoulder again. It's in a lot of little things: in a turn of phrase, in a glance, in the language that I came to know so intimately because somebody loved me and I loved her. It's this indefinable quality that I recognize now when I read a book by a writer from Amsterdam, things that I can't explain but that I know are merely words for most people in Belgium whereas I, like all people who've lived in Amsterdam for a while, sense a specific smell, see a room with a view of inner court-yards or identify an implied Amsterdam quirk. A random sentence might evoke for me the sound of words on a narrow staircase with bicycles hanging on hooks, the inextricable link between the chime of a doorbell and the cord used to pull open the front door from the upstairs landing; the kinds of things that people say while they're in a restaurant waiting for their reserved table to become available; or I recall that a drunken newcomer can benefit from remembering the phrase "Piet Koopt Hoge Schoenen" [i.e. Piet Buys High Shoes] as a mnemonic for remembering the order of the canals: Prinsen-gracht, Keisersgracht, Herengracht and Singel.

Stefan Hertmans, *Cities* [*Steden*] (1998)
translated from the Dutch by Laura Vroomen

✳ ✳ ✳

*Even a novel in which a demon visits Amsterdam
waxes lyrical about the city …*

Amsterdam, you've been the changing backdrop to the chapters of my life, I know your changing skies, Amsterdam, the drizzle on your glistening cobble-stones and the lights reflecting in the greenish, troubled water of your magnificent canals, your family men in shirt-sleeves, your street urchins, your mothers doing the washing, your tram with its eleven-cent fare and its transfers, I know your civil servants and your welfare offices, Amsterdam, your bankers, your tobacco merchants and your state schools, your brothels with their red lights, your intimate shopping streets and your rubbish bins, your traffic wardens, your fire brigade, your tobacconists and your urinals, I know your Jewish quarter, Amsterdam, with its rich butter cake, its sticky ginger buns, its cod liver and its slaughtered geese, its peddlers and the jokes of its market women. I know your feisty working-class girls, Amsterdam, your reading tables and libraries, your hospitals and your holding cells, your pawnbrokers, your social institutions and your whinging about the weather! But above all I know your ordinary lives, Amsterdam, your everyday existence, your anxious children with their dry wit and their secret dreams and desires. I possess none of your riches, Amsterdam, yet I'm totally possessed by you.

Marcel van Gestel, *The Demon of Amsterdam*
[*De demon van Amsterdam*] (1947)
translated from the Dutch by Laura Vroomen

✳ ✳ ✳

And the pleasures of a mild winter's day, by Nescio (Latin for 'I don't know'), the pen name of legendary Dutch writer Jan Hendrick Frederick Grönloh (1882–1961).

26 December (1951) Wednesday (Boxing Day). Spring-like morning, sun and blue sky and open windows all around the Linnaeushof. So mild. I went to get milk on the Nieuwe Weg and crossing the courtyard with my jug on the way back I expected to hear the blackbird.

On my bicycle at five o'clock in the evening. Last light of day, the days are starting to draw out again. So mild and still. Red and gold in the Ringvaart and the reflection of the streetlights and the houses ever so still. The five broom trees at the Colonial Institute and a trace of pale sky amid the branches. The evening star in the water where Mauritskade meets Alexanderplein; the star bobbed up and down a bit and yet the water was perfectly still.

The bright lights, golden yellow. Autumn is behind us now. The still autumn. First sun and stillness, then darkness and stillness, still damp and fog. Cosy Amsterdam during this still, damp open winter.

Nescio, *Nature Diary* [*Natuurdagboek*] (1997)
translated from the Dutch by Laura Vroomen

❊ ❊ ❊

The voluble narrator of The Fall, *by Nobel Prize-win-ning French author Albert Camus, has plenty to say about the diverse pleasures of Amsterdam.*

I like walking through the city of an evening in the warmth of gin. I walk for nights on end, I dream or talk to myself interminably. Yes, like this evening – and I fear making your head swim somewhat. Thank you, you are most courteous. But it's my over-flow; as soon as I open my mouth, sentences pour out. Besides, this country inspires me. I like this crowd of people swarming on the pavements, wedged into a little space of houses and canals, hemmed in by fogs, cold lands, and the sea steaming like wet washing. I like it, for it is double. It is here and elsewhere. [...]

For we are at the heart of things here. Have you noticed that Amsterdam's concentric canals resemble the circles of hell? The middle-class hell, of course, peopled with bad dreams. When one comes from the outside, as one gradually goes through those circles, life – and hence its crimes – becomes denser, darker. Here, we are in the last circle. The circle of the ... Ah, you know that? By heaven, you become harder to classify. But you understand then why I can say that the centre of things is here although we stand at the tip of the continent. A sensitive man grasps such oddities. In any case the newspaper-readers and the fornicators can go farther. They come from the four corners of Europe and stop facing the inland sea, on the drab strand. They listen to the fog-horns, vainly try to make out the silhouettes of boats in the fog, then turn back over the canals and go home through the rain. Chilled to the bone, they come and ask in all languages for gin at *Mexico City*. That's where I wait for them.

Till tomorrow, then, Monsieur *et cher compatriote*. No, you will easily find your way now; I'll leave you near this bridge. I never cross a bridge at night. It's because of a vow. Suppose, after all, that someone should jump in the water. One of two things –

either you follow suit to fish him out and, in cold weather, that's taking a great risk! Or you forsake him there and to suppress a dive sometimes leaves one strangely aching. Good night. What? Those ladies behind those windows? Dream, Monsieur, cheap dream, a trip to the Indies! Those persons perfume themselves with spices. You go in, they draw the curtains and the navigation begins. The gods come down on to the naked bodies and the islands are set adrift, lost souls crowned with the tousled hair of palm trees in the wind. Try it. [...]

But this evening I don't feel quite up to the mark either. I even find trouble expressing myself. I'm not talking so well, it seems to me, and my words are less assured. Probably the weather. It's hard to breathe; the air is so heavy it weighs on one's chest. Would you object, *mon cher compatriote*, to going out and walking in the town a little? Thank you.

How beautiful the canals are this evening! I like the breath of stagnant waters, the smell of dead leaves soaking in the canal, and the funeral scent rising from the barges loaded with flowers. No, no, there's nothing morbid about such a taste, I assure you. On the contrary, it's a deliberate act on my part. The truth is that I force myself to admire these canals. What I like most in the world is Sicily, you see, and especially from the top of Etna, in the sunlight, provided I dominate the island and the sea. Java too, but at the time of the trade-winds. Yes, I went there in my youth. In a general way, I like all islands. It is easier to dominate them.

Charming house, isn't it? The two heads you see up there are heads of Negro slaves. A shop-sign. The house belonged to a slave-dealer. Oh, they weren't squeamish in those days! They were self-assured; they announced: 'You see, I'm a man of substance; I'm in the slave-trade; I deal in black flesh.' Can you imagine anyone today making it known publicly that such is his business? What a scandal! [...]

Look it's snowing! Oh. I must go out! Amsterdam asleep in the white night, the dark jade canals under the little snow-covered bridges, the empty streets, my muffled steps – it will be purity, even if fleeting, before tomorrow's mud. See the huge flakes drifting against the window-panes. It must be the doves, surely. They finally made up their minds to come down, the little dears; they are covering the waters and the roofs with a thick layer of feathers; they are fluttering at every window. What an invasion! Let's hope they are bringing good news.

Albert Camus, The Fall (1956)
translated from the French by Justin O'Brien

✽ ✽ ✽

Author Richard Mason first visited Amsterdam in his early twenties – the perfect age to fall in love with the city. And he finds his appreciation deepening over time.

I first saw Amsterdam in my early twenties, at roughly the age my Afrikaaner ancestors were when they passed through it on their way to South Africa. I should confess I didn't spend much time imagining their experience of the place. Like the other foreigners who clog the cycle lanes and annoy the waiters, I threw myself headlong into sampling the city's delights. Oh the pleasures of a visit to a coffee shop after breakfast, followed by a wander along the Herengracht! It took me some time to realise that the central canals are not straight, and thanks to a poor sense of direction and a wariness of maps I'd often find myself arriving at my starting-point after a very long walk in search of my youth hostel. In those days, before I knew it better, Amsterdam was like a maze in a fairytale – full of unexpected challenges and treasures. I never understood how my Dutch friends were able to work or study, given the distractions on offer to them; and only very gradually did I come to understand that the city's plentiful temptations in fact encourage *restraint*, and not excess.

For a decade, I visited Amsterdam whenever I had the time and the money. I made Dutch friends, who treated me with tremendous kindness and hospitality. From them I learned how to balance on another person's handlebars and to conceal my shame when an entire dinner party lapsed into perfect English, merely to accommodate me. I learned where to buy cheese, and sweaters, and bicycle pumps; and to kiss three times on the cheek; and I began to delight in the quiet frankness of the Dutch, and their willingness to see things from other people's point of view.

I had already written my third novel, *The Lighted Rooms*, before I came anywhere close to appreciating the deeper possibilities of the city. I had come to Amsterdam with some hedonistic friends to celebrate the end of a book tour, and was thoroughly sick of talking about myself. A Dutch friend had borrowed a boat and took me and my party on a long, ambling tour of the canals, at the cusp of a mellow summer's afternoon. I won't ever forget that boat trip. As I lay on the deck, listening to the trickle of conversation and looking up at the buildings, I began to fall in love with the architecture – not the infatuation I had felt before, since infatuation by its nature is shallow and does not endure. I mean that the buildings began to provoke in me a powerful *love*; a devotion that endures as I write a novel called *History of a Pleasure-Seeker*, whose setting is Amsterdam, 1907, and whose central character is a glamorous young Dutchman charming his way through the city's elite. For the first time that day, I felt I was being initiated into the mysteries of the city; that I was beginning to understand the statements conveyed by its bricks and mortar and dazzling panes of glass.

Amsterdam shuns grandiloquence. But that doesn't mean that its buildings don't boast. They do. As we chugged up the Herengracht towards the Gilded Curve, I saw that the houses became subtly grander as we progressed – not the flamboyant grandeur of rich men's houses in Paris, or turn-of-the century New York; a subtler, more discreet assertion of wealth and sophistication. I began to appreciate the nuanced individualism of the canal houses: the uniqueness of a piece of wrought iron tracery above a door; the whispered message of an elongated window.

Now I understood that Amsterdam was not merely a pleasure-drenched refuge from the quotidian pressures of life in drabber cities. For the first time, I glimpsed what it could teach me as a writer. I began to visit more regularly, and to turn the miraculous completeness of the 17th century centre to my advantage. How I praised those brave citizens who insisted on the preservation of the canal belt in the mid–1800s! Who refused to submit to the demands of roads and grand thoroughfares, of the kind that decimated the ancient hearts of other European cities.

I experimented with music, and saw that the city can work as a time machine – that if one listens to a Baroque concerto, the glories of the 17th century gilded age spring to life; that if you choose a popular tune from the 1940s, Gestapo officers skulk in doorways, full of malevolent purpose. That the centre of Amsterdam has been in some fundamental way unchanged for more than 300 years is a wonderful gift to the story-teller: walking down the Keizersgracht, it is easy to imagine the dramas of the past; in fact, you cannot escape them.

One of Amsterdam's great achievements is that it is not a dead city, like Venice. Though the reality of the past is omni-present, that doesn't lessen the vivacity of the present. In an age of energy squandering, when New York skyscrapers blaze all night whether occupied or not, Amsterdam sets an example to the world by getting dark at night, and going to sleep. Suffi-cient space has been given to cars, but not too much; they must continue to skulk on the side of the canals, like uninvited guests. And though the twinkling of the street lights on the water is a magical sight, the city would be just as beautiful without them.

Shortly after the Stern report was published, warning the world of imminent climate catastrophe, I saw from my Amsterdam window a seductive and inspiring sight. Two couples were coming home after dinner. The men rode their bicycles; the women sat lightly on their handlebars – so elegantly, as though the manoeuvre cost no energy. (I know better!) They were laughing and continuing their conversation; they were going home, but having so much more fun than similar couples stuck in traffic jams in London.

And that's when I saw that Amsterdam has as much to teach us about the future, as the past.

Richard Mason, 'Amsterdam' (2009)

✳ ✳ ✳

Janneke van der Horst could go anywhere in the world, but – despite the city's little annoyances – prefers Amsterdam to anywhere else.

I was eighteen, finished with secondary school and I could go anywhere I wanted. To Eastern Europe, Rio de Janeiro, Asia, New York, Berlin. But instead I departed for the city that was just thirty kilometres north of my hometown, and moved into a rented room where I fought mice and rats and a creeping loneliness – in spite of the mice and rats and the lively cafés I frequented with good friends.

When I was twenty, twenty-three, twenty-five, I could still go anywhere I wanted. I knew someone in Israel, London, Moscow, and the mountains of Morocco. While in the Antilles I received a marriage proposal from the son of wealthy Venezuelan. I had casual boyfriends in Paris and Copenhagen, and I'd been to their homes.

But I stayed. I relocated within the city to a building on the quay, closer to the centre of the centre, where the view from the attic window looks like the illustration from a picture book. Here I live high above the rooftops, still higher above the canals, and just above the Nieuw Amsterdams Peil, that thing that marks the water level. No mice come here, or rats either, but pigeons cover my balcony with poop and clumsily settle their fat bodies in front of my window. I hiss 'kssst' and the pigeons fly away, frightened, and I hear them angrily cooing from my neighbour's roof, like aggrieved citizens on their soapbox.

Even worse than the pigeons are the herons, who keep an eye on me from their nests. With their long legs and long bills, they settle their differences out on the street. The noise from their breeding rites makes my teeth hurt. Sometimes, when I see one standing in the street, I bicycle a little further past.

Now I'm twenty-seven and I can still go anywhere I want. I don't have a full-time job, or a house of my own. All my goldfish are dead. On the Internet I sometimes look for bargain flights to Southern Italy and San Francisco, or cheap train tickets to Brittany. I know that it's raining today in Siena and that in St. Tropez the first bikinis of the season have been written about by happy columnists. Tomorrow they're expecting thunderstorms in Bangkok and a temperature of 28 degrees in Bloemfontein.

In Amsterdam it will be fifteen degrees and partly cloudy with a chance of rain. I know that won't stop the estate agents from propping their sunglasses on top of their heads. And yet I stay here, some thirty kilometres north of my hometown. Sometimes I dream I ring the necks of all the herons in the city, one at a time. Just the other day I was sure a pigeon winked at me. People say that no matter where you are in the city, there's always a rat within four metres.

Janneke van der Horst, 'Rats and Herons' ['Ratten en reigers']
Het Parool (20 April, 2009)
translated from the Dutch by Patricia Gosling

❊ ❊ ❊

Writer and multi-prize-winning translator (and intro-ducer of this anthology) Sam Garrett gives some sugges-tions about how to navigate the complicated structure of Amsterdam in his story, 'Cutting the Techno-Onion'.

It was late and it was raining outside. Someone in the back room of the café was bopping out a scat number, *a capella*, yowling and growling like an animal in heat. It sounded like a tribute to Ella Fitzgerald. The evening had taken an early turn towards black beer and something Tipp was recommending as 'Bengali temple ball', but I was still lucid enough to appreciate good music when I heard it. In fact, I had pretty much the whole bar swinging along with 'April in Paris' before I realized it was the barman's cat.

"Have you told them about cutting the onion?" The music had stopped and Tipp was suddenly there, back from the john or wherever he'd been, looming up behind me, risen from the plumbery depths and bigger than ever. His convex reflection in the brass rail around the bar made him look two hundred feet tall.

"It's up to you, man. No one's gonna do it *for* you. Quarter and slice an onion. Make them look at it. Before you know it … *voila*!"

I guess I'd been whining to Tipp about my problem, which was relatives, visiting American relatives to be exact. Back home they could navigate sweeps of high desert by the smell of wild garlic alone, but here, in a town not much bigger than their daughter's high school parking lot, their sense of direction had been thrown for a loop, compass needles spinning wildly at the heart of an experiential hurricane. And they were clinging to me, hating their helplessness all the while but gratefully saying nothing, the way drowning people will cling to a bloated horse.

Tipp was only trying to help. Tipp was also, as that oblique Dutch saying goes, 'stoned as a shrimp'. But he had a point. The gull's-eye view of Amsterdam, the rings of split oak, the metropolis as onion, quartered and sliced: these were the kinds of true-life models my family needed to help them find their way around. The mistake was a hopeful one, but it was up to me to shatter their illusions; no one had ever run a straightedge across this place and 'laid it out'.

Downtown Manhattan, London or Paris may contain more crushing mass, but they also contain the comfort of a rectilinear brand of logic. Amsterdam offers no such solace. Ultimately, the Bowery, the City and Montparnasse can all be navigated by means of cautious tacking maneuvers, by following streets and turning corners in ever-widening rectangles. I know, for I have lost my way in all of them; yet none of those trials ever brought on the dark night of the soul which descends on the traveler lost in Amsterdam's lower rings. It is a desperate man who first realizes that following his nose has not only failed to take him from point A to point B, but that doing so has – with the same, inflexible Euclidean force – cost him a perfectly good afternoon and taken him absolutely nowhere.

There's nothing so strange about it when you realize that, for the first six hundred years of its life, Amsterdam grew the way a mollusk grows, ring by ring. And the old city still has something of the tide pool about it. Big-eyed tourists washed into its inner circles watch as strange creatures come out to feed, lunging from the fissures between buildings, and disappear again without warning. Street markets in the rain are a hum and bubble of hunger, where eels are slapped into slime-covered crates and hooded housewives scuttle up, bumping their broad backs together, to take their pick.

With the pragmatism of the fisherman who casts his nets not where the water is loveliest but where the fish are most plentiful, Amsterdam has developed not as it should, but as it could. The centre opened onto the world's seas, the IJ the sluice through which the florins cascaded into the tills of the *burghers*. And the city kept its back, rounded and fortified like the mussel's, to the jealous interference of the outside world.

From this centre the old town has spread out in concentric arcs, slice by slice, rising to its present height during the course of several centuries before losing itself in the surrounding countryside. A map of Amsterdam as it was on the eve of the Industrial Revolution is a drawing of six-hundred years of calcified growth, a human coral reef shaped by the technological and economic currents in which it grew. For Amsterdam's original shape, the quarter onion, the expanding half-moon on the IJ, was given it not by regents and draftsmen, but by hydraulic engineers and dredgers, by technicians, technocrats and *douaniers*. Based, first and foremost, on the world's only true low-friction transport system: water.

Seen from five-hundred miles above water and land, the countryside around Amsterdam is bio-circuitry. From this vantage, SPOT 2 photographs the River Amstel as it squirms blackly through a microscopic hatching of flooded peat pits, waterways, roads and rails. Making its pass every twenty-six days, the weather-eye sends us pictures of the river dangling umbilically from the city's core. But turn the picture upside down, and the graceful Amstel goes on record as it rolls into town, lithely feeds the canals and – *voila*! – smacks into a brick dam.

Seen from the surface of the canals, three meters under the level of the North Sea, there is something claustrophobic about all this water held in check; if you think about it too long, it is as though the stone and earthen walls are only a greenstick fracture away from total deluge. Perhaps that silent threat is the river's revenge for its strictured dignity, for the interruptus imposed centuries ago on its fertile union with the sea.

The streets, alleyways and bridges around St. Olof's Chapel are among the city's oldest, the basal whorl where Amsterdam clings to the thirteenth-century wall of sand and clay. Close to the chapel, but immured now within the Golden Tulip/ Barbizon hotel and its cocktail-party references to the city's past, lay Amsterdam's first public cemetery. Somewhere behind the Brut dispenser in the hotel's basement lavatory is the final resting place of solitary fishermen and stray dogs, interred there more than three hundred years before Huygens discovered the regulatory power of the pendulum, at least that long before the Dutch East India Company shackled the Spice Islands to its side.

There beneath those bridges, in the black water that washes the sides of the old graves between the Oudezijds Kolk and Damrak, lies the seven-hundred-year-old seed onion, nestled up against the fundaments of the old sea dyke. The time traveller need only keep this microscopic heart of the city at his back; any line he follows then will lead him through ever-expanding rings to the present

It *is* a strange place, this bend in the river, this half-ring of concentric ripples still reverberating from the plunk in a thirteenth-century pool. Yet what other city balances so well on so many cutting edges, teetering between propriety and chaos, the chic and the chichi, between drowning and dry land?

Tipp was right: it was my town and I was in it up to my ears. If I wanted my family off my back, I had no choice but to impose sense on the unsensible. I would wrest direction from the mussel's rings; I would cut for them the techno-onion … .

Sam Garrett, 'Cutting the Techno-Onion' (2001)

'Water, water, everywhere ... '

Cees Nooteboom, one of the Netherlands' best known and loved writers, gives a lyrical portrait of the 'miracle' that is Amsterdam, a city painstakingly pulled from the ever-threatening waters to become one of the great jewels of Europe.

First of all the land. The North Sea beats against a row of dunes that resists it and rolls, green grey, brown grey, to the place where it finds a passage. From there it whips around the land, between the wall of islands, and becomes the Wadden Sea, then the Zuider Zee. Now it burrows with its mighty arm, the IJ, into the land on the other side. Between sea and sea lies a desert of peninsulas and salt marshes, always subject to the rule of water, protected by pitiful dykes of seaweed, between which the growth of reeds and weeds is burned down so that the land can be cultivated. A region of sparse farmers and fishermen, a population of water people between the streams, the mire, and the flows of water, living on the banks of rivers, on high ground, always threatened by the rising sea, by the settling of the peat, by storms and floods. Thus originates not only land but also a sort of people, a people that neither found its land nor received it, but rather created it. The farmers resist the pumping and pulling of the greedy sea, the everlasting attack, by laying sods of peat crosswise. Everywhere in the low lands the inhabitants lay down dams against the rising water from the east, build houses of loam and reed and wood, and through the first sluices they lead the now powerless water to the sea, which forever seeks to return. If they want to survive they cannot leave anything to chance; they organize themselves in hamlets that defend against the fluid, streaming enemy. The land is marshy and vulnerable under a high, ever-changing sky; the only mountains are the dunes in the west, the Dutch mountains. They have a sea in front of them and a sea behind them: North Sea, Zuider Zee. A river writes it way through the land of Amestelle. The counts of Holland and the bishops of Utrecht quarrel over this wet, uncertain peat bog in a remote corner of the realm of Nether Lorraine. *Stelle:* safe, protected place. *Ame:* water. The land gives its name to the drifting river. The river drifts around the high ground, dances and sways through the land that calls for straight lines; it poses as a slow-moving, baroque festoon. Where it ends in the Zuider Zee, the water is called IJ, and there the river invents a city, a city on the water. Now the game can begin.

The river leaves its sign upon the shore like a seal, writing its form therein like an accomplished calligrapher. Once you have seen it, there is no escaping it: over the centuries, the street map of Amsterdam has become an ever more complicated sign, a Chinese character that has kept spreading but always signifies the same thing. The land is the paper, the water the ink. Like an Oriental master, the river drew the first line, effortlessly, accurately, a sign of utmost simplicity. Now it is up to the people to continue writing. Together they are a calligrapher with a lot of time, all eight

34

hundred years, and the emblem that appears is a neat labyrinth of canals, concentric, crossing each other, a net of waterways and defensive bulwarks, a self-contained cosmos, a magical semi-circle that will leave its mark on the world. The pivot continues to be the river and the water in which it ends, and which connects the city to the world, but in between and along that water the city takes on the shape it has now. Every new line in the drawing is history – economic, political, cadastral. Every movement of the calligrapher's brush is dictated by power relations, wars, economic shifts, discoveries, greed, defense, consolidation. The ring of canals by the sea, forever perpetuating itself, becomes one of Europe's mightiest strongholds; the ships that leave the city and return after many years sail to the end of the known world, bearing the name and repute of the city to the tropics and to the barbaric ice of the northernmost seas and so contribute to the sign that grows. [...]

Everyone, it seems, had something to do with ships in those days; everyone belonged to the water, the same water that still stands dark and mysterious in the canals and that is so much wilder and murkier outside of town, the water of the ocean upon which ships came sailing right to the city's edge, "a forest of a thousand masts." On the old map by Cornelis Antonisz from the year 1544, the walker can see the city with her ships. Very few canals cut through the surface between city walls. The Golden Age has still not arrived, but the IJ is already full of ships. In the place where Centraal Station will one day rise, the smaller ships are able to sail into the city; the larger ones – tens of them – stay on the roadstead. The two large churches stand sheltered between the houses, each at its own side of the water – they are still there. The wide waters of the Damrak came to where the Royal Palace now stands and divided the small city in two: the old side and the new. He recognizes buildings, the layout of streets. The city has saved itself for him; he still walks every day where his house will be built in the seventeenth century and a red mill still stands, the green land encircling the city that keeps jumping over the next canal as it grows larger on every subsequent map. Larger because fame and prosperity rose with the new ships of the Companies. The canal of the *Heren*, gentlemen, that one first, confirming the might of the merchants, only then the *Keizers*, emperors, then the *Prinsen*, princes. And those other, transverse canals with names of trees and flowers, *Lelie, Egelantier, Roos*, and *Laurier*, in between which, in a district called Jordaan, lived ordinary people: the ship carpenters, the loaders, the sailors, the men with loud voices who brought the air of the great worlds into the narrow streets.

Cees Nooteboom, *The philosopher without eyes*
[*De filosoof zonder ogen*] (1997)

translated from the Dutch by Manfred Wolf and
Virginie M. Kortekaas

✳ ✳ ✳

As "the Venice of the north", it isn't surprising that water – both the canals and the sea – features prominently in writing about Amsterdam. One of the best novels on the subject is H. M. van den Brink's On the Water *(beautifully translated by Paul Vincent), telling the story of two young rowers, Anton and David, moving through the golden summer of pre-war Amsterdam, and into the Nazi occupation. In this extract, Anton conveys his fascination with and love of the waters of Amsterdam.*

The best part of the day was early in the morning when I left home. I set off in good time, so that I would be able to make a detour. I hurried round the corner. In Emerald Street I could already smell the river. I crossed the road and forced myself not to look too intently at the water, although of course I cast sideways glances and it was immediately obvious to me what state it was in, calm or troubled, quiet or busy. I didn't turn left towards the centre of town but right, until I got to the new bridge with the electric lamps. In the middle of the bridge I stopped and only then did I allow myself, with my arms resting on the wrought iron of the balustrade, to look properly into the water, first directly beneath me, black in the shadow of the pillars, and then slowly further away, where it became blue and white and began to shimmer, as far as I could see.

I took in everything: the freight barges on their way into the centre of town or on the contrary returning after delivering their cargo to the markets, the life on the houseboats, the flags on the larger ships, the washing hanging out to dry somewhere on board, a fisherman bent over his rod and in the distance the jumble of house fronts, masts and towers, the silhouette of the city. But even more than the life on and around the river, I studied the water itself, which was calm on most of these summer days, inviting, as though made to catch with our oars. I drank it all in and even that early in the day felt a bitter-sweet taste of nostalgia permeate my whole body, while my hands grasped the balustrade of the bridge and behind me the tram passed, cars growled, horses and carts trundled by. I had to tear myself away.

I walked on along the affluent side of the river, past the next bridge and past the club where no flag was waving this early, until I got to the third bridge, which would take me back to my everyday life, leading as it did directly to the bustle of the centre. I crossed, forcing myself not to look left too much, towards the inviting emptiness at the end of the city.

Late in the afternoon, after I had completed my last set of figures, I followed the same route in the opposite direction. The coolness had now given away to a fully saturated splendour of colours, as if it were no longer the wind that ruled the water but the humidity that had evaporated during the day. And I felt the same nostalgia, though sadder now, as if the invitation extended by the water belonged in the past and had lost its validity.

Every day that passes is irreplaceable. That was the message the river gave me. The figures on my desk with their unchanging meaning tried to assert precisely the opposite.

H.M. van den Brink, *On the Water* (1998)
translated from the Dutch by Paul Vincent

'Water, water, everywhere …'

* * *

Maarten Asscher's ingeniously titled H₂Olland
contains a fascinating exploration of the history of
Amsterdam and its waters.

Amsterdam, with its horseshoe-shaped, quadruple ring of concentric canals, is the most distinctive of all Dutch cities where you can live in close proximity to the water. Cities such as Haarlem, Dordrecht, Leiden, Utrecht, Delft, Alkmaar and smaller towns such as Hoorn, Enkhuizen and Edam can be seen as scaled-down versions of Amsterdam's seventeenth-century canal structure from which they derive – on a smaller and sometimes prettier scale – a similar atmosphere. Just as after a visit to Venice the island of Murano reminds you of a not yet fully grown version, a kind of adorable early stage of the bigger city, Edam looks like a scale model of Amsterdam, an innocent toddler beside its big, pretentious and perverted brother.

That is not to say that the canals in Amsterdam and elsewhere were constructed for aesthetic reasons. On the contrary, extremely practical considerations informed the city's expansion during its seventeenth century prime when, from its medieval heart by a dam in the river Amstel, it spread in all directions with ever-wider concentric canals. From 1612 the Singel was followed by the Herengracht, the Keizersgracht and finally – the longest of all – the Prinsengracht. In 1658 they were extended eastward which gave them their distinctive horse-shoe shape. The practical considerations initially concerned Amsterdam's defences, but later mainly the population explosion in the prospering city, the shipment of goods, removal of the city's waste and management of its water levels. The latter was regulated by a sophisticated system of locks, the relics of which can be seen scattered throughout the city.

Over the years I have come to know several sections of Amsterdam's main canals quite well, either by living or working there or by being a frequent visitor to offices or the homes of friends. In the early years, if I wanted to remember the order of the four main canals (from the outside in), I would often refer to the mnemonic Piet Koopt Hoge Schoenen ("Piet buys high shoes"), the first letters of which correspond to the initials of the four canals. You soon learn that each of these sections of canal forms something of a small neighbourhood and you discover landmarks: a church, a side canal, a shopping street, a distinctive corner building. But in fact even dyed-in-the-wool Amsterdamers get it wrong on occasion. You see, each of the Amsterdam canals features magnificent and less magnificent, expensive and less expensive, higher and lower rows of houses. Those who live in the so-called Golden Bend on the Herengracht (roughly between numbers 400 and 500) have a completely different kind of house – more of an urban palace – than those who live at the beginning of the Prinsengracht, where you'll find charming but more modest seventeenth century cottages. Of course both parties can say that they live by an Amsterdam canal.

The great urban planning tragedy of Amsterdam as a water-front city is the construction of Central Station, designed by the great architect Pierre Cuypers and built during the years 1881–1889, which cut the city off from its most important water's edge, its open access to the IJ. This large new station established a crucial connection between the Willemspoort Station west of the city centre (for trains towards Haarlem) and the south-eastern Rhijnspoor Station (towards Utrecht). But the IJ was Amsterdam's original link with the IJsselmeer (formerly known as the Zuiderzee) and later – via the North Sea Canal which opened in 1876 – with the North Sea. This vast, open expanse of water and the unique view of the old city that it offered were sacrificed to the era's dream of steam and iron: the train

Those who wish to picture seventeenth-century Amsterdam must begin by imagining all the filled-in canals excavated and refilled with water (and blocking out all the parked and passing cars of course) before visualizing the entire northern part of the old city – from the Haarlemmer Poort in the west to the Maritime Museum in the east – as a harbour front. This is where people used to arrive by ship and from where they could see the church spires, the town gates and the emerging silhouette of the Royal Palace on Dam Square.

With the decline of this erstwhile maritime perspective on Amsterdam, the city centre has become closed in on itself. In fact, the label "canal ring" has acquired pejorative connotations as a closed, self-absorbed clique of people with cultural and material pretensions, who feel superior to the rest of the city and indeed the rest of the country. It wasn't until the 1990s that the city began to capitalize on the town planning opportunities offered by the northern IJ banks, the old trading docks to the east and west of Central Station and the now deserted industrial estates on the IJ. In no time residential neighbourhoods replaced former shipyards, docks and warehouses. Housing and office complexes now border the railway lines separating the IJ from Amsterdam and prestigious cultural projects have been realized, including the Muziekgebouw, a concert hall for contemporary music, a public library with a floor area of 28,000 m2 and a music academy. But whether this side of town, with the water closed off by roads and railways, will ever have an urban heart again remains to be seen.

Despite repeated and major investment over the past century in the dock areas further north and west and in the waterways linking the city with the North Sea, Amsterdam has long since ceased to be a real port. Over the past decade, for example, aldermen for economic affairs have been at a loss what to do with a costly container terminal along the North Sea Canal which has failed to attract any custom from major international shipping companies. The cranes of this container terminal can be seen for miles around, like a monument to the tenacity with which Amsterdam clings to its historic seaport aspirations. A press release from Zeehavens Amsterdam, dated 20 August 2007, illustrates the perceived intensity of the competition between the capital and the now far bigger Port of Rotterdam. It states that a miscalculation in the Port of Amsterdam's half-yearly figures for 2006 had put the increase in transhipment at 9.2 instead of the actual 1.8 per cent. The truth is that the Port of Rotterdam tranships nearly five times as much as the ports of Amsterdam, Zaanstad, Beverwijk, Velsen and IJmuiden combined. One of the few port activities that Amsterdam can rightfully boast about these days is strictly tourist-related: the reception of large cruise ships. In 2007 the capital attracted 78; in 2008 their number will increase to around 120, carrying a total of more than 200,000 tourists.

In this day and age water in Amsterdam is mostly a picturesque affair, with canal tour boats, privately owned pleasure crafts with crates of beer on board and the ubiquitous Canal Bikes, leaving many tourists soaking wet, if not because of the rain then because of an ill-advised manoeuvre trying to avoid a canal tour boat that suddenly emerges from under a bridge. The most noteworthy water event in Amsterdam is Sail, a show held every five years. This extravaganza, featuring large numbers of historic sailing ships that lend the Amsterdam IJ the appearance of its bygone seventeenth century glory days, illustrates the extent to which our capital's port is a historical rather than a contemporary phenomenon.

Maarten Asscher, $H_2Olland$ (2009)
translated from the Dutch by Laura Vroomen

* * *

As in the earlier piece from On the Water, *this extract from Dirk van Weelden's* The World of 609, *links water and time in a piece that is both lyrical and pragmatic.*

Twelve o'clock (for minutes on end clocks and carillons cshime throughout the entire city) and the Amstel River glistens in the wintry light. The afternoon starts from zero. Just go over to the window, look left, past the bare trees where the Herengracht meets the Amstel under the bridge. Do you see how the river raises white quills to the wind? A fine sturdy stretch of water through which tour boats shoulder powerfully forwards. Through the window on the second floor of this mansion house, the winter's day is a spectacle; a constant stream of air, light, rain, dirty grey clouds, and in five hour's time, darkness once more. A carrousel of imperturbable states.

The only gods who may lay claim to eternity (and then only the limited eternity of planet earth) are the weather gods. The atmosphere, flowing and eddying, is the oldest being on our planet. At first it was a cauldron of poisonous primordial soup, volcanic lava and methane gas. Years of thunderstorms lashed the ferns, cockroaches and dinosaurs. Aquatic apes, Homo habilis, Neanderthals and Cro Magnons shared the same pleasure in inhaling the spring breeze and recognised the inky clouds announcing a rainstorm, just as we do.

It drizzled on Babylonia. The Greeks were bothered by drafts. The Huns had the wind against them. The Romans underestimated the thaw and sank through the ice. For thousands of years, ships all over the world have been going to Davy Jones's locker in a storm. Harvests spoilt by rain. Flocks frozen to death. Military campaigns foundering in rain, snow and mud. Emperors and beggars, irrespective of their rank, bombarded with dust, wind, rain, hail and lightning. There will always be people who think that they can order the right weather with certain songs, dance steps or child sacrifices. But there is no reliable method. And the scientific acumen that brought us brain surgery, Photoshop, the Hubble telescope and beta blockers has little to offer when a tropical hurricane approaches or a force 7 creates black ice. At those times the best thing to do is abandon our trains, planes, cars and bikes and crawl away for a while.

The weather comes and goes, it whirls past, unremitting in its complex movements. And in a pathetic way, that is why it is the most wonderful example of the law of eternal return. We'll be eternally creosoting; we'll be perennially putting Vaseline on our lips when a biting easterly gets up. Centuries of kindling and damping down, irrigating and pumping dry. The cruel sun will perpetually burn the necks of farmers toiling in the tropics, after which monsoon rains will cause rivers to flood and all that toil for nothing. Bridges, gates and bikes will rust forever.

The wind will demolish hairdos, umbrellas, parasols and the fruit harvest until the end of time.

For a cool four billion years the weather has been balderdash and yet it remains eternally topical. A living soul comes into the light on a bleak day with storms and sleet and is buried on a clammy overcast afternoon in September. I'm standing here with you in an empty house, a mansion on the Herengracht in Amsterdam and when that shower beats down presently (can you see it falling already over the Amstel station?) onto the sheets of zinc protecting the roof, it will be indistinguishable from a shower two hundred years ago. This house looks to be of respectable age, but on the time scale of the weather gods its three hundred and thirty-eight years are a mere blink of the eye.

Dirk van Weelden, *The World of 609* [*De wereld van 609*] (2008)
translated from the Dutch by Michele Hutchison

* * *

In Doeschka Meijsing's About love *(*Over de liefde*), the narrator – about to make a speech during a waterside meal with friends – manages to escape an event she is far from enjoying by taking an unplanned swim in the canal ...*

I got up and moved to stand behind my chair because you can use both hands to hold comfortably onto the back during your speech, but I forgot to push it under the table. I got caught behind a leg of the chair, tried to correct my position by making a quarter turn, got my heel stuck in the low railing put there to prevent the cars parking there from going over the embankment, lost my balance, and fell backwards into the water.

After coming back up, spitting out the canal water and wiping it out of my eyes, I got my bearings. Thank goodness I had fallen between the bow of a fishing boat and the stern of a small old sailboat and had not broken my legs or my back. Treading water, I turned around slowly. There was the light of

Prinsengracht with the long tables at the water, farther down the parked cars. There was Jula with her girlfriends. Several of the women were lying flat on their stomachs over the rail, their hands extended. These were the rowers who had some experience in pulling someone out of the water. It wasn't until then that I heard their voices that sounded loud and reassuring.

"Don't worry, Pip, we'll easily pull you up."

"Grab our wrists, grab our hands."

"Come up, Pip," shouted Jula.

I looked at the scene from my dark place in the depth. And suddenly I realized that I was no longer in the mood for all that light and all those blond women who were strong, not for Jula, especially not for Jula, my angel, my Judas. All in all I was no longer in the mood for that life at the water's edge, the tables with lemon ice cream with vodka, conversations with people, not for going shopping and working on an article, not for life.

I turned around and swam away.

The water of Prinsengracht wasn't too cold; the sun had beaten down on it all summer long. It should stink, but I smelled nothing. I wasn't afraid of rats – they would be more afraid of me. I used the breast stroke to swim from in between the two boats until I seemed to be in open water. It was too late at night for tourists on the water; the surface was as smooth as glass and reflected the moon. It was quiet and calm in the middle of the canal. I had the place to myself.

I veered to port and started to swim. My breast stroke had always been unusually powerful. If I competed with one of Jula's rowing friends, or with Jula herself, I would win. I'd win against Maret, but I didn't let that count because Maret was lazy in the water. I beat everyone. It was the only stroke that I had mastered; others were fast in freestyle or the butterfly; I find the latter exceedingly ridiculous. They had never been interested in the breast stroke – that was for the elderly. But to their great surprise I beat them.

I took pleasure in swimming with big strokes, in working my way through the city like this, in the dirty water where the sorrow of the big city had been dumped. All that sorrow behind all those front doors – the water received it silently and carried it out of the city, to the IJ, to the sea, where it dissolved in the perpetual movement of the tides. I swam upstream. I didn't know where I would swim; I concentrated on the liberating movements of my arms and legs. I had left my summer shoes somewhere in the water.

I approached a bridge. For a moment I hesitated, but then I decided to continue swimming underneath the bridge – afterwards the moon would suddenly be high in the sky again. Under the bridge the water was much colder. And it was dark there. Now I also saw the rats that were chasing each other like maniacs on the underside of the bridge. It became nasty – now I had really ended up in filth, and I was ready to scramble ashore. Once I reached the other side of the bridge, I saw the façade of De Duif, the only baroque church façade of Amsterdam, restored fairly recently. That's where I wanted to climb ashore, on that spot I would start anew.

On the church façade it said *In loco iste dabo pacem* – I knew that from the countless times that I had looked at it from the square. I didn't know where it said that in the Bible or who had said it – perhaps Jesus of Nazareth; it was the kind of text that was likely to be attributed to him, even though I suspected that it was medieval Latin. *In this place I give you peace*. There was no mention of the source. A strange need to believe what it said came over me. *That's* where I wanted to climb ashore, in that place I would start anew.

I had just found a clear space between the houseboats where there was a high wall, when I noticed that there was no peace and quiet next to the canal. In swimming so far away from ordinary life I'd become unaware of human activity. I saw something that looked like a fire engine with several firemen around it. Flawless Jula! She had called in the fire department. The bright beam of a floodlight was directed at me after a short search across the water. I shielded my eyes with my arm.

Completely unexpectedly, the head of a fireman covered by the smooth hood of a wetsuit suddenly surfaced next to me.

"Don't be afraid, we'll pull you up," he said.

I wasn't afraid; by using the houseboats, I could easily have climbed onto the embankment, but in the Netherlands you can't disappear just like that – help appears whenever and wherever. Here you can't be a Perelman who walks from his mother's kitchen table straight into thin air. I wasn't afraid for a moment, but I did get colder and colder. At first the water of Prinsengracht may have felt almost lukewarm, around sixty-one degrees, but underneath the bridge it had probably been fifty-seven degrees. The wine, which had initially offered me some protection, had worn off, and I suddenly started getting very cold. My teeth chattering, I could only emit unintelligible sounds to my neighbour with his encased head; I wanted the *pacem* that was promised here, I wanted out of the water, I wanted warmth.

Doeschka Meijsing, *About Love* [*Over de liefde*] (2008)
translated from the Dutch by Jeanette K. Ringold

❊ ❊ ❊

Unsurprisingly, a darker view of the water is given in this later part of H. M. van den Brink's On the Water *now that Amsterdam has become an occupied city.*

Almost no lights are lit in the Eden Hotel these days. In fact, the paper on the panes no longer serves any purpose. There are no newspapers on the polished table in the lobby and no one sits in the plush armchairs waiting for someone. Everyone's waiting, but for no one in particular. The city is waiting, with its empty shop windows and its hollow people. Not because it has a date, but because it can't do much else but wait and think of the past. Under the window of my room, three floors below, is the canal. Black and dead as a cesspool, a stinking pond from which any instant poisonous bubbles can come bubbling up. You hope it will never start moving again, and it probably won't, it is too tired.

46

Only at the edges does it still lap spitefully at the houses, which are gradually being undermined by it. The process of decay and putrefaction has been going on for hundreds of years, it began when the first piles were driven into the mud and became saturated with moisture. But it wouldn't surprise me if this winter were to be the last, if the ulcer were now to burst and the whole terrace with all its memories of pleasure and sin were to topple forwards, slowly, in slow motion as in a modern film, vanishing into the depths and never floating to the surface again. The city goes under and submerges us in a dome of water. The river, curious, no longer keeps aloof. It overflows its banks, it ripples over the remains of roofs and walls, it washes away the exhaustion with it. [...]

Even when I approached the river, I could still not smell it. It suddenly loomed up in front of me. No moon. I could just make out the silhouette of a bridge. But I didn't cross yet. I kept walking in the shadow of the houses, with the water on my left, until I reached the new bridge, our bridge, the one with the electric lamps, which were removed long ago. The iron of the balustrade was a blazing strip of cold through the night. I touched it for a moment and had to withdraw my hand almost immediately. I slid from lamp to lamp in stages. I had never counted them. I was able to find the middle without difficulty. And because I had the feeling that nothing could happen to me any more, I stopped.

Water beneath me, moving restlessly, stretching and swaying as if it knew it was soon to freeze.

H.M. van den Brink, *On the Water* (1998)
translated from the Dutch by Paul Vincent

❊ ❊ ❊

The narrator of Adrian Mathews' novel, The Apoth-ecary's House, *is living in a houseboat on the Prinsen-gracht ... which has some unsavoury realities among its obvious advantages.*

From her berth on the Prinsengracht, she had a view down the Bloemgracht canal. The morning sun hung above the water like a pale levitating apricot. It pinked the air and trees with its fruity bloom, lending a glamorous fluorescence to the step gables of the Keyser Foundation building.

A low soup of fog still clung to the water, the odd gossamer wisp tearing itself away. […]

She sat like a bosun on the edge of the gunwale and surveyed her domain.

In theory, seawater was pumped into the canals from the IJsselmeer and the dirty water streamed into the North Sea during low tide at IJmuiden. The reality was that the canal system was a seventeenth-century open sewer, just one of the functions it was designed to fulfil in the first place. The houseboats, vessels and arks were gradually being connected to the modern sewage system. In the meantime, it was not exactly a life on the ocean waves. A few lumps of raw sewage were bobbing and rolling in the water right now and – she noticed – some colourful new graffiti had materialized on the galley hatch. All the same, the odour of tar and the whiff of wood smoke from her stove's chimney rescued her good humour.

A boat was a boat and there was a heck of a lot to be said for it.

In this country it was the land that was precarious, not the water, a subaqueous plain that would completely vanish if the sea level rose by twenty metres. The words 'sea level', in fact, were rarely used in polite conversation. One said 'NAP' – normal Amsterdam level – instead. 'NAP' was user-friendly. 'Sea level' meant up to your gizzard in water. 'Sea level' meant breathing brine. Remember that, ye putrid landlubbers! All things considered, and given Amsterdam's reputation as a modern Sodom and Gomorrah, having an ark handy was not such a bad idea in the end …

Adrian Mathews, *The Apothecary's House* (2005)

'Water, water, everywhere …'

* * *

Frozen canals are a frequent feature of novels set in Amsterdam. Here are three examples – the first a seventeenth-century scene depicted by Sarah Emily Miano, then two modern skating episodes by Sue Rann, and Adrian Mathews.

The sky is a pale-green curtain. A raven flies overhead. Snow fleeces the rooftops and edges the thin branches of barren trees which line the frozen canal. People skate and gather on the ice: a young man pulling an old woman on a handmade sled; a girl offering a hand to her companion who toddles behind; a skinny dog with a curly tail shivering near a hole; three children in a circle playing a game of dice; a stall selling food and drink; a pair of lovers skipping along in clumsy harmony; one woman in a red coat, having lost her balance, sits on the ice, and no one is helping her up …

Sarah Emily Miano, *Van Rijn* (2006)

* * *

Oude Schans was wide as well as long, a stubby extension of the docks poking south-west into the city streets. Even with houseboats clustered three deep along its edges, there was a broad swathe of ice out there, and it would be thinner towards the middle of the canal, weakened by the passage – yesterday or the day before – of tourist boats and other water traffic.

The city up above carried on with its winter-evening amusements, heedless of snowstorms or incipient murder. Music gusted past my chill-numb ears with the flurrying of snowflakes. Jazz closest to, a heavier house beat stabbing out from a club somewhere in the nearby streets. In one of the boats I passed, someone played the guitar, a rich dancing sound, and I heard laughter.

I peered out from under the prow of yet another steel-built scow. It was like a city within a city down here. A tight-packed, unplanned town of squat black walls and clusters of lighted windows like strings of coloured lanterns. The snow heaped along gunwales and deckhouse roofs only added to the sense of cosiness.

I sneezed and wiped water out of my eyes. The snow was falling fast now, big wet flakes. My hair was soaked. I turned my jacket collar up and gripped an ice-crusted rope with one hand to steady myself. [...]

The bridge was just up ahead – in fact, it was the only thing I *could* see up ahead. A flat dark cutout shape at the end of the last brick-walled corridor, topped by the tall stalks of street-lights. Prins Hendrikkade.

Snowflakes jerked and tossed in the orange spotlights, fairy-lighted oblongs of trucks rumbled past. A snow-plough whisked westwards towards the railway station, blades gouging two perfect arcs of glittering powder.

Beyond the deep blue shadow of the bridge, everything was white: a portal to the North Pole. Fragments of ice stuck up, broken and trapped, re-frozen. Through the whirling storm I could just see the blue-green, floodlit shape of the newMetropolis, sticking up like a failed attempt to raise the *Titanic* in the middle of Oosterdok.

Nothing moved on the rumpled plain. The man had vanished. My eyes ached from searching. I pulled off a glove to rub cold fingers over my closed lids.

'This is stupid,' I repeated aloud – as if I needed reminding. 'Stupid, stupid, *stupid*.' I'd lost him.

I walked up the white trough towards the bridge. I couldn't go any further, the ice wouldn't be safe underneath. It never froze properly under cover like that.

Stupid was right, Carlson. You were so close and you blew it. My throat tightened. I should just go back to the boat.

The ice under my feet thrummed. The sharp tang of snow was overlaid down here with algae and rust and brackish water. The wind had tidied the snow into smooth, concave drifts.

I went the last few steps to the shadow's edge – just so that I could tell myself, later, that I had done everything I could do.

My right foot kicked something heavy. I jumped back with a yelp of fright, slipped, pirouetted in a flurry of limbs, and headbutted the ice.

Sue Rann, Looking for Mr Nobody (2003)

✳ ✳ ✳

She crossed the street and followed the Keizersgracht till she came to some worn stone steps that descended steeply to the frozen canal. She sat on the top step, pulled on her skates and laced them up tightly. […]

Skating on the canal, you had to be careful. It wasn't like a rink. Flotsam and jetsam locked into the structure of the ice, potential hazards for dreamy skaters. Then there were chains and cables from the houseboats, arks and barges, not to mention natural irregularities where the water had hardened with a finish like roughly hewn quartz. On top of that, kids threw stuff onto the ice to watch it skid and, when it finished skidding, it just stayed where it ended up – stones, branches, Coke cans, even bicycle wheels – adding interesting features to the obstacle course. Luckily, the street lamps cast a lateral glow that grazed the surface, defining a clear, skateable channel down the middle and picking out the debris between the dense shadows of boats, trees, cars and the canal banks themselves.

She took it easy, skating with long, leisurely strides, her gloved hands clasped behind her back in the time-honoured tradition.

From down below, you had a different perspective on the city. Ruth was a purblind, burrowing creature that had scrabbled its way up through the frosty crust of darkness to find a big bold world of alien activity above.

51

Then the snatched glimpses through houseboat portholes – a man reading a map, a child brushing down a dog – and the strange, hollow resonance of her skate blades, knives drawn in long clean movements across a whetstone.

With a slick thrust of the right skate, she turned into the Singelgracht and swept under the façade of the de la Mar theatre, beneath the shadow of the bridge and past the Leidseplein, where the chandeliers sparkled like diamond fountains in the casino, then alongside the dour, stolid frontage of the Rijksmuseum. She pulled a long face when she came upon it, as if she'd done her best to make it laugh, but there was nothing doing.

My ex place of work ...

But, as she passed the old Heineken brewery and, further on, the Nederlandse Bank, her insouciance gave way to a growing sense of pleasurable tension and focus. It was a tingly sensation, rousing her, like the blue electric sprites you get touching a door handle, shaking someone's hand, after scuffling along a nylon carpet.

She felt fit, reckless and invincible.

Was it the adrenalin that did that? Part of her – the wise Ruth, the god in the machine – advised caution, but the strange wellbeing that blew through her like a spring breeze didn't listen.

Life was good. Life was strong.

How could anything spoil this sweet rush of vitality?

Then all of a sudden the broad expanse of the Amstel opened up ahead of her under a starry gasp of sky.

Here it was perilous to skate mid-river. There was no telling what flaws and infirmities lay hidden beneath the seamless brittle expanse of ice. To underscore the warning, there were no other skaters in sight.

She stuck close to the bank, skirting the moored boats, occasionally grabbing at rusty bolts and projections from their hulls when she fancied she heard a creak or sensed a titling motion beneath her feet. Her knees and ankles began to ache with the effort. And suddenly she was a little girl again, wobbling on the first pair of chalk-white skates her father had bought her when she was seven. The flashback was picture-perfect, neatly puncturing the hermetic cell of the memory so that it flooded her brain with its details.

By the time she reached the Magere Brug, she was edging forward on her skates at slower than walking pace. The white struts of the wooden drawbridge were as bright as old bleached bones in the darkness. People walked briskly across overhead. A couple leaned on the white barrier, above the red stop light for shipping, taking in the view, their warm talk vaporizing around them.

Now she melted back into the shadows.

In the dim light she tried to pinpoint the solitary individuals, on the bank or on the bridge, who looked as if they had assignations.

No one fitted the bill.

She slipped under the bridge and pawed her way along the dark, damp brickwork.

She came out on the other side and looked up again. There were one or two potential candidates, but the angle was too steep. She could make out nothing more than vague silhouettes. In all probability, they were getting a better view of her.

She skated to the nearest steps, put her skates into her shoulder bag and changed back into her boots. She climbed up to street level. Her feet felt heavy and the drop in stature had an equivalent diminishing effect on her spirits.

Adrian Mathews, *The Apothecary's House* (2005)

✳ ✳ ✳

Moving on from the more picturesque aspects of the city's waters, Jan Donkers – famous as a radio DJ, journalist, and author of many books – describes the north side of the IJ river.

It is not difficult to say when such a thing existed as an Amsterdam on the other side of the River IJ and that was at the beginning of the twentieth century. Before that time, Amsterdam-North did not exist. From around 1200, the city was bordered on the north side by the IJ and on the other side of that lay Waterland, a region inhabited by god-fearing fishermen, seafarers and merchants. I imagine that throughout the centuries Waterland must have looked the same as Durgerdam now when you approach it from the water, or Zuiderwoude as sighted in the distance from the road to Uitdam. An area of grassland that was too marshy for arable farming, and where the wind in the hinterland had free reign over the villages of Zunderdorp and Ransdorp and the prosperous Buiksloot, as well as the villages arranged in a short tercet on the dyke along the body of water: Nieuwendam, Schellingwoude, Durgerdam.

The sixteenth-century historian Wilhelmus Gaudamus wrote of this area: 'Waterland, lying within sight of Amsterdam, possesses great riches. The inhabitants do not only cultivate the soil but also the sea. In the summer they set sail to the East and to the West: fetching salt from here, taking it there, and importing various other materials. The land is fielded, with ditches running through it, so that a common man can keep twenty cattle. To generalize about their morals: if Good is to be found anywhere in the World, it is here in this corner. They are a labour-loving folk, partaking of milk and cheese, they drink Whey not because they hate Wine, they like to eat well and are of prosperous build. A Waterlander is powerful when he catches and strikes; he is fed on cow's milk, from which his strength is derived.'

A description, methinks, which does not strictly differ from what a contemporary anthropologist would observe about the inhabitants of this region.

Jan Donkers, *On Amsterdam's Doorstep*
[*Zo dicht bij Amsterdam*] (2008)
translated from the Dutch by Michele Hutchison

'Water, water, everywhere … '

* * *

And two visits to the dock areas, first with Ruth, the protagonist of The Apothecary's House, *getting off the tram at the end of the line on a foggy day …*

The vibration lulled her into numbness. She let her body go limp and sway with the tram's motions as it trundled alongside the Oosterdok. Then, sooner than she'd expected, it clanged to a stop and the doors opened. The driver killed the motor and announced the terminus.

They were just off Piet Henkade.

She descended with the last few passengers and continued east along the IJ Haven.

Metallic spars and structures loomed out of the air – derricks, conveyor pipes, elevated jetties, booms and marker lamps. They were made of the same dream stuff as the fog itself, standing out like embossed hieroglyphs on a grey card background. She heard the clamour of a big dog yelping and straining at a choker chain behind a warehouse door as she passed.

The rare phantom vessels that passed sounded their foghorns, each one a sacred 'Om'.

There were residential streets to her right, a cold sweat of damp on their walls and cobbles, but nobody was about. These odd thoroughfares stopped abruptly at the water's edge, where the mast of moored sailing ships bristled at jumbled angles and made eerie clicking and whirring noises. The fog denatured them further. It was poison gas. All the inhabitants were done for, quietly expiring behind dull sash windows and dripping gutters and downpipes in a latter-day Pompeii.

The Ersthaven, then a bridge over the Amsterdam-Rijn Kanaal, and she was heading out to Zeeburg and the IJmeer.

There were busy roads nearby – she could hear the cautious growl of traffic.

She stuck, wherever possible, to the dockside.

The temperature dropped the further she strayed from the city. This marginal place belonged to the stevedores and merchant seamen. When the weather broke, they slouched off the freighters and tankers and container ships, into the flop-houses or hot little corner bars that cropped up now and then with banknotes from around the world tacked to their ceilings and coins superglued to the floor, glowing electric clocks in the shape of beer glasses, jukeboxes, satellite TVs on wall brackets and bar football. Frankly, she felt safer on the streets. The bars were boozy little global villages of nomadic men, killing time and brain cells in the accepted matelot ways.

Adrian Mathews, *The Apothecary's House* (2005)

✳ ✳ ✳

And an equally bleak visit to the docks with Chris Ewan.

I walked on from my street the short distance to the Ooster-dokskade Bridge, at one end of the Oosterdok. To my left was the grand red-brick façade of Centraal Station, nexus of the Dutch train system and home to raggedy-clothed vagabonds and glassy-eyed druggies, hookers who couldn't afford the overheads of a lighted glass booth and western students bent-double with the weight of the ruck-sacks on their backs. To my right was the bleak expanse of the eastern dock area, rain drops ticking onto the surface of the water from the bridge railings I was leaning against. The dark, petroleum-laced currents undulated listlessly, nudging the flotsam of discarded city litter against the concrete edges of the dock. Commercial vessels were moored all around – tugs, transporters, sightseeing barges and even a dated cruise ship that had been transformed into a floating youth hostel. A few decrepit houseboats awaiting refits or the scrap yard were dotted here and there, along with the odd rubber dinghy.

The edges of the dock were bordered by anonymous pre-fab warehouses where nameless industrial processes were undertaken or complex chemicals stored. Between the warehouses I saw bare concrete yards, with stacks of wooden palettes and mini forklift trucks parked beside the gleaming BMWs and Mercedes of the factory owners. Occasional manual workers, dressed in faded boiler suits and heavy duty work boots, smoked cigarettes or talked into two-way radios beneath plastic hard hats.

The docks were a large, open area and the biting wind that had followed the storm showers swooped across the surface of the water unhindered, cutting into me, seemingly passing right through the fabric of my overcoat and woollen hat and gloves. I blew warm air onto my hands and rubbed them together as I walked, pulled my chin down against my chest to stop the wind getting at my bare neck, and battled the cold for quite some time before I found the buildings I was looking for.

The complex of stone-built warehouses lined the curved area near the mouth of the harbour, at the point at which the dockland water met with the expanse of tidal water that separated central Amsterdam from its northernmost district. There were three warehouses in all, linked by raised walkways positioned on the fourth floor of the six storey buildings. All of the warehouses were empty and looked as if they'd been that way for a number of years. Most of the single-glazed panels in the windows fronting the dock had been smashed or blown through and on closer inspection, the bottom floor of each building was nothing more than a vast concrete carcass, while the yards that adjoined them were filled only with wild-grass and abandoned metal cages and the burnt-out remains of a Renault 19.

Chris Ewan, *The Good Thief's Guide to Amsterdam* (2007)

> *But let's redirect our steps back to the centre of the city and a final reminder of the beauty of Amsterdam's waterways. To celebrate her recovery from a serious illness, the American writer of this diary entry decides to cross the Atlantic and visit her favourite European cities, starting with Amsterdam.*

April 16

Here, in the centre of Amsterdam, I have fallen in love with water all over again. The awful grey sea is behind us – that belittling sea and the docks with their ugly rustiness – and water is 'civic' again. Civic. Civil. Civilised. I prefer Nature under control: not mountains and oceans but, as here, the pleasing and useful canals that pull down strips of the sky onto themselves. Just enough sky to make you forget its vastness and enable you to say 'It's a beautiful day' without so much as looking up into the endless blue of it.

I once saw a very beautiful Japanese film in which those who died had to decide on the moment from their life that they wished to become their eternity. One such moment that I would give serious thought to happened this morning: we stood in the centre of a bridge over the Herengracht, the spring sunshine on our faces, our arms around each other's waists, enjoying the beautiful houses on either side and laughing at a little white cloud going for a swim in the canal.

Simona Luff, Diary (2006)

Must see

Who better to introduce us to the 'sights' of Amsterdam than world-famous travel writer Geert Mak. His Amsterdam: A Brief Life of the City is an absolute must for anyone seriously interested in the place. Like many great cities, Amsterdam constitutes "a small nation inside a larger one", but is unlike so many others, says Mak, in being relatively 'unmonumental'.

Amsterdam is a city, but it is also a country by itself, a small nation inside a larger one. Moreover it is a city that spreads out progressively across the country. For a first impression it is best, as always, to drop in on the neighbours for a cup of coffee. Foreigners are often more interested in us Amsterdammers than we are in ourselves, decent and modest as we are. […]

Amsterdam […] is almost an anti-monument turned flesh. The city tried once to express its wealth and its power in a building but that was bargained away to the royal court in the Hague. The architecture of prestige has largely passed

Amsterdam by, apart from the Rijksmuseum and the Palace of People's Industry, although the latter burned to the ground in 1929. In the late twentieth century, the combination of Town Hall and opera house resulted in a massive, cumbersome building – the Stopera – born out of thriftiness and with all the grandeur of an Ikea chair. The modern business district, which lacks the least display of planning vision, is hidden away on the south-eastern outskirts of the city.

For some reason, monumental buildings do not work in Amsterdam. Whether such buildings are the result of the plan to lure the Olympic Games to the city, or of the plan to make the banks of the IJ (an arm of the IJsselmeer) something that would be noticed abroad, or of the town-hall-and-opera idea which brought about the Stopera, the city's answer is nothing but mockery and sniggering. The monumentality of Amsterdam exists only in the heads of its inhabitants, not on the streets.

Amsterdam is not proud; indeed, it is even unproud in a proud sort of way. The wealthiest Amsterdammers have clung stubbornly to the sobriety of their seventeenth-century forefathers, with the result that a cityscape has emerged untouched by the grandeur of absolutism, and uncut by the broad avenues which might have been driven through the city in the nineteenth century. Even the proud Amsterdam of the Golden Age was, in its time and according to the norms of the day, the very anti-image of a modern city: traditional in outlook, oriented towards individual citizens rather than a powerful aristocracy. Its wealth has always been quiet and discreet. There is a direct line from the eighteenth-century "Widow Pels on the Herengracht", who, although the richest inhabitant of the Amsterdam of her day, employed no more than five servants, to the senior manager from the city who recently asked in a weekly magazine whether the KLM airline could not tone down the service in its Business Class a little: "A cheese sandwich and a glass of milk are more than enough as far as I am concerned."

The explanation for the modesty of this civic pride lies in the simple fact that Amsterdam has already existed for a very long time as a city state, and the quiet self-assurance our medium-sized European city derives from this fact is not to be underestimated. Amsterdammers, in other words, have for centuries felt no need of boastful tombs, palaces, statues, avenues.

Geert Mak, *Amsterdam: A Brief Life of the City* (1995)
translated from the Dutch by Philipp Blom

✳ ✳ ✳

For a first quick tour of the city we join first-time Amsterdam visitor Kelvin Whalley and his wife as they give in to the temptation to join the locals and get on those bikes ...

The first thing that strikes you about the city is the vast number of push bikes. Every road has a cycle lane. Every set of traffic lights has a separate symbol dedicated to cycles and every lamp post and railing has an abundance of bikes chained to it. The ringing of cycle bells is everywhere.

After breakfast on our first full day, we caught the tram to Dam Square where the dam in the river Amstel was constructed, giving the city its name. In the square is the National Monument built in 1956 to honour those who perished in World War II. Walking down Raadhuisstraat toward the Anne Frank House, the variety of people cycling past was both surprising and entertaining. Business men in suits with black leather brogues, secretaries in smart attire and stilettos, mothers towing toddlers in trailers, workmen with tool boxes attached displaying their trade, young couples sharing one bike ... Then, seeing streams of yellow bikes in convoy on a guided tour, we decided to hire bikes ourselves.

Mounting a bike for the first time in twenty years, I decided we should get up our confidence in a deserted car park. But, like swimming, cycling is something you never really forget, and we were soon ready to join the army of cyclists on the streets.

To combat cycle theft most Amsterdammers ride vintage models of the "Mary Poppins" type with proper mudguards and a basket on the handlebars. These old bikes are of little value to a thief. Our hired bikes were of a similar style: no gears required, no hills to climb. Built on reclaimed marshland, Amsterdam is very flat, its many canals earning it the label "the Venice of the North".

Although you can't let your attention wander too much in Amsterdam's traffic, we did begin to get the general feel of the city, stopping now and then to consult the guide book, discovering, for example, the rationale behind the design of those characteristic Amsterdam houses – most of which are joined together, like English terraces. A tax used to be levied on each house dependent on its width. Because of this, most of the old houses are very narrow and tall, with three or four floors, the smallest house being just two metres wide. A hoist positioned on the outside wall above the upstairs window allows furniture to be winched into the house via the façade, the stairs being too narrow.

When we finally turned towards the Red Light District, I got off the bike, intending to meander along and maybe glance in the odd window and smile at the ladies behind the glass. My wife, however, had other ideas. She pedalled swiftly past the windows, forcing me to jog to keep up. I tried to explain I was just curious to sample the diverse cultural nuances that make Amsterdam simultaneously traditional and racy ...

Consulting the map we headed next for the Vondel Park in the Museum Quarter. Named after a famous Dutch poet, it was used in the late 60s as an open-air dormitory by followers of the flower-power cult. Today, the park is a haven for buskers, skaters, joggers and of course an abundance of cyclists. No lycra shorts or brightly-coloured helmets, just hundreds of old bikes being ridden by ordinary folk. Mounting her metal stallion, my wife blended in and moved as one body with the other riders. I, on the other hand, laden with rucksack and carrier bag, wobbled somewhat, nearly causing a pile-up. If she was riding a stallion, then I was on a donkey! We stopped at the Film Museum within the park where we ate lunch al fresco, on the terrace, studying the map over our cappuccinos and planning the next stage of our route.

From the balcony of our hotel room that evening, we looked out over the city. Coloured lights danced on the canals as the pleasure cruisers continued their perfectly choreographed movements and we recalled the high points of our day. Cycling around Amsterdam had enabled us to see far more than would have been possible on foot. An added bonus: with no time for shopping, the contents of my wallet were still intact … I slept well that night.

Kelvin Whalley, 'Cycling Amsterdam' (2009)

❊ ❊ ❊

As we move through the winter-time city with the protagonist of The Apothecary's House, *we catch a glimpse of some well-known Amsterdam sights.*

Outside, the Entrepotdok canal was frozen hard, scattered and skidmarked with slats and splinters of ice where kids had thrown them. She tugged her black woollen beret down over her ears, did up the top toggle on her navy duffel coat and blew into the conch of her cupped hands.

At one end of the road was the long façade of the Oranje-Nassau barracks, at the other the square tower of the General Union of Diamond Workers.

Apart from a muddy salted channel on the pavement, a glassy crust of snow clung everywhere. She made a small geisha shuffling motion on the sea salt, then headed off.

Opposite the Hortus Botanicus, the entrance to the Wertheimpark. Two winged, smiling sphinxes, each with an iron lantern poised above its head. On the spur of the moment, she slipped in and jogged along the winding gravel paths, from which the snow had melted away. She touched her toes, clapped her hands together and slapped her sides. She trotted past the glass memorial, 'Nooit Meer Auschwitz', and round the ugly dry fountain, a brown marble column rising out of a dish on legs. [...]

A number fourteen tram trundled up to its stop. She boarded, gripped her coat sleeve and rubbed a porthole into the miasma of human breath on the window to watch the familiar landmarks roll by: the unremarkable modern Stopera concert hall, the flamboyant Blauwbrug bridge, the Rembrandtsplein – seedy but endearing – and the bleak wind-tunnel of Rokin, leading up to old Dam Square.

When they reached Mint Tower, where the Singel and Amstel rivers met, there was a sharp explosive crack. The tram jumped a few centimetres sideways and came to a rough, shuddering halt. A fat woman lurched forward over the wheels of a pushchair and bumped her head on a handrail. The baby in the pushchair began bawling. The driver clambered down and inspected the wheels of the tram, the trolley boom and overhead power cables. [...]

'You might as well all get off,' said the driver. 'We're not going anywhere now.'

Ruth lived on a houseboat in the Jordaan. The walk was not unwelcome. She set off through the shopping precinct of Kalverstraat, then took a left – on impulse – into the maze of transverse side streets, away from the Saturday throng, the clearance sales, the piped music and the aromas of coffee, hot chestnuts and warm poppy-seed bread.

She thought she knew Amsterdam, but it was precisely at such moments of unshakeable conviction that the city sprang its surprises – and now was no exception.

She came out onto an unfamiliar street corner, where a busy 'brown' café, its windows plastered with ads for Hoegaarden,

Grolsch, Ridder and Kriek, plied its trade beside a humpback bridge. Here, in the hot heart of the city, the waters of the canal had not yet curdled and clotted into ice. The sky was marbled with the tints of encroaching night: lavender, foxglove, heather, amaranth. The colours ran down and soaked into the deep mulberry shadows of basements and alleyways.

The old-fashioned street lamps flamed into life as she stood there. Instead of chasing them, the intimate artificial light lent greater depth and secrecy to the shadows. A festive arch of light bulbs tripped on along the lower rim of the bridge, forming a flaming circus hoop with its swaying reflection in the canal.

Ruth hesitated a moment and tried to get her bearings.

Adrian Mathews, *The Apothecary's House* (2005)

✳ ✳ ✳

And now for the beautiful Vondel Park, in the company of Geert Mak, H. M. van den Brink, Chris Ewan, Martin Bril and Remco Campert.

Only the one part of the city escaped the blandness of most nineteenth-century developments: the area around the Vondel Park. When the Plantage recreation ground was swept away to make way for houses, members of the Stock Exchange and bankers set up a fund for the establishment of a large, new park. The Vondel Park would enable Amsterdam once again to compete with other great cities. The founding fathers, however, had bought far more land than was needed for the park, in order to finance it with the profit from selling the unused ground. When this land was auctioned off, the same restrictions were applied as during the building of the canal belt: private individuals were permitted to use it as building ground, as long a no worker's lodgings or factories were built on it. Thus, another area of the city came into being, a spacious area of stately villas, intersected by quiet, broad and shady avenues, the Vondelstraat and especially the Willemsparkweg, the beginnings of what was to become Amsterdam Oud-Zuid. Important institutions found their home in this semi-rural environment: the Manege (1881), the Concertgebouw (1883), and the Rijksmuseum (1885), this last being, quite literally, the gateway to another world.

Geert Mak, *Amsterdam: A Brief Life of the City* (1995)
translated from the Dutch by Philipp Blom

✽ ✽ ✽

Summer began early that year and, though we didn't know it yet, was to last an infinity. On one of the first warm days, a Sunday, my reconnoitring took me in the direction of his house. I knew where it was, in a street by the park, close to one of the richly decorated entrances, and I'd noted down the number of the house. The fine weather had lured the inhabitants of the town into the park and they were still there now, as evening fell, in large numbers. No longer as they had been earlier in the day, amusing themselves exuberantly, pushing each other and commenting excitedly, as though the sun were a special offer, an exceptional bargain in the sales that would never be repeated. By now, the mood on the paths had become sedate. People were still walking around enjoying themselves, but through it all a deep weariness was also perceptible. Walking sticks tapped. There was the crunch of a pram. Voices were hushed. It had been almost too much, a day off and marvellous weather into the bargain. A brass band played waltzes under a white dome and now even the waltzes seemed tired and sluggish.

I entered the park on the eastern side, close to a tram stop, and hesitated to leave it again. I thought that the light would stay longer in the wide avenues outside than here under the dark-green leaves. I sought out the tall trees, avoiding the open lawns and meadows, walking along the edges of the park. Only when I saw the lamps lighting up did I walk outside again and then I was immediately in the street where David lived. No more than a few metres from his house.

All the houses here were tall and imposing. Those on the park side were also wide, with verandas and wooden extensions, and some even had little fairy-tale towers. On the other side of the street, however, the houses formed a closed front and had grey steps and white ornaments. They differed from each other in those ornaments: sometimes tableaux of tiles containing a reference to the profession of the resident, but the houses also showed in the way in which the bricks were joined that they were there in the first instance for their own benefit and for that of their residents, not to serve a greater whole. Often two or three were built in the same manner, but undoubtedly not because the design of the street required it. It was rather as if in their occasional uniformity they were giving a polite nod to each other or offering a small token of respect. Those who lived here did so because this dignity suited them like a coat designed especially for them. And just as happens with good clothes, the dignity of the buildings reflected on the residents. That was how you achieved harmony – not through forced uniformity, but through an intimate embrace of differences. In all its variety, this street seemed to have a greater unity than ours, where you couldn't guess who belonged behind which house front. Where it didn't matter.

In the monumental villas which adjoined the park, the lamps had already been lit. I walked further into the street. The light hadn't lasted longer there than in the park, but the heat had. The stones retained it better than the grass and the trees. The grey granite of the steps and doorways especially still glowed with the heat. A church bell rang. I looked up at the spires. It was half past eight. I stopped opposite David's house, under the overhanging branches of a large tree. Anyone looking out of the windows of the first floor in the summer would scarcely realize that they lived in town, the covering of foliage was so thick and extensive. The windows of the house were mirror-smooth and dark. I tried to imagine what the rooms looked like. The lamps, the paintings in their sparkling frames on the walls, the gleaming table and the comfortable chairs and sofas on their islands of Persian carpet. The stairwell with its thick red carpet and yet the echo of marble floors and tall white walls. The garden behind the house on to which David's bedroom would look out, with gravel paths, box hedges, large roses and white hydrangeas at the corners, and at the back perhaps, yes almost certainly, a green summerhouse with a slate roof, for the pleasure and amusement of his elder sister. Those born here had no need to fear anything.

H.M. van den Brink, *On the Water* (1998)
translated from the Dutch by Paul Vincent

✳ ✳ ✳

Even though it was a weekday afternoon in winter, the park was still busy. People on rollerblades and rusting bicycles zipped past me, couples strolled along arm-in-arm, groups of back-packers sat together on rucksacks, smoking candy-smelling joints, and the occasional freak show walked by – one girl had her face pierced with countless metal rivets and the man she was with wore nothing more to protect himself from the cold than a pair of fishnet stockings and a leather jockstrap.

I dragged my weary bones as far as the Blue Tea House, where I took an outside table, settled into a rubber-strung chair and ordered a Koffie Verkeerd. I smoked some more of my cigarettes and drank my coffee, letting the caffeine and nicotine and the icy breeze battle against my fatigue and the sore ache in my eyes. Then I ordered a second coffee and sat there drinking it and smoking another ciga-rette until finally the chill and the nicotine became too much for me and I buried my hands in my pockets and continued my walk.

I walked right around the perimeter of the park and it took me close to an hour. By that time my toes were feeling the cold too and my nose had started to numb. My mind felt clearer, though, and I seemed about as awake as I was likely to get.

Chris Ewan, *The Good Thief's Guide to Amsterdam* (2007)

* * *

We found ourselves in the Vondel Park for the Saint Maarten celebrations, where several hundred children and their parents were following a silent man who, wearing a dark cloak and riding a slowly swaying horse, represented the saint.

It was the first time we had gone electric. Our lantern – a construction made of milk cartons, iron wire and crepe paper – hung from a plastic rod with a Duracel battery inside the handle and a cord at the end from which a fresh bulb dangled.

You just hook the lantern onto it.

The bulb inside did its work without flickering, smouldering or unexpectedly going out; let alone the whole lantern going up in flames in a gust of wind, something that any normal child should experience at least once. Now that we had gone electric, it was no longer a possibility.

Progress.

There were still some acoustic lanterns, if you want to call them that, but looking at the parents squatting in the damp grass fiddling around with matches to try to get them going, you could see that they would be going electric next year too. Hard to say whether we watched them with malicious pleasure or admiration.

Nostalgia.

That much was sure.

Martin Bril, *Show-window Legs* [*Etalagebenen*] (1998)
translated from the Dutch by Michele Hutchison

* * *

It was busy in the park. Naturally there were a lot of mothers with high wheeled prams, in which the babies weren't visible, unfortunately, or fortunately – you couldn't tell, wrapped as they were from head to toe in knitted outfits despite the heat, and buried under fluffy covers, and further obscured from passing baby enthusiasts by rattles, cuddly toys and bags of sweets. The mothers of the babies were wearing floral dresses and white shoes and carrying large imitation-leather bags. The fathers were absent in spirit and sometimes physically as well.

There were ageing couples too, who had sought to make new acquaintances by means unaccustomed to them – replies in confidence – and succeeded. They included nurses, former revue stars, retired builders and members of religious sects.

Between the adults, children with grazed knees and an untamed scruffy look chased around, trying to tackle each other to the ground. The newly-besotted and the long-engaged, having no place of their own, lay down on the grass, felt their clothing pinch, and uttered long sighs. Stray cats crouched in the bushes, prowling for sparrows and loose shoelaces.

Goggle-eyed families hawked documents written in curiously wooden language, announcing the end of the world. A mentally handicapped boy with a sloping head full of brackish water, unzipped his flies in front of a litter bin with faltering, jerky movements and kept the park tidy by peeing into it.

Underneath a weeping willow next to yet another pond, Panda descried two American soldiers on leave. They wore red and green checked shirts and light green trousers. They leaned against the trunk of the weeping willow and gazed out to sea. No one had wanted to paint them like that since the overrated Van Gogh had caused European painting to take a wrong turn. Now the sunlight added gleaming accents to their cropped corn-coloured hair with the hand of an old master, and the half empty whisky bottle resting in the grass at their feet was a beautiful example of illumination. A duck, descending for a moment before rising again, left an unreadable and immediately erased signature on the wet paint surface of the water.

Remco Campert, *Life is Deeeluscious* [*Het leven is vurrukkulluk*] (1992)
translated from the Dutch by Michele Hutchison

✳ ✳ ✳

*And for those who love city markets, Dubravka
Igresic suggests something for your itinerary.*

The Albert Cuyp Market is the largest and most famous in
Amsterdam. It is located in the Pijp, a former working-class
district. Its stalls, of which there are said to be over three
hundred, come out every morning and don't come down until
late in the afternoon. The idea of buying fish, fruit or vegetables was only a rational cover for the vague magnetism that
would draw me towards the market, engulfed as it was in a
mist of pollen and the strong scents of spices from beyond the
seas – cinnamon, cloves, nutmeg – shot through with wind and
salt. The air fairly sparkled with the bolts of rich silk and thick
plush, of exotic jewels, of gold and beads, of the mother-of-
pearl of immodestly open shells, of the glittering silver of fresh
fish. The apples in my marketplace had a golden lustre all their
own; each grape glowed like a tiny lantern; the milk was as rich
and white as a Vermeer woman's skin.

There were times, however, when the magnetism lost its
force, when a dead fish lay heavy on the stand and the apples,
though still red, and the lettuces, though still green, had lost
their sheen. There were seedy vendors of cheap clothing, the
air around them electrified by the synthetic fabrics; vendors
of bric-à-brac one would be hard put to find names for: cloths
that might be dusters, plastic brushes of various shapes and
sizes, nylon chignons in all colours, wooden backscratchers
with plastic fingers, packaged snack foods; vendors of soap,
shampoo, face cream, shabby handbags, artificial flowers,
shoulder pads, patches, needles and thread, pillows and blan-
kets, prints and frames, hammers and nails, sausage and cheese,
chickens and pheasants, moth-eaten scarves ...

Wandering among the stands, my heart full of Gypsy
shrapnel, I chanced upon something that immediately caught

my eye: a plastic bag with red, white and blue stripes – Ana was right: I paid only two guilders for it – and like a wound-up mechanical toy, I made for the butcher's called Zuid, South, a code word to the local Yugos, who were its principal patrons. The butcher's window proudly displayed jars of pigs' knuckles, and the shelves were lined with a modest selection of Yugon-ostalgic delicacies: Macedonian ajvar, sausage from Srem, olive oil from Korcula, Plasma Biscuits (whose ridiculous name made them an instant cult item the moment they appeared on the market), Minas coffee (which of course came from Turkey) and Negro Chimney-Sweep toffee (it too a cult item because of the name). I bought a jar of ajvar and some toffee. It was a ritual purchase, purely symbolic: I hated ajvar and the toffee was bitter.

> Dubravka Ugresic, *The Ministry of Pain* (2004)
> translated from the Croatian by Michael Henry Heim

✳ ✳ ✳

Kees 't Hart takes a trip down memory lane as he visits a recently refurbished Carré Theatre, twenty-five years after he used to work at the famous establishment ... when conditions were very different.

A listless river flows between me and the theatre. The remains of a complex of locks are visible in the middle of the water: a couple of piers, green huts, the wooden spokes of ancient wheels that were used long ago to open and close the now absent sluice gates. The theatre is a radiant white cake, a pink blush blustering through the white. It was recently refurbished. The name was stuck in large red letters to the side of a structure on the edifice's massive curved roof. I used to live to the rear of the place, in the attic of a house that can't be seen from here, but then it was a dilapidated building with a dirty white facade, bare and musty dressing rooms, and a backstage stench of horse manure.

Twenty-five years ago, when I had a temporary contract with the revue, the administrative offices were housed in the two canal-side houses to the right of the theatre where I collected my wages every Wednesday between eleven and twelve in a room that could only be reached via a maze of corridors, stairs and doors. De Miranda led the way the first time and pointed out where the director had his office, behind a glass door in a room with brown chairs and posters of famous magicians. The room had a large window that looked out onto the river. He's often there on paydays, he said, and you can always stop for a chat. We're one big family here and everybody's welcome, take it from me. The secretariat was a brightly lit room with uncomfortable wicker chairs, which I didn't dare use at first. Our wages were distributed in brown envelopes.

A bateau mouche murmurs past, water splashes restlessly against the bank. I pick up the plastic bag I had rested between my feet and walk towards the antique white drawbridge nearby. The floorboards bob up and down when cars drive over it. I recognise nothing. There are only a few boats left where there used to be many more, and the riverside houses have been smartened up. I'm afraid someone will see me. I steal past the theatre, past a circus poster and one of a dancing, short-haired woman holding a luminous white violin. I hesitate in front of the glass entrance doors, which are flanked on either side by pillars bearing masks of laughing and crying faces. I press my face against the glass. The floor of the reception hall is tiled with shiny reddish-brown marble. Nothing has changed. In the background, the corridor embracing the auditorium also looks the same. I continue on my way, past the buildings that used to house the administrative offices of the revue, past the basement eatery and the concrete office block on the corner. It has moss on its walls. I cross the street, to the café.

Kees 't Hart, *The Revue* [*De revue*] (1999)
translated from the Dutch by Brian Doyle

* * *

One of Amsterdam's most popular tourist destinations is the Anne Frank House. We accompany three overseas visitors, each with their own particular 'take' on the experience – Indian writer and journalist Salil Tripathi, Spanish politician and writer César Antonio Molina, and American satirist David Sedaris.

Anne Frank's story is now a legend. A child in a close-knit family, forced to live in hiding for years, unable even to step out and play, she had kept a diary in which she wrote of her hope in humanity. Her house, facing the canal, is now a museum.

I recall walking through its corridors, looking at pin-up photographs of the film stars young Anne had stuck on a wall. There is a half-finished board game, which she may very likely have played. Her handwriting can be seen in notebooks and pads. It begins as a lazy scrawl, but grows into a solid firmness which, while not necessarily calligraphic, certainly looks determined and cursive: the way a teenage girl would write in a journal she hopes only she would read. We do this; we know friends who do this, and then discover those adolescent fantasies decades later, while clearing an attic. In Anne's case, she didn't live long enough to rediscover her writing.

There is an ordinariness about her house, its quotidian nature, which makes the experience chilling. There is a banality about that street, but as Hannah Arendt was to say when Adolf Eichmann went on trial in Jerusalem, there is banality in evil, too.

The real horror about Anne is that her home does not stand out in any way, just the way the Jewish community was apparently integrated in pre-war Amsterdam. Looking identical to other houses from the outside, the view you get from inside is quite different. In a brilliantly conceived part of the museum, I see a tall window, and I see outside a tranquil canal, its water turning dark, and a few pedestrians walking by. A cyclist moves past, clad in a glowing leotard, pedalling furiously, as if late for a yoga class. But take several steps back from the window and the translucent screen turns opaque, and you see the scene as Anne would have seen it. Suddenly the colours disappear and a hazy greyness covers the window now, and you see a large, black-and-white image of goose-stepping Nazi troops. It is a frozen frame, meant to shock, and the black-and-white imaging accentuates the sharpness of the tragedy.

Almost everyone I see in the museum is moved; nobody speaks. This is the story of one family, but that family has become the microcosm of what visited millions of families, in different ways.

Anne Frank has a way of emerging in Dutch debates, rattling Dutch conscience at odd, unexpected times. Amsterdam is a tolerant city, with its cafés selling drugs openly, and its red light area legal and safe. And yet, in 2004, film-maker Theo van Gogh was murdered by a Dutch-born Muslim of Moroccan origin, because the assassin was upset over a film he made which was critical of Islam's treatment of women. Ayan Hirsi Ali, a Somali immigrant and later Dutch parliamentarian, had written the script.

For her outspokenness, Hirsi Ali, too, faced the death threat. She got protection initially, but after the government found that she had misrepresented her history while seeking refuge in the Netherlands, the authorities threatened to take away her citizenship (which refugee does not lie about her – or his – past?). Hirsi Ali left the Netherlands for the US (she is now back in Europe), pointedly reminding the Dutch that they had let down another young woman –Anne Frank – half a century ago.

Salil Tripathi, 'Visiting the Anne Frank House' (2008)

❖ ❖ ❖

After crossing the bridge over the Keizersgracht canal, behind the Prinsengracht which leads to Anne's house, we saw a monument to persecuted homosexuals: a breakwater in the shape of a triangle. The girl (I still hadn't asked her name) pointed out the Westerkerk tower. 'It's the tallest in Amsterdam. I think it's about ninety metres high.' I looked up at the small dome; a lightning rod and weather vane rose above it. 'It was the only thing Anne and Peter could see through the skylight in the attic at the back part of the house. That great swathe of sky, and the clouds revelling in their freedom.' [...]

Anne's house, silent and closed for the night, lay in front of us. The queue of people hoping to visit had turned back towards Westermarkt. A guard told us that the staff entrance was at number ten. We went to look for it and, at number six, found a plaque saying that the French philosopher René Descartes had stayed there for a year in 1634. It quoted a letter that he sent to Balzac [i.e. Jean Louis Guez de Balzac] in 1631: '*Quel autre pays ou l'on puisse jour d'une liberté si entière*' ('In what other country can one find so complete a freedom?') The plaque was dated 1920, so the Frank family, or at least the father Otto, must have read it. At the porter's lodge they confirmed my name and told me that the director was coming to greet me and accompany me on my visit. [...] Director Jan Erik was a charming young man. He took me from the foundation headquarters, a modern neighbouring building, into the house. We passed by the last visitors on their way out and as we went up the floors our solitude became more and more noticeable. The storeroom, Otto's private study where they listened to the radio and where Anne sometimes wrote her *Diary*, the kitchen, the revolving bookshelf that was a hidden entrance into the house behind, and now the bedrooms. There were the marks on the wall that Anne and her sister Margot had made to measure how much they had grown and some photos of film stars which she had stuck on the walls of the room that she shared with Fritz. Jan Erik left me alone. Everything was quiet, the sink and the blue Delft ceramic toilet were the only furniture.

Through half-drawn blinds which opened onto a large interior patio, I saw the sway of a centuries-old oak tree and heard the rustle of its branches just as they must have seen and heard them.

César Antonio Molina, *Waiting for Years Past* (2007)
translated from the Spanish by Kit Maude

✳ ✳ ✳

On our first afternoon we took a walk and came across the Anne Frank House, which was a surprise. I'd had the impression she lived in a dump, but it's actually a very beautiful seventeenth-century building right on the canal. Tree-lined street, close to shopping and public transportation: in terms of location, it was perfect. My months of house hunting had caused me to look at things in a certain way, and on seeing the crowd gathered at the front door, I did not think, *Ticket line*, but, *Open house!*

We entered the annexe behind the famous bookcase, and on crossing the threshold, I felt what the grandmother had likened to being struck by lightning, an absolute certainty that this was the place for me. That it would be mine. The entire building would have been impractical and far too expensive, but the part where Anne Frank and her family had lived, their triplex, was exactly the right size and adorable, which is something they never tell you. In plays and movies it always appears drab and old ladyish, but open the curtains and the first words that come to mind are not "I still believe all people are really good at heart" but "Who do I have to knock off in order to get this apartment?" That's not to say that I wouldn't have made a few changes, but the components were all there and easy to see, as they'd removed the furniture and personal possessions that normally make a room seem just that much smaller.

Hugh stopped to examine the movie-star portraits glued to Anne Frank's bedroom wall – a wall that I personally would have knocked down – and I raced on to the bathroom, and then to the water closet with its delft toilet bowl looking for all the world like a big soup tureen. Next it was upstairs to the kitchen, which was eat-in with two windows. I'd get rid of the countertop and of course redo all the plumbing, but first I'd yank out the wood stove and reclaim the fireplace. "That's your focal point, there," I heard the grandmother saying. I thought the room beside the kitchen might be my office, but then I saw the attic, with its charming dormer windows, and the room beside the kitchen became a little leisure nook.

Now it was downstairs for another look at the toilet bowl, then back upstairs to reconsider the kitchen countertop, which, on second thought, I decided to keep. Or maybe not. It was hard to think with all these people coming and going, hogging the stairwell, running their mouths. A woman in a Disneyland sweatshirt stood in the doorway taking pictures of my sink, and I intentionally bumped her arm so that the prints would come out blurry and undesirable. "Hey!" she said.

"Oh, 'Hey' yourself." I was in a fever, and the only thing that mattered was this apartment. It wasn't a celebrity or a historical thing, not like owning one of Maria Callas's eyelashes or a pair of barbecue tongs once brandished by Pope Innocent XIII. Sure, I'd *mention* that I was not the first one in the house to ever keep a diary, but it wasn't the reason I'd fallen in love with the place. At the risk of sounding too koombaya, I felt as if I had finally come home. A cruel trick of fate had kept me away, but now I was back to claim what was rightfully mine. It was the greatest feeling in the world: excitement and relief coupled with the giddy anticipation of buying stuff, of making everything just right.

I didn't snap out of it until I accidentally passed into the building next door, which has been annexed as part of the museum. Above a display case, written across the wall in huge, unavoidable letters, was this quote by Primo Levi: "A single Anne Frank moves us more than the countless others who suffered just as she did but whose faces have remained in the shadows. Perhaps it is better that way. If we were capable of taking in all the suffering of all those people, we would not be able to live."

He did not specify that we would not be able to live *in her house*, but it was definitely implied, and it effectively squashed any fantasy of ownership. The added tragedy of Anne Frank is that she almost made it, that she died along with her sister just weeks before their camp was liberated. Having already survived two years in hiding, she and her family might have stayed put and lasted out the war were it not for a neighbour, never identified, who turned them in. I looked out the window, wondering who could have done such a thing, and caught my reflection staring back at me.

David Sedaris, *Dress Your Family in Corduroy and Denim* (2004)

✳ ✳ ✳

Some observations on the old Jewish Quarter from Ian Buruma.

On the far side of the Nieuwmarkt is an old section of the city whose narrow, densely populated streets were once lined with higgledy-piggledy row houses, some dating back to the early seventeenth century. Almost all those houses are gone now, replaced by buildings of the 1980s, whose slick white modernity makes them stand out in the historic heart of Amsterdam. It used to be known as the *jodenhoek*, Jews' corner. [...]

This part of the city, with its seventeenth-century Portuguese and German synagogues and its lively street markets, had long been populated by Jews, most of them poor. Rembrandt lived there too, however, and picked the models for his biblical paintings from the streets around his studio. Before the German occupation more than eighty thousand Jews resided in Amsterdam. By the end of the war about five thousand had survived.

After the last cattle train to "the east" had left in 1943, the *jodenhoek* was like a ghost town. The houses, emptied of their inhabitants, had been looted for wood to stoke the fires of Amsterdammers during the icy "hunger winter" of 1944–45. And so for three decades after the war they remained, gutted and increasingly falling apart, often with the Jewish family names of abandoned shops still faintly showing on crumbling walls. Many of the houses were later demolished, leaving large gaps filled with rubbish. People preferred not to think about the reasons for this urban ruination. The remains of a human catastrophe were simply left to rot. The few houses that were still there in the 1970s were taken over by young squatters, until, finally, around 1974, the last remnants of the *jodenhoek* were swept away to build an underground railway station and a new opera house.

But first the squatters had to be removed from their improvised homes. What followed was a kind of grotesque re-enactment of the historic drama. Not that the Dutch police, using batons and waterhoses to flush out the squatters, had anything in common with the Nazis, or that the squatters were destined to be murdered. It was just that the spectacle of uniformed men dragging people from their homes, while we watched the action behind fortified barriers, conjured up images I had only seen in blurry photographs taken on that very spot three decades before.

Before remembering the Holocaust, in memorials and textbooks, became an almost universal Western ritual in the late 1960s, only two monuments in the *jodenhoek* stood as reminders of what happened there. One, a relief in white stone, was erected in 1950. It is called the monument of "Jewish Gratitude" – gratitude to the Dutch people who stood by the Jewish victims. The other, built two years later, is a sculpture of a burly workingman, with his head held high, and his meaty arms and large proletarian fists spread in a gesture of angry defiance. The Dockworker is a monument to the two-day "February Strike" of 1941, when Amsterdam stopped working in protest against the deportation of 425 Jewish men to a concentration camp. The men had been brutally rounded up in plain sight of many gentiles shopping at the popular Sunday market. Word spread quickly: city cleaners refused to collect garbage, mail was not delivered, trams stopped running, and the port of Amsterdam was silent for forty-eight hours.

Ian Buruma, *Murder in Amsterdam* (2006)

✽ ✽ ✽

The experience of the Jewish population in Amsterdam over the centuries has been a mixed one, ranging from freedom from persecution (when persecution was the norm elsewhere in Europe) to the tragic elimination of a huge percentage of the city's Jewish residents during the Nazi Occupation. In Stav Sherez's novel, The Devil's Playground, *the protagonist visits the city's wonderful Jewish Museum. (Visitors should also try to see the famous Portuguese Synagogue.)*

The rain stopped as he wound through the thin, clasping alleys of the red-light district, avoiding the hustlers and early-morning wrecks. Out of an alley he emerged into the sudden explosion of space that is Nieuwmarkt. He had to stop, take in the space, the open vista stretching across the square. Out of the dark huddle and into the light. He lit a cigarette and stared at the Waag, the weigh-house that looked like a medieval castle, almost arbitrarily located at the centre of the square. He looked around. It was early, the city, sleepy and slow, was still shuttered and shrouded in the aching movement of waking. The cobblestoned and unadorned square was empty, stretching beyond the Waag and to the tall buildings on the other side. The castle with its round medieval towers, its slitted windows and garrets, seemed an afterthought, as if to compensate for the massive emptiness of the square. Here he could breathe, see the sky as more than a strip painted between roofs. He enjoyed standing around, no one to hassle him here, only a few feet from the district but also in another world.

The Jewish quarter lay to the east of the Waag, a long boulevard that wound down to the museum. He sat in a café, only just opening, the waitress bleary-eyed and tired, and ordered an espresso. He wanted to delay things for a bit. He knew the museum was waiting for him. [...]

He crossed the canal and headed towards the museum. Everything around him was new, the demolished medieval buildings of the Jewish Quarter nothing but unremembered ghosts. Everything modern and shiny. The massive buildings, the streets uncobbled now, the great white expanse of the Operahouse. He came to a stop by the black granite monument that stood at the edge of the land, almost dangling between the confluence of the wide, raging Amstel and the quiet Zwanenburgwal, the place where the city spills open. He stared up at it. The inscription in Hebrew and Dutch. The way the black reflected the scuzzy sun and the swirl of the canals behind it. It looked like a monolith from the film *2001*. Some pre-natural signifier stranded here in another empty square, the sterile, dead concrete fields of the Operahouse stretching out in every direction, bounded only by the restless canals and the memory of what used to be.

The Jewish Historical Museum had once been four separate synagogues, greatly frequented by the many Jews of Amsterdam. After the war, there being not many Jews left, the buildings lay empty until the 1980s where they were converted into one composite structure that now served as Amsterdam's memory of its Jews. Four synagogues, from the ancient stone of the Grote, built in 1671, to the stark brickwork of the Nieuwe, built a hundred years later, to the functional spaces of the extended gallery appended in 1987. All together now. Linked by a feat of architecture even more impressive for the fact that it was almost invisible. Four synagogues, merged and buttressed, under one roof, a sort of homogenizing of past and present, the kind of thing this city was so good at. [...]

He smiled, gave the old man the entrance fee and set off into the cool high-vaulted spaces of the museum.

He walked by the Torahs and scriptures as if they were alien relics, the strange backward language and tradition into which he had been only partly initiated. Nineteenth-century Passover tables, neat, exact and somehow sad, ensconced in their glass cages. The sun slanting in from above, illuminating great, huge, frazzled Bibles, mysterious marks etched into the parchment. [...]

He slowly and painstakingly read every piece of printed literature tacked up to explain the exhibits. He stared at the black ribbed shofars, like artefacts from an alien civilization, the gold menorahs, elegant and out of time. He knew that in this place he was a gentile, someone who needed interpretive guides for the objects on display, a stranger with no sense of God or belief, only a nagging curiosity as to what the objects were, their material meaning and function. He stared at the Tefillin, the small black boxes containing Bible verses that the reverent fastened to their left arm and forehead, straps of leather going round the skin like snakes. He understood little of the ritualistic artefacts on display, not having participated in such ceremonies, not knowing even what they signified in the minds of believers. He felt a little ashamed at his ignorance and was glad that he hadn't told the old man at the counter that he was Jewish. What if he'd asked him some innocent question? He would have been shown to be the impostor he now felt, someone who'd lost their right to claim their hidden heritage.

In the next room were ancient, gloomy canvases filled with huddled men from previous centuries. Even the bright halogens of the modern age were not enough to illuminate the dark-ness that surrounded them like soup, enclosing them in some terrible secret, so dark that it was hard to make out individual figures. Next to them lay fake Torah scrolls, made out of plastic, with a video monitor at their centre where the text should be. He stopped and stared, watching on the screen the old, liver-spotted hands of a man painstakingly scratching the strange figures that populated the scrolls, that mysterious writing, the dead traditions.

In the next room he saw the photos of people herded out of their houses and into the streets. Saw the misery and fear in their faces and knew he'd reached the Holocaust section. [...]

There were countless documents on display here, letters of transit, faked postcards from Auschwitz, children's identity cards, different types of yellow stars and bills of receipt for human cargo. The neat handwriting on the latter made him feel queasy. He wondered what it would be like to see your own name on one of those bills, a record of your slaughtered family, up for display now to anyone who paid the entrance fee. There was a certain intrusion of privacy inherent in such exhibitions, even if the people were all dead.

He came back to the first photo he'd seen, the one of the men lined up against the wall, and it seemed especially cruel to have fixed their images as such, their faces smeared with fear and anxiety. Surely these were once proud citizens who would have been aghast at the idea of being displayed in their moment of weakness.

The photograph had its own narrative thrust beyond and across the scene that it presented. The look on their faces and the abject way in which they stood against the paint-splattered wall told a story beyond that moment, no less horrifying than if they had chosen the next shot, the inevitable mound of bodies and smiling officers. These men died in their best suits, Jon thought, in the middle of the day and in front of a camera. In front of a fucking camera. [...]

At the end of the exhibit, on a small table, was an old leather-bound book of comments. Jon stepped up to it, wanting to write something, to make concrete his feelings but nothing came and instead he began flicking through the previous pages, reading the comments of other men and women who had passed through here. He deciphered handwriting that would flummox a cryptographer, skimmed through messages of hope and fear.

Stav Sherez, *The Devil's Playground* (2004)

✳ ✳ ✳

Finally, let's loiter on the Rozengracht for a while and maybe have our spirits well and truly lifted, like those of the anonymous man in this extract from Martin Bril's City Eyes *[Stadsogen], by the extraordinariness of the ordinary on the city's streets.*

The Rozengracht lay there like only the Rozengracht can. It was the end of the afternoon. To the west the sun was setting in the bend the De Clercqstraat takes to the right, the sky was as pink as candyfloss.

On the corner at the junction with the Akoleienstraat a man stood waiting. Just a normal man. He was wearing a raincoat and had a paper under his arm; he was forty or thereabouts.

He'd started by killing time looking at the Breitlings in the window of Jan Steen's jewellers, but now he had sauntered away from the shops and was gazing down the short street.

At the end of it there was a narrow, dilapidated building, its doors clad in graffiti. Above it on the façade, large white block letters spelled out RADIO & GRAMOPHONE FACTORY. The letters hadn't been touched up for years. The weather had got to them, some were barely legible.

The man looked at his watch. A full tram 18 rattled past and stopped at the corner by the Marnixstraat. People got in and out. A few crossed over and walked towards the man, but the person he was waiting for wasn't amongst them. Two young women who passed him were discussing the fate of a mutual acquaintance. She'd just given birth.

'What was it actually?' one of them asked.

'A boy,' the man heard the other say.

'Cor. Great. What's his name?'

'Abel,' came the answer.

'Nice name,' the man just caught, and a smile played over his lips. He too was momentarily touched by the beauty of Abel's name.

An old Opel stopped on the other side of the street, outside the Persian supermarket 'Roze', next to the Roothaanhuis, where a young Russian woman who stank of sweat used to sell unbranded vodka, and a middle-aged woman got out. There was an uncanny moment of silence. 'Well, bye darling … ' the waiting man heard, loud and clear. And as the mother stepped onto the pavement, her son joined the traffic that was suddenly present and in full force.

The waiting man strolled a few feet towards the city centre. He looked at the Turkish delicacies in the window of Madurak patissiers, his gaze catching that of an old Turkish man who sat eating in the Hilal grill next door. Something connected the two men and an absolute peace reigned between them. Although it passed in the blink of an eye, it seemed to last an aeon.

It was, after Abel and the mysterious logic behind that moment of silence just now, already the third time the man had felt truly blessed in his waiting. All of his senses were alert. He heard the words 'I need to let that sink in for a while' from a passing cyclist with a mobile telephone.

And that was precisely how it was.

Martin Bril, *City Eyes* [*Stadsogen*] (1999)
translated from the Dutch by Michele Hutchison

Art seen in Amsterdam

*Along with Paris, Amsterdam is probably the North
European city most associated with painting. No visit
to the city is complete without a visit to the magnificent Rijksmuseum, Van Gogh Museum, the Stedlijk
Museum of modern art, and a quick look in at the
Rembrandthuis. But can we reach the true essence
of a city and culture through the images it creates of
itself in paint? Alain de Botton has some thoughts on
the subject in response to ideas expressed by the character Des Esseintes in French writer Joris-Karl Huys-
man's famous novel of 1884, À rebours.*

There was one other country that, many years before his
intended trip to England, Des Esseintes had wanted to see:
Holland. He had imagined the place to resemble the paintings
of Teniers and Jan Steen, Rembrandt and Ostade; he had antic-
ipated patriarchal simplicity and riotous joviality; quiet small

87

brick courtyards and pale-faced maids pouring milk. And so he had journeyed to Haarlem and Amsterdam – and been greatly disappointed. It was not that the paintings had lied, there had been some simplicity and joviality, some nice brick courtyards and a few serving women pouring milk, but these gems were blended in a stew of ordinary images (restaurants, offices, uniform houses and featureless fields) which these Dutch artists had never painted and which made the experience of travelling in the country strangely diluted compared with an afternoon in the Dutch galleries of the Louvre, where the essence of Dutch beauty found itself collected in just a few rooms.

Des Esseintes ended up in the paradoxical position of feeling more *in* Holland – that is, more intensely in contact with the elements he loved in Dutch culture – when looking at selected images of Holland in a museum than when travelling with sixteen pieces of luggage and two servants through the country itself.

Alain de Botton, *The Art of Travel* (2002)

✻ ✻ ✻

American Paul Auster's The Invention of Solitude *features both the Rijksmuseum and the Van Gogh Museum – the latter reminding the protagonist of his youth and the inspiration Van Gogh provided for his early poems. The reflections of his older self, however, are more sombre.*

He thinks, in particular, of a painting he saw on his trip to Amsterdam, *Woman in Blue*, which nearly immobilized him with contemplation in the Rijksmuseum. As one commentator has written: "The letter, the map, the woman's pregnancy, the empty chair, the open box, the unseen window – all are reminders or natural emblems of absence, of the unseen, of other minds, wills, times, and places, of past and future, of birth and perhaps of death – in general, of a world that extends beyond the edges of the frame, and of larger, wider horizons that encompass and impinge upon the scene suspended before our eyes. And yet it is the fullness and self-sufficiency of the present moment that Vermeer insists upon – with such conviction that its capacity to orient and contain is invested with metaphysical value."

Even more than the objects mentioned in this list, it is the quality of the light coming through the unseen window to the viewer's left that so warmly beckons him to turn his attention to the outside, to the world beyond the painting. A. stares hard at the woman's face, and as time passes he almost begins to hear the voice inside the woman's head as she reads the letter in her hands. She's so very pregnant, so tranquil in the immanence of motherhood, with the letter taken out of the box, no doubt being read for the hundredth time; and there, hanging on the wall to her right, a map of the world, which is the image of everything that exists outside the room: that light, pouring gently over her face and shining on her blue smock, the belly bulging with life, and its blueness bathed in luminosity, a light so pale it verges on whiteness. To follow with more of the same: *Woman Pouring Milk, Woman Holding a Balance, Woman Putting on Pearls, Young Woman at a Window with a Pitcher, Girl Reading a Letter at an Open Window.*

"The fullness and self-sufficiency of the present moment."

It was Rembrandt and Titus who in some sense lured A. to Amsterdam, where he then entered rooms and found himself in the presence of women (Vermeer's women, Anne Frank), his trip to that city was at the same time conceived as a pilgrimage to his own past. Again, his inner movements were expressed in the form of paintings: an emotional state finding tangible representation in a work of art, as though another's solitude were in fact the echo of his own.

In this case it was Van Gogh, and the new museum that had been built to house his work. Like some early trauma buried in the unconscious, forever linking two unrelated objects (this shoe is my father; this rose is my mother), Van Gogh's paintings stand in his mind as an image of his adolescence, a translation of his deepest feelings of that period. He can even be quite precise about it, pinpointing events and his reactions to events by place and time (exact locations, exact moments: year, month, day, even hour and minute). What matters, however, is not so much the sequence of the chronicle as its consequences, its permanence in the space of memory. To remember, therefore, a day in April when he was sixteen, and cutting school with the girl he had fallen in love with: so passionately and hopelessly that the thought of it still smarts. To remember the train, and then the ferry to New York (that ferry, which has long since vanished: industrial iron, the warm fog, rust), and then going to a large exhibition of Van Gogh paintings. To remember how he had stood there, trembling with happiness, as if the shared seeing of these works had invested them with the girl's presence, had mysteriously varnished them with the love he felt for her.

Some days later, he began writing a sequence of poems (now lost) based on the canvasses he had seen, each poem bearing the title of a different Van Gogh painting. These were the first real poems he ever wrote. More than a method for entering those paintings, the poems were an attempt to recapture the memory of that day. Many years went by, however, before he realized this. It was only in Amsterdam, studying the same paintings he had seen with the girl (seeing them for the first time since then – almost half his life ago), that he remembered having written those poems. At that moment the equation became clear to him: the act of writing as an act of memory. For the fact of the matter is, other than the poems themselves, he has not forgotten any of it.

Standing in the Van Gogh Museum in Amsterdam (December 1979) in front of the painting *The Bedroom*, completed in Arles, October 1838.

Van Gogh to his brother: "This time it is just simply my bedroom ... To look at the picture ought to rest the brain or rather the imagination ...

"The walls are pale violet. The floor is of red tiles.

"The wood of the bed and chairs is the yellow of fresh butter, the sheet and pillows very light lemon-green.

"The coverlet scarlet. The window green.

"The toilet table orange, the basin blue.

"The doors lilac.

"And that is all – there is nothing in this room with closed shutters ...

"This by way of revenge for the enforced rest I have been obliged to take ...

"I will make you sketches of the other rooms too some day."

As A. continued to study the painting, however, he could not help feeling that Van Gogh had done something quite different from what he thought he had set out to do. A.'s first impression was indeed a sense of calm, of "rest," as the artist describes it. But gradually, as he tried to inhabit the room presented on the canvas, he began to experience it as a prison, an impossible space, an image, not so much of a place to live, but of the mind that has been forced to live there. Observe carefully. The bed blocks one door, a chair blocks the other door, the shutters are closed: you can't get in, and once you are in, you can't get out. Stifled among the furniture and everyday objects of the room, you begin to hear a cry of suffering in this painting, and once you hear it, it does not stop. "I cried by reason of mine affliction ... " But there is no answer to this cry. The man in this painting (and this is a self-portrait, no different from a picture of a man's face, with eyes, nose, lips, and jaw) has been alone too much, has struggled too much in the depths of solitude. The world ends at that barricaded door. For the room is not a representation of solitude, it is the substance of solitude itself.

And it is a thing so heavy, so unbreatheable, that it cannot be shown in any terms other than what it is. "And that is all – there is nothing in this room with closed shutters ... "

Paul Auster, *The Invention of Solitude* (1982)

✳ ✳ ✳

In his introductory essay to American artists Ed Kien-holz and Nancy Reddin Kienholz's amazing 'Hoeren-gracht' installation (representing Amsterdam's red-light district) at London's National Gallery, Colin Wiggins gives us an insight into the hidden meanings of some of the great paintings of the Dutch Golden Age.

Amsterdam's red light district has been around for centuries. Early in the seventeenth century, after winning independence from the Catholic Spanish Hapsburg Empire, the Protestant United Provinces of the Netherlands rapidly established themselves as a major global power. Amsterdam became one of the biggest ports in Europe and all kinds of businesses prospered there, the respectable and the less so. This period of rapid expansion and prosperity is reflected in the artistic production of the time, which has become known as the Golden Age of Dutch painting. Although many grand paintings were made to decorate public buildings, the majority of the paintings were intended for intimate domestic settings. Portraits of newly prosperous burghers and views of native Dutch landscapes abounded, but detailed descriptions evoking everyday life – known as genre scenes – are perhaps the most distinctive feature of seventeenth-century Dutch painting. [...]

The subject of seduction or courtship was one of many standard themes for Dutch genre painters. Traditionally music was associated with love – young gentlemen or young ladies are regularly shown playing music to an attentive audience. These pleasantly romantic paintings were extremely popular among the picture-buying public of the time. Often artists would add little hints to their pictures that implied all was not as pure and morally correct as it might be. [...]

Steen's paintings are full of lewd jokes and puns. *The Interior of an Inn ('The Broken Eggs'* [c.1665–70]) is a tavern scene where a lively customer paws drunkenly at the skirt of a serving woman. The frying pan handle, the pipe, and the gesture of the man filling it are all crude indications of his intentions. The broken eggs and empty mussel shells that are liberally strewn about the floor are all indicative of a disorderly house and less-than-moral behaviour. [...]

The subject of prostitution crops up in quite surprising places. It is even found in the cool beauty of the Delft interiors of Johannes Vermeer. When we look into *A Young Woman seated at a Virginal* we see the lady at her keyboard with a viol-da-gamba placed in the foreground, turned towards the viewer. A picture hangs on the background wall – so far, so innocent. But the picture on the wall behind has other implications. It is a scene from a brothel: a leering man pays an old madam for the services of a much younger woman who plays a lute. Dirck van Baburen painted the original version of this painting and it seems likely that Vermeer, in his capacity as art-dealer, owned it for a time. Perhaps Vermeer's demure lady is inviting the viewer to take up the viol-da-gamba and perform with her. By placing Baburen's brothel scene right behind her, maybe Vermeer is suggesting that this performance might go beyond the merely musical.

Colin Wiggins, The Hoerengracht: Kienholz at the
National Gallery, London (2009)

❊ ❊ ❊

Deborah Moggach's novel Tulip Fever *shows us, as well as an obsession with the production of tulips, a seventeenth-century painter trying to paint the portrait of a well-healed Amsterdammer and his*

> *wife, such a portrait helping to establish that such a man has 'arrived', socially and (it being Amsterdam) commercially.*

'My hand should be here, on my hip?' Cornelis half turns towards the painter. His chest is thrust out and his other hand grasps his cane. He wears his brocade coat and black stove-pipe hat; he has combed his beard and waxed his moustache into points. Today he wears a ruff – deep and snowy white. It detaches his head from his body, as if it is being served on a platter. He is trying to conceal his excitement.

'You know the proverb, *you cannot dam a stream for the water gushes forth elsewhere*? Though we have whitewashed our churches, banning holy images from within them –' He inclines his head in my direction. 'Here I must beg my wife's pardon, for she is a Catholic – though our Reformed church has withdrawn its patronage from painters, their talent has bubbled up else-where and we are the beneficiaries, for they paint our daily life with a luminosity and loving attention to detail that – without being blasphemous – can border on the transcendental.'

The painter catches my eye. He raises his eyebrows and smiles. How dare he! I look away.

'Madam, please keep your head still,' he says.

We are being painted in my husband's library. The curtain is pulled back; sunlight streams into the room. It shines onto his cabinet of curiosities – fossils, figurines, a nautilus shell mounted on a silver plinth. The table, draped with a Turkey rug, carries a globe of the world, a pair of scales and a human skull. The globe represents my husband's trade, for he is a merchant. He owns a warehouse in the harbour; he imports grain from the Baltic and rare spices from the Orient. He sends shiploads of textiles to countries that are way beyond my small horizon. He is proud to display his wealth but also, like a good Calvinist, humbled by the transience of earthly riches – hence the scales, for the weighing of our sins on the Day of Judgment; hence the skull. *Vanity, vanity, all is vanity*. He wanted to rest his hand on the skull, but the painter has rearranged him. [...]

Two weeks pass before the next sitting. Cornelis is a busy man, he is always out and about. He has his warehouse to run, down in the harbour. At midday the Stock Market opens and he hurries down to the Bourse. Amsterdam is awash with capital and dealing there is brisk, often frenzied, because the place closes at two. In addition to this he has civic duties for he is a prominent citizen, a man of substance in this burgeoning city. It is 1636 and Amsterdam is thriving. The seat of government is in The Hague, but Amsterdam is the true capital of the Republic. Trade is booming; the arts are flourishing. Fashionable men and women stroll along its streets and the canals mirror back the handsome houses in which they live. The city is threaded with mirrors. They reflect the cold spring sunshine. Copper-coloured clouds lie motionless beneath the bridges. The city sees itself in its own water like a woman gazing into a looking-glass. Can we not forgive vanity in one so beautiful.

And hanging in a thousand homes, paintings mirror back the lives that are lived there. A woman plays the virginal; she catches the eye of the man beside her. A handsome young soldier lifts a glass to his lips; his reflection shines in the silver-topped decanter. A maid gives her mistress a letter ... The mirrored moments are stilled, suspended in aspic. For centuries to come people will gaze at these paintings and wonder what is about to happen. That letter, what does it say to the woman who stands at the window, the sunlight streaming on to her face? Is she in love? Will she throw away the letter or will she obey it, waiting until the house is empty and stealing out through the rooms that recede, bathed in shafts of sunshine, at the back of the painting?

Who can tell? For her face is serene, her secrets locked into her heart. She stands there, trapped in her frame, poised at a moment of truth.

Deborah Moggach, *Tulip Fever* (1999)

✣ ✣ ✣

*The story of Rembrandt's descent from fame and
wealth to bankruptcy is well-known. In Sylvie
Matton's novel,* Rembrandt's Whore, *we see the
bailiffs arrive.*

A keeper at the Chambers of Distress always visits the house of
the debtor and makes an inventory. The possessions described
on the list no longer belong to him; he can keep them, see them
on his walls every day, but they already belong to the Chamber
of Insolvents. So he can get used to the idea, you say. After the
sale (the 'liquidation', says Thomasz Haaringh), the creditors
can't make any more claims, even if they haven't been paid
back everything they're owed. I understand that it's the least of
the evils. I can't get used to the idea; to make myself remember,
I go through the rooms of the house with you, looking for the
walls between the paintings, while I wait for the words to turn
into a nightmare.

Early this morning, when it was still dark, a man knocked
three times. Rembrandt was quicker than me: he got up and
opened the door. In the shadow against the freezing wall, I saw
the man in black, the crow that never stops looking for the whore.
Almost the same black beak. He's not alone; the man behind him
holds a book and a quill pen. They came here two days in a row,
went round every room, looked at everything without seeing the
beauty: walls, tables, cupboards, drawers and coffers. And every
box of drawings. The man in black asks the question, always the
same one: 'What's the name of this? … ' or 'What do you call
this? … ' and you reply, sometimes enjoying the joke of giving
so many details the two men can't think straight any more. They
didn't ask what a giant's helmet was.

The list the second man makes is turning into a last work
of art: a description of your years of collecting, of the years of
love for these objects you'll never see again, sold and dispersed.

This list brings them together forever, for an eternity that will outlast the sale and our lives.

For two days the quill pen scratched away at the paper. A landscape by Rembrandt; another landscape by same; a trifling work touched up by Rembrandt; a painter's studio by Brouwer; a little landscape by Hercules Serghers; three little dogs painted from life by Titus van Rijn; a plaster head; four Spanish chairs covered in Russian leather; a little metal cannon; sixty Indian pistols, as well as arrows, javelins and bows; an Annunciation; the head of a horned satyr; a head by Raphael; a book of very rare engravings by same; five antique hats; the skins of a lion and lioness; the statue of the Emperor Agrippa; a statue of Tiberius; a Caligula; a Nero; a child by Michelangelo; a giant's helmet.

Transparent in the shadows, I seethe at the hands that point, the hands that lift, weigh, open and rummage, turn things over in the sunlight – they're filthy hands. They wipe out the beauty in your house, your works, your collections, your life. Maybe it's grief, maybe it's the cold, I don't know but I'm shaking. In answer to their questions, you even remembered your three shirts, six handkerchiefs, three table rugs and twelve serviettes, as well as a few collars and sleeves still at the dyeing mill, where Judith's husband works. As if my clothes have been torn off and I'm suddenly naked, I cross my arms and legs and huddle over my modesty, over what I want to hide from thieving hands.

Sylvie Matton, *Rembrandt's Whore* (1997)
translated from the French by Tamsin Black

❊ ❊ ❊

In seventeenth-century Amsterdam, painting had not yet acquired the Romantic associations with 'tortured genius': it was a job more-or-less like any other potentially profitable enterprise.

Jacob is an ambitious young man. He knows that he is going to go far. Though he is only sixteen he has his life mapped out.

By the age of twenty-five he plans to be an established painter, with his own studio. He will specialise in portraits, for here in Amsterdam there is an unlimited supply of potential clients who wish to see themselves immortalised on canvas. By the age of thirty he will have made his name with a major commission – a militia painting, a guild group, a Civic Guard banquet. Not only is one paid by the individual portrait – head-and-shoulders so much, full-length more – but the picture then hangs in a public place and ensures that one's fame spreads abroad.

His role model is not Jan, about whom he has mixed feelings. Those he admires are Nicolaes Eliasz and Thomas de Keyser, successful portraitists at the height of their fame. They are commissioned, paint to a reliable standard and deliver their canvases on time. After all, painting is a trade, like any other; those who succeed are those who give good value for money. His other idol is Gerrit Dou, a past pupil of Rembrandt van Rijn. How different is Dou from his erratic and temperamental master! Dou's fine detailing means that his paintings are in high demand. The collector Johan de Bye owns twenty-seven of them; the Swedish ambassador in The Hague pays a thousand florins a year – *a thousand* – simply for the promise of first refusal. Dou's is the style to which Jacob aspires. Neatness and order, not the baffling self-indulgence of Rembrandt or the florid brushwork of the Antwerp phenomenon, Peter Paul Rubens. Jacob likes to be in control.

Painting is a job, not a gamble.

Deborah Moggach, *Tulip Fever* (1999)

* * *

A painter who has been associated with the idea of 'tortured genius' is Vincent van Gogh – though recent re-assessments and the fascinating exhibition of his letters to his brother goes some way to correcting this extreme and very 'marketable' version of Van Gogh.

He can now be appreciated as a profoundly informed painter: what he produced were not the wild daub-ings of a disturbed epilectic but the carefully and sensitively constructed pictures of a great mind. César Antonio Molina takes us on a thoughtful visit to the Van Gogh Museum.

The Van Gogh museum in Amsterdam is very close to the Rijksmuseum. The main building was designed by the architect Gerrat Rietveld and opened in 1973. In 1999 a second building, designed by the Japanese architect Kisho Kurakawa, opened to hold special, temporary exhibitions. In between these three buildings is a large park. The collection consists of more than two hundred paintings, five hundred and eighty drawings, four sketchbooks, and seventy-five letters, most of which were sent by Vincent to his brother Theo. It also has the brothers' collection of works by contemporaries which they acquired through purchases, exchanges and gifts. A new acquisition programme has been adding to this collection. Vincent's works were originally Theo's property; his older brother was an employee at one of the best Parisian art-dealers and also the person who most took care of him. When they had both died, Theo's widow Johanna, moved to Holland and set herself to promoting the work of her brother-in-law, keeping the legacy almost completely intact until on her death she passed it on to her son Vincent Willem, an engineer, who eventually donated it to the Dutch state. Like Vermeer and Rembrandt, Van Gogh died feeling that he had failed as a human being and an artist. In 1890 he abandoned a mental asylum in Saint-Paul-de-Mausole and moved to a town close to Paris, Auvers-sur-Oise, thirty kilometres to the north of the capital, where Cézanne, Pissarro, Daubigny and Daumier had all once stayed. In one letter Vincent says to his brother: 'I feel a failure, I think that that is my destiny and I accept it.' That same year he shot himself in the chest and agonized for two days before dying. Half a year later, Theo would also die. Had he lived longer he might have been able to make his brother's work more famous and witnessed the beginnings of his recognition.

I walk through the rooms of the museum, which open on to a large central patio, looking for some of my favourite works. *The Potato Eaters* is the counterpoint to the great Dutch portraits of the sixteenth and seventeenth centuries, in which the wealthy bourgeoisie showed off their well-fed faces and magnificently-clad bodies. The faces of peasants from Brabant are gaunt with hunger and the fatigue of their worn-down, rag-covered bodies is there for all to see. However, they maintain their dignity in spite of their shabby surroundings. The potato which one of the five figures in the painting holds in their hand is like a soft heart, it becomes a symbol of generosity.

From the Arles period, *The Bedroom* and *The Sunflowers* catch my attention. I've seen *The Bedroom* reproduced on innumerable occasions but in person it's easier to see the various superimposed layers. In spite of its apparent simplicity, the great attention to detail the painting pays to the room turns it into another psychological self-portrait. Everything is organized so that each object is in its own pool of shared soli-tude. It's not the intensity and complementary nature of the colours; red, green, yellow and brown, blue and orange, that attracts my attention but the silence that emanates from the composition. I feel the same thing when I see *The Sunflowers*. A still life full of movement, of gestures and, perhaps, futile protest. The flowers are full of life, but they're dead too, trapped in the vase.

From the Saint-Rémy period, *The Reaper* is a dark painting full of symbolism. The wheat is being harvested. The sun is still out, but about to descend. It has lost its force and colour and is soon to be devoured by the mountains. The peasant, a small figure, barely relevant in the midst of the nature and the landscape holds a sickle in his right hand. He is at the centre of a sea of wheat. Yellow takes up almost the entirety of the canvas excepting the fence and the background, with its brown hills, expressing the extreme heat of the day. Solitude and silence once again. I don't know which I prefer from the Parisian period: *Vase with Irises* or *Vase with Gladioli*. The yellow of the background and the blue of the petals of the first compete with the more faded blue background and intense red of one of the stalks in the second. Van Gogh used still lifes to develop his studies of colour, experimenting with different combinations.

Vincent painted expansive fields, with birds flying over them, in all the seasons imaginable. In Paris he had already painted an idyllic impression of a *Wheat Field with a Lark* and later in Auvers he produced the unsettling *Wheat Field with Crows*. What intrigues me most about the painting is not the subdued yellow wheat field, nor the dark blue sky, nor even the dozens of flying crows, but the humble path that crosses everything and disappears before reaching the horizon. Van Gogh was always obsessed with being recognized and success, but if it had worked out like that would he have painted the way he did?

César Antonio Molina, *Waiting for Past Years*
translated from the Spanish by Kit Maude

❊ ❊ ❊

But an acerbic observation on the tourists leaving the museum from Chris Ewan.

I got as far as the end of the road, then turned left and left again, until I found myself stood opposite the entrance to the Van Gogh museum. It was closing time and the last visitors were wandering down the concrete steps at the front of the building, many of them carrying poster tubes. No doubt most of the tubes contained yet more prints of those damn sunflowers. They seem to be in every tourist shop window in the city. The image is available on postcards, on T-shirts, on tea towels and on coffee mugs. You can buy it on mouse-mats or baseball caps or as a jigsaw puzzle. It's a wonder the average visitor knows that Van Gogh painted anything else.

Chris Ewan, *The Good Thief's Guide to Amsterdam* (2007)

✻ ✻ ✻

And a young artist of today takes his ambition for a walk through the city …

When I got to Amsterdam I didn't take the tram but walked home. It was still the afternoon, but twilight was setting in already.

– Just you bloody well wait …

My words were directed not only at my teachers, but also at those petty-minded slugabeds without a scrap of talent or creativity who screw things up for artists like me.

I barged on, my painting equipment rattling away in my suitcase. I passed the cafés steeped in golden light where people enjoy themselves. Just you wait, I thought again and I was speaking to the couple closest to the window, a man and a woman in a clingy embrace. The man was a neckless freak with thin brown hair, an inconsequential snub nose and the small deep-set eyes of a pig. And she was no pearl amongst women, but she was pretty enough for you to wonder what she was doing with a guy like that. They were indulging each other with kisses. One day, I thought, you'll be sitting there, all tangled up like a pair of mating worms and you'll look up and say, 'Look – there! See that young man walking along, the fiery-eyed one? That's Gonzales, the half-Spanish great master.' I'd leave a trail of unreturned gazes behind me. I decided to go through the Spiegelstraat. The galleries were already closed but the paintings lit up in their windows told me enough. As usual, most of the works being puffed were Henri Roggeveen's. Roggeveen the celebrated painter. The fantastic, incredibly successful

Roggeveen. And I floated along that street, I rose above it all – Roggeveeen's daubery, the nudes, the still lifes, the portraits, the landscapes – I drifted through the air for the entire length of the street, like a contented albatross.

After the Rijksmuseum, I turned left, into the Pijp. I went to sit on a bench in the park next to my house, the suitcase on the ground between my feet. In the distance, I could hear the rumble of trams and the whoosh of cars. I gazed out over the water, but after a few minutes I couldn't make out the ducks swimming there – night had fallen, the greenery became darker, the houses transformed into yellow-eyed silhouettes.

I tried to imagine how my father would respond to this whole matter. I pictured him standing there, a stocky man who, struck dumb by my decision to leave the academy, might lose his grip on his perpetual cigar. A heart attack couldn't be ruled out.

Victor Meijer, *A Misunderstood Genius* [*Miskend talent*] (2008)
translated from the Dutch by Michele Hutchison

The Amsterdam-nation

Amsterdammers, it is said, are a nation within a nation: like many dwellers in great cities, their lives and outlooks can sometimes differ significantly from those of the majority of the country's population. But how to sum up Amsterdammers? All we have space for here are some portraits of well-known residents and visitors of the past and present, a few fictional Amsterdammers, and some ordinary people who make their home in the modern city. We start with the great philosopher Baruch Spinoza (1632–1677), referred to by his nickname, 'Bento', in this extract from Matthew Stewart's lively study of Spinoza and Leibniz, The Courtier and the Heretic.

As a merchant of Amsterdam, Bento frequented the city's mercantile exchanges, its warehouses, and the port. He worked alongside brokers, bankers, fellow merchants, and shipmasters.

A number of the open-minded, spiritually hungry gentiles he first met in the course of his business activities in fact became lifelong friends. Jarig Jelles, for example, who would write the preface of the philosopher's posthumous works, was a successful grain merchant who retired in early middle age in order to pursue wisdom.

On one of his forays into town, the young trader made his first, fateful visit to a bookshop. Amsterdam in the seventeenth century was a city of bookshops. There were at the time as many as four hundred establishments dedicated to spreading the printed word. Under the tolerant eye of the civil authorities, authors from across Europe sent their wares to Holland for publication, and, as a result, Dutch publishers outproduced their continental rivals in several languages. An important part of the Amsterdam adventure for intellectual visitors as diverse as Leibniz and John Locke was a visit to one or more of the city's bookshops, where one had the opportunity not just to browse the aisles for contraband literature, but also to sniff out new ideas among the freethinking bibliophiles, who with the stimulus of coffee and Dutch-made pipes – for smoking had become a national sport – would while the afternoon away discussing novel theories, plotting revolutions, and bantering about the latest developments in the republic of letters.

It was in this nicotine-laced atmosphere of intellectual excitement that Bento one day met Frans van den Enden. Bookseller, Latinist, medical doctor, amateur thespian, champion of radical democracy, outspoken advocate of free love (until caught *in flagrante*), ex-Jesuit (erroneous beliefs), author of the play *Lusty Heart* (banned from the stage), accused of "sowing the seeds of atheism" among the youth of Amsterdam (guilty as charged), van den Enden was the bad boy of the early Dutch Enlightenment. One pupil who later repented his own youthful errors described him as "entirely without God." A widower at fifty, he raised his brood of children according to his own, unorthodox principles of education. His eldest daughter, Clara Maria, was among the very few young women in Europe at the time who could claim to be a master of Latin, music, painting, and theatre. "She was rather frail and deformed," says Colerus. "But she made up for it with her keen wit and outstanding learning." She was just the kind of girl, perhaps, who would have attracted the eye of a young philosopher.

When van den Enden's bookshop went out of business in the late 1640s, he decided to set up a school in his own house, offering instruction in Latin, Greek, and other subjects. Despite his eyebrow-raising reputation, Frans managed to lure students from good families, some coming from as far away as Germany. In order to foster the thespian spirit among his students, he organized them into productions of Roman comedies and other plays.

Frans introduced Bento to a thrilling world of learning he had hitherto glimpsed only from a great distance. It was Frans, no doubt, who told the young man that "it was a pity that he knew neither Greek nor Latin." Having devoted much of his childhood exclusively to the Hebrew Bible, Bento must have felt left behind in the tumultuous progress of the wider republic of letters. The aspiring scholar promptly enrolled in van den Enden's school for scandal, accepting Clara Maria as his tutor in Latin. At some point in his early twenties, Bento moved in with Frans and his family. Now a master of Latin in his own right, he offered tutorials in exchange for his room.

By all accounts, Bento exhibited a ruthless passion for learning. The focus of his intense desire to know was Descartes, the great French philosopher whose ideas had sparked controversy throughout the European intellectual world. Descartes resided for two decades in Amsterdam before his death in 1650, and possibly Bento saw the philosopher himself strolling along the canals. With his short stature and unusually unprepossessing face, the Frenchman cut a recognizable figure in city life. In any case, Bento soon established a reputation as a formidable expositor and critic of the Cartesian philosophy. According to Colerus, he adopted as his guiding maxim the words of his French master: "That nothing ought to be admitted as True, but that which has been proved by good and solid reasons." It wasn't long before he concluded that this maxim ruled out most of the Bible, not to mention Descartes's own philosophy.

The young radical was drifting ever farther from the Jewish community in which he was raised. Back on the other side of the Houtgracht, the tongues wagged. Some of Bento's peers began to whisper that the wandering merchant was retailing some truly execrable ideas. They said that he believed that the books of Moses were made by man; that the soul dies with the body; and that God is a corporeal mass. For Jews of this time, just as much as for Christians, such notions were frightening heresies.

Matthew Stewart, *The Courtier and the Heretic* (2005)

✳ ✳ ✳

For many Amsterdammers, singer Ramses Shaffy was Amsterdam – both in the songs he sang and the way in which he sang them. (See his moving performance of 'Het is zo stil in Amsterdam' on YouTube.) When he died, on 1st December 2009, this is how a report in Het Parool *recorded the nation's response.*

A long line of mourners moved past the plain casket that held the body of Ramses Shaffy, who died Tuesday.

From our reporter Peter de Graaf

AMSTERDAM 'It's so quiet in Amsterdam,' croons a guitarist in front of the doors of the Carré Theatre. A group of five women hum *Op de dam*. They've come all the way from Amersfoort and Baarn to bid farewell to Ramses Shaffy, who is lying in state in a closed casket in the Amsterdam theatre. Marian de

107

Ridder: 'That man had such charisma. It's almost as though you can feel his charisma right through the casket.'

Hundreds of people are queuing up Monday afternoon to pay their last respects to the deceased musician. 'He was such a versatile singer and composer,' says Marie-José Boot. 'And he was such a presence in the city. You would always run into him, from early in the morning until late at night, whether in the Gelagkamer, the terrace of the Café Hoppe or here in the American Hotel. Amsterdam misses him.'

Sicco Kingma: 'It was a delight to identify with those songs. You often had the feeling they were about you. Sometimes I saw myself in every word.' His nine-year-old son Byrd Ramses – named indeed after the great Ramses himself – stands next to his father in the long queue. His favourite song is 'Sing, confess, cry, pray', he says. Kingma: 'The most beautiful songs about Amsterdam were written by Ramses.'

Pim Burgers still remembers the time her father wrote a poem for her mother, Annemie, who was suffering from nervous exhaustion: 'Look up, Ammie, look up high, Ammie.' It was the first time she realized that her father really loved her mother. Burgers: 'I found it so amazing that even my conservative father knew Ramses Shaffy.'

'He was always able to put into words that Amsterdam feeling,' says Jan Fraijman. Sometimes I used to get up at four in the morning and ride my bike around the city just to manifest that Ramses Shaffy feeling.'

Boot: 'He did all the things that were impossible or not allowed. He was an icon of the roaring sixties and seventies.'

After a half hour the waiting crowd shuffles into the Carré Theatre. The plain wooden coffin is covered with an enormous bouquet of red roses.

Photos of the young Ramses and the older Ramses are projected onto two screens and alternate continuously. A huge pile of roses and flower bouquets visibly grows. Someone has left behind a symbolic half-empty bottle of rosé.

The fans bow their heads in tribute, touch the casket or make the sign of the cross. Ramses Shaffy will be buried today in a private ceremony.

Peter de Graaf, 'In the presence of Ramses – one more time', *Het Parool* (2009) translated from the Dutch by Patricia Gosling

✳ ✳ ✳

A very different kind of musician – and man – from Ramses Shaffy, legendary American jazz trumpeter Chet Baker is now inexorably linked with Amsterdam because of the dramatic nature of his death in the city. James Gavin describes Baker's tragic end.

Sometime on that balmy spring afternoon he had shown up in the Prins Hendrik's small lobby. A female employee spotted him there, carrying his trumpet case. "I thought, 'Oh, my God, what an old man!'" she said. "I didn't know it was Chet Baker." The desk clerk found him "a little nervous" as he registered. Baker settled into a tidy room with bright yellow walls, a double bed, a night table, and a TV. The two windows, which started at knee level, looked out onto a winding network of streets surrounded by hotels and restaurants. Trolley cars whizzed through, and the chiming of bicycle bells filled the air. Baker locked the door behind him.

He stayed hidden away until approximately 3:10 a.m. on Friday the thirteenth. At that time, a man leaving a bar on Zeedijk saw a body on the narrow sidewalk in front of the Prins Hendrik. It lay curled in a foetal position under a full moon. The passerby banged on the door to the lobby, which was dark; at night the entrance was locked, and guests needed a key to enter. According to a police report filed later, the sole clerk on duty was in another part of the hotel and didn't hear the knocking. But an American guest did. He went downstairs, but when he saw the agitated figure at the door, he assumed a drunken vagrant was trying to get in. The guest went back to his room.

Moments later, the police at Warmoesstraat, a street in the adjacent red-light district, received a phone call, probably made by the man who had discovered the body. Officers arrived at the Prins Hendrik minutes later. What had looked like a passed-out junkie or wino proved a grislier sight up close. The man lay next to one of the short concrete posts that lined the streets, his face covered in blood and his skull bashed in. He wore a short-sleeve shirt and a pair of pinstripe trousers, caked in blood. Beside him were a pair of spectacles and a heavy steel pin of the kind used to prop open Dutch windows. Finding that, the police concluded that he had fallen from one of the hotel rooms and struck his head on the post. The corpse was wrapped in a white sheet and delivered to the morgue on Warmoesstraat. Lacking any identification, the body remained anonymous. Its face was obscured by dried blood, but the condition of the body led police to think they had picked up a thirty-year-old man.

On Friday morning at about eight, Rob Bloos, a young inspector, arrived for work at the Warmoesstraat station. Learning about the new corpse at the morgue, he wasn't too concerned. "It was just like the other ones," he said. "At that time we had in this neighbourhood a lot of junkies – German guys, Italian guys. They used a lot too much. And died."

Nevertheless, he brought two colleagues to the hotel and began a meticulous investigation. His report, which filled more than thirty pages, included a diagram of the room, a complete inventory of its contents, and interviews with hotel staff. Checking the registry, Bloos saw the signature of Chet Baker, a name he had never heard. He found the door to the empty room locked from inside, indicating that no-one else had been there. Nor was there any sign of a disturbance. A glass containing traces of heroin and coke, and another with a needle in it, were on the table, along with less than a gram of heroin. The only luggage was a trumpet case, later rumoured, inaccurately, to have been found beside the body on the street. In it were a trumpet, a watch, fifty guilders, a bracelet, a cigarette lighter, and a piece of paper with the name Chet Baker on it.

James Gavin, *Deep in a Dream: the Long Night of Chet Baker* (2002)

❊ ❊ ❊

The name of Miep Gies will be familiar to anyone who knows the story of Anne Frank and her family: Miep was the brave person principally responsible for hiding the familiy and keeping them supplied with food during the German Occupation. And after the family were betrayed and deported to the camps, it was Miep who found and kept Anne's diary, presenting it to her father when he returned, the sole survivor of the family. Her death in January 2010 elicited many appreciative obituaries; here is one from the Guardian.

Miep Gies, who has died aged 100, wrote towards the end of her life: "I am not a hero. I stand at the end of the long, long line of good Dutch people who did what I did – and much more." She was, however, the material from which the truest, most decent, most steadfast heroes are made. She found, and at great personal risk, preserved the diary of Anne Frank for posterity in 1944 after the girl and her family were caught in hiding by Germans.

More than that she was, earlier, the friend who looked after the Frank family in their now world-famous Amsterdam annexe. She shopped for them, watched out for them, cheered them up and gave the adolescent Anne her first – and only – pair of high-heeled shoes. Without Miep, the family's two years in hiding would have been impossible.

After their capture, she tried to buy the people of the annexe back from Gestapo officers, only to be called *"schweinehund"* and thrown out. When Anne's father, Otto, returned from the camps as the Franks' only survivor, he lived as one of her family for some years.

In the 1950s, as the diary began to win a reputation, Miep was one of a wide range of people investigated on suspicion that she had betrayed the Franks to the Nazis. Otto stopped the investigation with a sentence: "If you suspect Miep, you suspect me."

She was the last human link with the concealed but intense life in the secret building on the Prinsengracht canal, now known as the Anne Frank House, which attracts about a million visitors a year.

Like the Franks, who were German Jews, Gies was not Dutch. She was born Hermine Santruschitz, in Vienna, Austria. But, because her body became wasted through undernourishment during the first world war, she was sent with other Austrian workers' children to be revitalised in the Netherlands. She took to Holland, reached the top of her Dutch language class within months and was happy when her stay was prolonged. By agreement with her natural parents, she was adopted by a middle-class Dutch family, the Nieuwenburgs, while keeping her Austrian citizenship – it was the Nieuwenburgs who nicknamed her Miep.

As an adolescent, she read Baruch Spinoza and Isaac Beeckman, kept a diary and – like Anne – had "a deep longing for an understanding of life". In 1933, she answered a newspaper advert for a job in Otto Frank's firm, which sold pectin, for home jam-making. After a few weeks on jam-making duties, she was given an office job, dealing with customer complaints. In 1941, after the German occupation of Holland, Miep became a Dutch citizen by marrying Jan Gies, a social worker. The Frank family provided their wedding breakfast and Anne, then 12, gave them a silver plate.

In June 1942, Anne's elder sister, Margot, was sent papers ordering her to report for forced labour in Germany. The Franks, with others, went into hiding in the annexe with a concealed entrance accessible from Otto's office. Jan, active in the Dutch resistance, got them forged ration cards. Miep, with 10 mouths to feed in a time of increasing scarcity, did so by cultivating relationships with black-market shopkeepers.

Her memoir, *Anne Frank Remembered* (1982), gives a unique glimpse of Anne's intentness as a writer. Interrupting her at work without meaning to, Miep saw "a look on her face I'd never seen before – of dark concentration, as if she had a throbbing headache. The look pierced me and I was speechless. She was suddenly another person, writing at the table. It was as if I had interrupted an intimate moment in a very, very private friendship."

On 4 August 1944, the police came. Miep heard the sound of the fugitives' feet as they were led down the annexe staircase like "beaten dogs". According to her book, the investigating German officer was about to arrest Miep as an accomplice when she noticed his Viennese accent. She mentioned the link, and after some thought he said, "From personal sympathy ... from me personally, you can stay. But God help you if you run away. Then we take your husband." Later, Miep retrieved Anne's clothbound diary and shawl. In June 1945, Otto returned alone from Auschwitz. Margot and Anne had died in the Belsen concentration camp of typhoid weeks before the liberation.

Each year, on 4 August, Miep and her husband would stay silently at home, marking the day of the family's arrest. Only when the diary was published in 1947 could Miep bring herself to read it. She realised that if she had known its contents before liberation she would have had to destroy it. It gave too many people away. In 1950, when she had a son, Miep used Anne's shawl to keep her baby warm.

During the Victory in Europe commemoration in 1995, Miep came to London for a joint Jewish and Christian memorial service for Anne Frank mounted at St Paul's Cathedral by the Anne Frank Educational Trust. She said the diary had done much good, but she still wished daily that the family had survived instead. "A human being is more than a book." She possessed a straightforward, unshakeable sense of her human duties and carried them out whatever the rigours and the fear.

Miep and Jan continued to live in Amsterdam until Jan's death in 1993. On her 100th birthday she asked that the many "unnamed heroes" who helped Dutch Jews to escape deportation and death should be remembered: "I would like to name one, my husband Jan. He was a resistance man who said nothing but did a lot. People like him existed in thousands but were never heard."

She is survived by her son, Paul, and three grandchildren.

Miep Gies, secretary and resistance worker, born 15 February 1909; died 11 January 2010

John Ezard, *The Guardian*, 13th January 2010

❊ ❊ ❊

Another Amsterdam death: the murder of the controversial cultural icon Theo van Gogh by Mohammed Bouyeri (ostensibly for making a film critical of Islam's treatment of women) leads Ian Buruma to consider the city's debate about what kind of monument would be appropriate to this particular hero of 'freedom'.

Should a memorial be built on Linnaeus Street, on the spot of the murder, or in the neighbouring park, or perhaps in the centre of Amsterdam, or maybe not at all? And what kind of monument should it be? *Het Parool*, a newspaper founded by the Dutch resistance under Nazi occupation, invited its readers to come up with ideas for the most appropriate memorial: a two-meters-high cigarette, suggested one reader, from which puffs of smoke would emerge at regular intervals; a sculpture of a great happy pig, said another, on whose pink flanks people could write their opinions. Many liked the idea of a sculpture in the form of a giant cactus – a cactus, in the words of one reader, employing their quaintly old-fashioned jargon of postwar novels about war heroes, "that was just as big and strong as Theo, as a beacon of prickly power, as an inspiration to stand tall, proud and undaunted."

The cactus had become something of a trademark for Van Gogh. He would always end his television talk shows by kissing one, after inviting his guests to do the same. One of his guests, Roman Polanski, refused. Van Gogh, who idolized Polanski, said he loved kissing cacti. Polanski replied that everyone has to be good at something.

Erecting monuments to their own bravery and suffering during World War II had become so prevalent a Dutch practice in the late 1940s and early '50s that people spoke of a "monument rain." The largest and most famous one, a kind of fluted stone phallus with reliefs all around of suffering Dutch humanity in chains, is the National Monument on Dam Square, opposite the royal palace in Amsterdam. The Queen lays a wreath there every year to remember World War II – not the Holocaust, which was hardly an issue in the 1950s, but the suffering of the Dutch people under German occupation. It is where the nation feels most sorry for itself. (It is also where the world's young gathered in the 1960s and '70s to strum guitars, make out in their sleeping bags, and smoke dope.)

One of the readers of *Het Parool* took the view that the National Monument should make way for a cactus monument that would be just as large and imposing. In the eyes of such people, van Gogh had finally become what he had aspired to be: the symbol of Dutch resistance, the national hero who stood tall, a freedom fighter who did his uncle and grandfather proud.

The cactus idea won. A decision was made by the borough council of East/Watergraafsmeer to erect the stone cactus in the park where Mohammed Bouyeri was arrested, not far from the place where he killed van Gogh.

Ian Buruma, *Murder in Amsterdam* (2006)

❋ ❋ ❋

One of today's best-loved Amsterdammers is famous travel-writer Cees Nooteboom. Spanish writer and politician César Antonio Molina allows us to share a visit to his distinguished friend.

Whilst my friend paid and said goodbye to his companions, I went inside the café De Zwart. It was tiny but lovely. The man behind the bar, a gentleman of a certain age, asked me where I came from. When I told him he said 'Mr Noteboom is very important. It's a shame that he doesn't come here more often but he's always travelling. He travels more than me and I spend the whole day walking in circles around this bar.' He shook hands with me, laughing. Cees took my arm and after crossing the alley in front of the establishment we went out onto the Singel and walked along it towards the sea.

'This is the city of my absences, anyone who's constantly travelling like I am never stays in the same place, so I am always absent. I'm somewhere else, I mean I'm nowhere, but really I am, I'm in myself. It annoys me when people ask "Why do you travel?" I think that I'm trying to get away from myself even though travelling only serves to help you get to know yourself better. The people who are really fleeing are the ones who let themselves get stuck in a daily routine, because they can't stand the bitter knowledge that travelling imparts. This constant movement has brought me the necessary calm in which to write. Movement and tranquillity balance each other in a union of opposites, the world is itself a traveller within an endlessly travelling universe. At the beginning of my book *Nomad Hotel*

I quote Ibn Arabi's phrase "Movement is the origin of existence. This means that immobility is impossible within existence because, if something is immobile it will return to whence it came: to Nothing. That's why the voyage never ends."'

Starting from number 319, which was the Antiquariaat Brinkman, an antiquarian bookshop, we walked along the odd-numbered side of the street, passing by an antiques shop which had a collection of Tintin figures in the window, the café Dante, the Boeken bookshop, which specializes in oriental literature, and a Greek restaurant. [...]

We had arrived in Roomolen Street where his house was. Simone greeted us as soon as we opened the door. She was younger than her husband and walked more easily up and down the five steep flights of stairs. The kitchen was in the basement. There were books everywhere. Next to the entrance was a small study where Cees showed me dozens of translations of his books in an infinity of languages. The living room was on the second floor. The bedrooms, with suitcases always packed ready to go, were on the third. The fourth and last, or fifth, if you counted the cellar, was where he usually worked. Cees showed me some manuscripts, the most treasured volumes in his library and one of the red, hard cover books in which he kept his diary.

'Once I lost a diary that I had been writing for years on the street in Catalonia. It was stolen along with our suitcases. We went to the police station but they didn't care. They made an inventory of all the things we had lost, giving each one an economic value and when they got to the diary they put "no value". For me, as you might imagine, it was priceless.'

'Haven't you been able to remember it?' I asked ingenuously.

Simone, who had been discretely quiet up until then, interjected:

'It's impossible to reconstruct the day to day things. There are details, subtleties, feelings, that are impossible to rewrite. I feel as if we've lost a child. Who has it? What will they do with it?'

'Don't worry!' said Cees. 'They must have burned or ripped it up. Why would they want a book written in a language no-one knows?' [...]

Simone had accompanied Cees on his travels for more than two decades and, as a photographer, had illustrated some of his books. I insisted on seeing her work and as she had the photos in a studio outside the house, we set out to the street once more. We walked down Brouwersgracht, crossed various bridges and came to an area very close to the sea. All the houses had heraldic shields illustrated with fantastic animals and the dates they were constructed on their lintels. They were almost all from the seventeenth century. Simone stopped in front of one, took out a key and opened a door. The place wasn't very large but the space was well used. This was where she had installed her photographic studio and archive. She showed us some photos and I noticed a series in black and white that focussed on stones. She had captured their shapes, their faces, their eternity. I asked her to let me take them to Madrid to see if I could set up an exhibition. She agreed with pleasure and put them into an envelope one by one. On the way back, Cees had us go into the Papist's Island café, Papeneiland, on the corner of Brouwersgracht and Prinsengracht. He greeted a large part of the clientele, some of them were old friends whom he hadn't seen for years. It was there that I came to understand his cosmopolitanism. Travelling across the whole world, an incorrigible nomad, he enjoyed the occasions when he temporarily returned home.

César Antonio Molina, *Waiting for Years Past* (2007)
translated from the Spanish by Kit Maude

✳ ✳ ✳

Moving on to fictional characters associated with the city ... starting with a reminder that that Tobias Smollett's Peregrine Pickle experienced the pleasures – and dangers – of Amsterdam in the eighteenth century.

The only remarkable scene in Amsterdam, which our company had not seen, was the Spuyl or music-houses, which, by the connivance of the magistrates, are maintained for the recreation of those who might attempt the chastity of creditable women, if they were not provided with such conveniences. To one of these night-houses did our travellers repair, under the conduct of the English merchant, and were introduced into such another place as the ever-memorable coffee-house of Moll King; with this difference, that the company here were not so riotous as the bucks of Covent Garden, but formed themselves into a circle, within which some of the number danced to the music of a scurvy organ and a few other instruments, that uttered tunes very suitable to the disposition of the hearers, while the whole apartment was shrouded with clouds of smoke impervious to the view. When our gentlemen entered, the floor was occupied by two females and their gallants, who, in the performance of their exercise, lifted their legs like so many oxen at plough and the pipe of one of those hoppers happening to be exhausted, in the midst of his saraband, he very deliberately drew forth his tobacco-box, filling and lighting it again, without any interruption to the dance.

Peregrine being unchecked by the presence of his governor, who was too tender of his own reputation to attend them in this expedition, made up to a sprightly French girl who sat in seeming expectation of a customer, and prevailing upon her to be his partner, led her into the circle, and in his turn took the opportunity of dancing a minuet, to the admiration of all present. He intended to have exhibited another specimen of his ability in this art, when the captain of a Dutch man-of-war chancing to come in, and seeing s stranger engaged with the lady whom, it seems, he had bespoke for his bedfellow, he advanced without any ceremony, and seizing her by the arm, pulled her to the other side of the room. Our adventurer, who was not a man to put up with such a brutal affront, followed the ravisher with indignation in his eyes; and pushing him on one side, retook the subject of their contest, and led her back to the place from whence she had been dragged. The Dutchman, enraged at the youth's presumption, obeyed the first dictates of his choler, and lent his rival a hearty box on the ear; which was immediately repaid with interest, before our hero could recollect himself sufficiently to lay his hand upon his sword, and beckon the aggressor to the door.

Notwithstanding the confusion and disorder which this affair produced in the room, and the endeavours of Pickle's company, who interposed, in order to prevent bloodshed, the antagonists reached the street; and Peregrine drawing, was surprised to see the captain advance against him with a long knife, which he preferred to the sword that hung by his side. The youth, confounded by this preposterous behaviour, desired him, in the French tongue, to lay aside that vulgar implement, and approach like a gentleman. But the Hollander, who neither understood the proposal, nor would have complied with this demand, had he been made acquainted with his meaning, rushed forward like a desperado, before his adversary could put himself on his guard; and if the young gentleman had not been endued with surprising agility, his nose would have fallen a sacrifice to the fury of his assailant. Finding himself in such imminent jeopardy, he leaped to one side, and the Dutchman passing him, in the force of his career, he with one nimble kick made such application to his enemy's heels, that he flew like lightning into the canal, where he had almost perished by pitching upon one of the posts with which it is faced.

Peregrine having performed this exploit, did not stay for the captain's coming on shore, but retreated with all dispatch, by the advice of his conductor; and next day embarked, with his companions, in the skuyt, for Haerlem.

Tobias Smollett, *Peregrine Pickle* (1751)

* * *

One of the most influential Dutch books of the nine-teenth century was Max Havelaar, *by Multatuli (the pen-name of Eduard Douwes Dekker). Exposing the horrors and exploitation of the colonial system, it caused a storm at the time and led to vigorous campaiging for change. Even those who have never read the book may be familiar with the name of Max Havelaar in connection with Dutch 'Fair Trade' coffee (it was the first ever 'Fair Trade' mark). Here, at the very beginning of the book, Max introduces himself.*

I am a coffee broker and I live at No. 37 Lauriergracht, Amsterdam. I am not in the habit of writing novels or things of that sort, and so I have been a long time making up my mind to buy a few extra reams of paper and start on the work which you, dear reader, have just taken up, and which you must read if you are a coffee broker, or if you are anything else. Not only have I never written anything that resembled a novel, I don't even like reading such things, because I am a businessman. For years I have been asking myself what is the use of them and I am amazed at the impudence with which a poet or story-teller dares to palm off on you something that never happened, and usually never *could* happen. If I, in *my* line – I am a coffee broker and I live at 37 Lauriergracht – gave a statement to a principal – a principal's someone who sells coffee – which contained only a small portion of the untruths that form the greater part of all poems and novels, he would transfer his business to Busselinck and Waterman at once. They're coffee brokers too, but you don't need to know their address. So, then ... I take good care not to write any novels, or make any other false statements. And I may say that I have always noticed that people who go in for such things generally come to a bad end. I am forty-three years old, I've been on 'Change for twenty years, so I can come forward if anyone's called for who has experience. I've seen a good many firms go down! And usually, when I looked for the reasons, it seemed to me that they had to be sought in the wrong course most of the people had taken in their youth.

Truth and common sense – that's what I say, and I'm sticking to it. Naturally, I make an exception for *Holy Scripture*.

Multatuli, *Max Havelaar* (1860)
translated from the Dutch by Roy Edwards

* * *

Most big cities have acquired their resident (or visiting) fictional detectives. Nicholas Freeling's Inspector Van Der Valk arrives in Amsterdam, driving past some of the most famous sights but harbouring a typical crimi-nal-hunter's thoughts about the people who live there.

Van der Valk had the car ready; without speaking he threw it into gear and headed towards the town. It is not possible to avoid the mid-afternoon traffic in Amsterdam; progress is fitful. The lights on the Muntplein were against them; Martin stared at the bell tower and the corner of the Singel with a new eye. Being in the half-world of the police gave a new definition to people. All these people, staring at Vroom's window display by the antheap where the Kalverstraat begins; all those others heading with an alert, expectant look towards the other antheap of the Reguliersbreestraat, as though in the Rembrandtplein they would be given a lovely present; who were they? People with no idea in their head except business – for if the motto of Germany is *Befehl ist Befehl* (Orders are orders) that of Holland is quite surely *Zaken zijn zaken* (Business is business). And some innocent little pleasures too – coffee and a nice big creamy chunk of tart in Doelen or Polen. What about the people taking a quick connoisseur's sniff at the weather – cold now and lowering from a yellowish leaden sky? Snow soon, doubtless, and ice perhaps, and the children asking for their skates. Were they thinking only of pea soup in ten thousand homes, and curly kale with boiled sausage in ten thousand more? Looking forward to the days soon when *Sinterklaas* would be coming with his *knecht*, and the bakers would all be displaying initials made of puff pastry stuffed with frangipane?

There were murderers among them, frauds, perverts, thieves, *souteneurs*. Psychopaths, many of them, no doubt: poor old men who followed little girls in parks. But many too were criminals, who enjoyed seducing virgins, who poisoned their wives, who would as soon steal from the poor as from the rich, especially as it was generally easier, who lived unworried and secure on the profits from the nasty little follies and meannesses of all the mass. Parasites, gamblers, pornographers. Victims. Van der Valk's professional eye was upon them too.

Nicholas Freeling, *Love in Amsterdam* (1962)

✳ ✳ ✳

In this extract from May the Sun Shine Tomorrow *[Laat het morgen mooi weer zijn], Abdelkader Benali creates the unforgettable healer Malik Ben and his basement office in the heart of Amsterdam. (And it's impossible not to love him!)*

Malik Ben weighed 300 pounds on the day he decided to have his name removed from the Yellow Pages. Lugging all that weight around day after day had gotten to be a chore, which is what prompted his second resolution: to go on a diet.

Malik had dark features. Black hair, which took on a reddish sheen–a kind of auburn he rather liked–whenever he spent too much time in the sun. Brown eyes, the same shade of brown as in the paintings of the old Dutch masters. Pupils that sometimes glowed with visionary intensity. Tawny, leathery skin, tough as birch bark, which served as a visual reminder of his parents–children of high deserts and mountains, where rattlesnakes slithered across the sun-baked soil and goats leapt from ledge to ledge. It was the kind of skin that would still be firm in old age. Malik used his hands a lot when he talked. He was delighted when his hands assumed the leading role halfway through a conversation and did the talking for him. They'd been made for the job. Hadn't the Spanish Lady told him so?

Malik Ben was a healer. He healed people who were no longer in touch with their true, authentic selves. He referred to himself as an "authenticity healer." His job was to help people recover their lost souls. It was a task he had taken upon himself. In the past, poets had been entrusted with the soul's welfare. But since no one believed in poets anymore, Malik had felt compelled to assume this responsibility.

Thanks to his verbal skills, Malik made contact with others quickly and easily. But he was also a good listener – a quality his clients valued even more. It was his listening skills that paid the bills.

Malik's office was in the heart of Amsterdam, in the basement of a nineteenth-century town house a stone's throw away from Leidseplein. Callers were obliged to ring a bell that jangled loudly. Even before they stepped inside, Malik could tell what was on their minds by the expression on their faces.

Land was expensive in Amsterdam, so every inch of space was put to optimal use. Malik's cubbyhole couldn't have measured more than 80 or 90 square feet, but it served his needs: his occupation didn't require a whole lot of space. The elm trees lining the street added an air of majesty, though the roots had gradually pushed up through the paving and cracked the sidewalk in several places. Drivers and pedestrians had never been heard to complain. The gnarled roots had a certain charm. People were used to them. Every once in a while somebody tripped over one, but it was usually a tourist, who scrambled to his feet and went on his way without noticing the beauty of the street.

Malik, down in his basement, stared all day long at shoes – sneakers, boots, pumps and high heels – as they strolled, stumbled and scurried past. He never tired of the scene. Sometimes the shoe-wearers came inside and were given a face and a name. They shook Malik's hand, sat down and told their stories. [...]

He was frequently asked at parties to explain his chosen line of work. "What do you actually *heal*?" It was then that he discovered that people had been given tongues to make life difficult. Your body might be in perfect shape and your cheeks cleanly shaved, but your tongue got so twisted up that nothing came out right. His few well-meaning stabs invariably trailed off into incoherent babble. His usual eloquence let him down just when he needed it the most. What he wanted to say, with studied casualness, was, "I try to restore the self-confidence of successful people who have lost their nerve." But it never came out casually. His tongue refused to cooperate. Instead, he usually said something like, "What's wrong with wanting to give people back their self-confidence?" It sounded defensive. It sounded like a counter-attack. And that had nothing to do with entertainment, much less clowns.

Faced with such a cryptic explanation, people usually looked at Malik as if *he* were the one who needed help. At that point, he would resort to an even simpler explanation. "I'm a kind of mental coach. I give my clients a psychological boost." That's how low he'd stoop in an effort to appear open and intelligible.

It takes a lot of energy to make yourself completely understood at parties. When Malik could bear the puzzled looks no longer, he'd make use of his last option: he'd slip quietly away. On the way home he'd feel empty and misunderstood, but the feeling never lasted long. Walking past his office was all it took to restore him to his usual good spirits.

Abdelkader Benali, *May the Sun Shine Tomorrow*
[*Laat het morgen mooi weer zijn*] (2005)
translated from the Dutch by Susan Massotty

❋ ❋ ❋

125

Moving on from fiction, we meet some of Amster-
dam's general population. First, Maarten Spanjer
recalls a 'colourful' encounter with Miss Willy White,
a show-girl in a 1960s club.

In the sixties and seventies the Rembrandtplein and Leidseplein were both awash with hostess bars. These dodgy establishments tended to be frequented by men from out of town, conveniently lumped toge`ther under the label "peasants" by native Amsterdammers. Photos of women with ample bosoms, decked out in fishnet stockings and suspenders, used to be plastered all over the windows to lure in the unsuspecting passer-by.

In the bar a few ladies who were approaching their best-before date would prop up the bar, looking bored and bearing little resemblance to the models in the photos. Once inside, the unfortunate peasant would be ambushed by one of these hyenas who, in exchange for a steady supply of piccolos – small bottles of fake champagne that were discreetly emptied into the flower boxes – showered him with compliments.

"Hi honey, you're looking great today! Where did you get that tie?" was a popular one from the repertoire. Such places always had a small stage, where second-rate magicians and strip-tease dancers could show their pathetic little tricks. One of them was Wil from the Goudsbloemdwarsstraat in the Jordaan.

She had been an acrobat in the circus in her day, but many years and many pounds later she had washed up on the night-club circuit around Rembrandtplein. Wil was still an attractive woman, providing German camp commandants were your thing. In the hostess bar where she performed night after night she would be announced as "*The famous Miss Willy White, straight from London, only tonight in our city.*" An acquaintance of mine who had been told me that she would emerge topless from behind a red velvet curtain to loud cheers and start attaching plastic windmills to her nipples in time to the music. By ingeniously shaking her breasts she would get the windmills to rotate in opposite directions. And as she increased the tempo to an accelerating roll of drums her jaw would drop as if she herself was astonished by the act. Once these windmills were spinning at top speed, she would ease herself into the splits with a pained expression on her face. Applause and curtains!

One night, egged on by the acquaintance, I decided to go and watch this tour de force with a couple of mates. We had to admit that he hadn't been exaggerating. When her act reached its climax I pulled a pillowcase from under my coat and ripped it in two in synch with her splits. With surprising agility Miss White, *straight from London*, jumped up, walked to the edge of the stage and snarled at me in a broad Amsterdam accent: "I'll be right with you, you twit. That's something for the whores on the Zeedijk." After a grumpy bow she disappeared behind the curtain.

Back at the bar I was the hero of the hour to my mates. Bursting with pride I held the ripped pillowcase aloft for the umpteenth time. But then suddenly Willy White appeared behind me and lashed out: "Here, take that!" was the last thing I heard before I tumbled off my barstool and the lights went out.

Maarten Spanjer, *Maarten Makes Friends*
[*Maarten maakt vrienden*] (2006)
translated from the Dutch by Laura Vroomen

✳ ✳ ✳

Staying with the 1960s, Belgian writer Geert van Istendael describes his experience of a very annoying Amsterdam 'hippie' of the period.

It was the year 1969, a chilly evening in April, and I was walking down the Marnixstraat in Amsterdam. I was twenty-two and wearing a grey jumper made of some dodgy material and an even greyer pair of polyester trousers worn so badly they were actually getting wrinkled. My hair was extremely short. As was my blue nylon anorak. A fellow my age asked me for a light for his cigarette.

127

I did have a light, although I only smoked pipes myself. We walked together for a bit. His cigarette had a peculiar smell. Hash and marihuana had already made it as far as Belgium, but I was afraid to ask. He wore an ankle-length coat and his tight little curls came down to his shoulders. The sentences he uttered were longer than the hair, but featured only a limited number of words. I had never heard anyone talk like that, and never have since: so monotonous, so muffled and yet so self-assured.

He'd embarked on a chemistry degree, he told me. This statement took him about a hundred yards, I reckoned. But he had dropped chemistry and switched to sociology. In the space of that one word you could have stored Max Weber's collected works. I was close to finishing the same degree; in fact, I was in Amsterdam for my dissertation. Over the years I had taught myself to stretch my short Flemish vowels into longer Dutch ones. He, on the other hand, said soooociooooloooogyyyyyy. Mind you, that's a radically abridged version of the real thing.

There were other parallels between us. His parents were Roman Catholic, as were mine. He was through with this faith, as was I. But quite unlike me he was reeeeaaaally tooooleeeeerant, y'knoooooow. While he laboured on these three words, I had plenty of time for a bit of soul-searching in true Roman Catholic style. I discovered that I was extremely resentful of Rome but decided, hypocrite that I was, again in true Roman Catholic style, that this was none of his business. There it was, at long last, the final syllable. His good parents were funding his studies, which afforded me a fresh insight into his open-mindedness. I hoped for their sake that their tolerant son studied faster than he spoke.

He pointed out a dusty old shop where you could buy wooden beads and joss sticks and, if memory serves, even prayer wheels. I'd opted for sociology because all my teachers had said that I should definitely do something with languages and because for

English I'd read *The Hidden Persuaders* by Vance Packard, an American journalist who was causing quite a stir at the time. Packard's book exposed the carefully constructed lies of the ad men that make consumers rush out and buy all kinds of things they don't need.

So to me, this guy with his long jacket, long hair and long words was an idiot for buying all this paraphernalia just because it happened to be in fashion. Idiot? I'm sure the feeling was mutual. The only difference between us was that he'd have the guts to say it because he was a Dutchman – I mean, an Amsterdamer – whereas I kept my mouth shut because, being Belgian, I was consumed by an inferiority complex. Maybe I really was an idiot as I'd always feared deep down in the anguished recesses of my soul. Absolutely everything about me was wrong: my short hair, my short coat, my answers, my sense of duty. I wanted to get to bed at a decent hour, because the library and my half-finished dissertation were waiting for me in the morning.

Pathetic, that's the word. Why didn't I listen to him? I could've been smoking pot and dropping acid and shagging mystical maidens. But I was already in a steady relationship with a sociology student; a marriage and a divorce later I would throw myself into the arms of a research chemist. Why didn't I ditch that half-baked hippie at the Leidseplein and head straight for the red-light district? "Looking for a good time? Just follow your nose," grinned a local barman the following evening when I politely asked for directions to the red-light district. I didn't ditch the hippie because I was far too timid in those days.

We decided to have a quick drink in a café next to the Stadsschouwburg. The place was called Café Reynders and it was virtually empty. He fancied the drink that everywhere in the world, and certainly in my mind, symbolized the worst of American capitalism. I wanted to order a jenever. But even though most of the customers had left – and we could clearly see a waiter in the back – nobody made a move in our direction.

Then the Amsterdam hippie did something that made me cringe; even today I'd be hard put not to make a quick exit. He started hurling abuse at the waiter, probably thinking that this was the right time to stage a demonstration. Completely unfazed, the injured party made his way to our table. I thought, He's going to throw us out – and who could blame him? Bye-bye jenever. The hippie carried on unabated: It's always the same with you waiters! You're bloody well paid more than enough. Who the hell do you think you are? And so on and so forth. In a last-ditch attempt to salvage my gin, I asked the waiter why he'd kept us waiting. I'll never forget what he said, not to me but to the hippie. "Long after you've turned into a little bourgeois git, this gentleman here will still be able to think for himself."

He wasn't referring to himself, but to me.

He and his colleague had of course divided the room into zones – one side for you, the other for me – and we evidently fell outside his designated area. Our waiter had nipped in the back because there weren't any customers on his turf and of course this guy wouldn't dream of crossing the line.

I gave the man a handsome tip. I couldn't care less about being hip, but I've rarely encountered a worldview more compelling than that of the Amsterdam waiter. And whenever I'm in Amsterdam, I have a jenever in honour of the shrewd waiter from Café Reynders. Even though the place has now been turned into a hideous Irish pub, I keep going back. In fact, I can highly recommend it. It broadens your worldview.

Geert Van Istendael, *My Netherlands* [*Mijn Nederland*]
translated from the Dutch by the 2005 Translation Summer School

✳ ✳ ✳

The fashion for 'human statues' as a form of street entertainment in the world's cities is taken up in

*this delightful piece by one of the most innovative
and interesting young Dutch writers, Thomas Olde
Heuvelt. Such statues have the perfect vantage point
for observing the city's population, as well as the time
to let their imaginations get to work on them ...*

Today I'm a harlequin. A green bronze harlequin with my
magnificent hat, motley costume and *batocchio* stuck in my
belt. The right statue in the right place can get you at least a
hundred and fifty euro on Saturday afternoons and offers you
many hours of quiet people watching.

I get to Dam Square early and stand in front of the National
Monument. I wave at Pantalone, the Iranian dandy with his
velvet jacket and suitcase filled with prayer books and magic
potions, who stands in his usual spot in front of Madame
Tussauds. Pantalone is made of gold. Once, we played a game
to see who could stay in the same position longest, looking
each other in the eye without laughing. That last bit was easy,
because we were more than 250 feet apart. It ended in a draw.
When we went home, early that evening, we were both as stiff
as boards and we'd made hardly any money, because everyone
had thought we were real.

Today there's plenty to marvel at. On the steps of the
monument the leather bracelet seller unwraps his packed
lunch. The pigeons try to snatch his olive bread away. A
rich, mature woman stumbles out of the Krasnapolski Hotel,
fumbling with her husband's cases. I stick out my tongue at a
little girl who's pulled along by her father. She laughs and tries
to catch his attention, but he's more interested in the breasts
of a student passing in a wheelchair. I'm sure that the city's
aroma is lost on all of these people, but I smell it, as always,
because it's mine. Have you ever hovered just inches above the
asphalt? I have. I'm capable of identifying every single aspect:
last night's rain, the vapours of the canals, the coffee and
ventilated warmth at the entrance to the Bijenkorf department

store and the salty, fishy smell because the fishmonger's wife is cleaning oysters.

Thinking of the herrings and eels lying there oily and disembowelled in trays, I imagine how only a few days ago they were still swimming in their fish universe, clueless about the world above. Standing on my base without so much as blinking an eye, I spot an almost invisible line falling from the sky and hovering in front of the bracelet seller's nose. Attached to it is a piece of freshly baked olive bread. The bracelet seller rises to the bait and is immediately yanked up in the air. His merchandise rolls down the steps of the monument. Last thing I see is the hook ripping his cheek into a grin, then he's gone. Nobody sees him disappear. Nobody, except me.

And me, I'm all pounding heart. I'm blind to the Japanese tourists taking pictures of me and trying to catch me out. To convince myself that it was just an illusion I blink, but the steps remain empty. It really happened, and soon after my suspicions are borne out when the entrails of the filleted bracelet seller hit the pavement with a warm splash.

Suddenly the sky over Dam Square is a black tangle of fishing lines. They swoop from the clouds like kite strings, only there's no Tinker Bell but a curved pirate's hook at the end. To each their own bait. The rich woman with the cases bites into a garlic sausage, bobbing her head like a turkey. The student in the wheelchair drools over a slice of chocolate fudge cake. The Japanese throw themselves onto a fillet of raw salmon like a pack of wild animals. And all around me people ascend, dangling from their hooks and forced to look up at the clouds in which they, one by one, disappear.

Not much later it starts raining, a scarlet rain, like a bleeding heart on Valentine's Day.

Thomas Olde Heuvelt, 'Harlequin on Dam Square' (2010)
translated from the Dutch by Laura Vroomen

✳ ✳ ✳

*Dubravka Ugresic gives us an insight into the lives of
East European immigrants in Amsterdam – the literal
and psychological difficulties of being an outsider in
the city. Allocated a basement flat in a poor district,
she begins to enjoy some of the local eccentrics.*

They coped. Most of them 'played tennis'. Playing tennis in their
group slang meant house-cleaning. It paid fifteen guilders an hour.
Some worked as dishwashers or waiters in restaurants. Ante picked
up small change playing the accordion in the Noordermarkt. Ana
sorted mail in the post office every morning. 'It's not so bad,' she
would say. 'I feel like the dwarf in Capek's *Postman's Tale*.'

But the best paying job you could get without a work permit
was a job at the 'Ministry'. One of 'our people' found work at a
place where they made clothes for sex shops and soon the whole
gang was working there. It wasn't strenuous: all you had to do was
assemble items of sadomasochist clothing out of leather, rubber and
plastic. Three times a week Igor, Nevena and Selim went to Regula-
teurstraat in Amsterdam Nord where the Atelier Demask, purveyor
to the many-faceted Dutch porno industry, was located. There was
an S/M porno club in The Hague called The Ministry of Pain, and
my students took to calling their porno sweat shop the 'Ministry'.
'Those S/M types, Comrade, they're real snappy dressers,' Igor
would joke. 'They don't think the most beautiful body is a naked
body. I wouldn't forget that if I were a Gucci or Armani.' [...]

I couldn't get over the number of signs and signals – finger-
prints – by which the inhabitants of the city made it clear that
they belonged. I thought the signals childlike and consequently
touching, like the breadcrumbs Hansel and Gretel sprinkle
behind them to guide their way home. Every one of them –
the figurines of cats climbing the fronts of old houses, the
flags hanging out of the windows, the posters and even family
photos, especially of newborn babes, inscriptions and slogans,

tiny sculptures, toys, teddy bears, African masks, Indonesian vajang dolls, models of ships, miniature replicas of typical Amsterdam houses – had one and only one message: 'I live here. Look! I live here.' [...]

The Refugee Department found a flat for me on the Oudezijds Kolk. It was a small canal with only a few houses, one end opening onto Amsterdam's Central Station, the other, like the sections of a palm frond, branching into the Zeedijk, a street known for its Chinese population, and the Oudezijds Voorburgwal and Oudezijds Achterburgwal, two canals running through the red-light district. It was a basement flat, and small, like a room in a cheap hotel. Apartments were very hard to come by in Amsterdam, or so said the departmental secretary, and I resigned myself to it. I liked the neighbourhood. In the morning I would take the Zeedijk in the direction of the Nieuwmarkt, stopping off at The Jolly Joker, Ther or Chao Phraya, the cafés overlooking the old De Waag. Sipping my morning coffee, I would observe the people stopping at stalls displaying herring, vegetables, wheels of Dutch cheese and mounds of freshly baked pastries. It was the part of town with the greatest concentration of eccentrics, and, since it was also where the red-light district started, it was a hang-out for small-time pushers, prostitutes, Chinese housewives, pimps, drug addicts, drunks, leftover hippies, shopkeepers, peddlers and delivery boys, tourists, petty criminals and the jobless and homeless. Even when the sky (that famous Dutch sky) descended and spread its pallor over the city, I would revel in the leisurely rhythm of the various passersby. Everything looked slightly squalid, the worse for wear, as if the sound were down or the picture in slow motion, as if there were something dodgy about it all, yet it all seemed to hold together in the name of a higher wisdom.

Dubravka Ugresic, The Ministry of Pain (2004)
translated from the Croatian by Michael Henry Hein

* * *

When Nicholaas Matsier achieves the privilege of moving from the suburbs to 'the edge of the centre', he discovers that neighbours can be friendly and helpful – though living at such unaccustomedly close quarters to others can leave one feeling somewhat exposed.

It still has something ragged about it, the neighbourhood where I live, at the northern edge of the Jordaan. Central market, cemeteries, allotments, gasworks, water tower, city gate, arterial road, railway line, fairground – they're all nearby. As is the city centre, which has a centre of its own, and an edge. This is a neighbourhood on the edge of the centre. I love the edge.

I remember the awe I felt when, having always been a resident of the suburbs myself, I heard that other people lived 'in the centre': to me it felt like a privilege that was reserved for the fortunate few. I'm now proud, and also slightly shocked, to have lived here for twenty years. Have I gained the status of neighbourhood resident in that time? That's a complicated question.

My first day, around twenty years ago. We'd just moved into our flat and were busy cleaning and painting and doing DIY. I'd dashed out without my keys on some errand or other, to buy work gloves or something. And now I was standing there, ringing the doorbell, with the new work gloves in my hand, and wondering – okay, just give the bell another ring – why my girlfriend wasn't opening the door.

On the other side of the street, which was a filled-in canal and therefore pretty wide, a window slid open, with an old-fashioned sound that's becoming increasingly rare: the simultaneous rattle and squeak of the rapidly spinning wheels that the ropes of the window weights run over. They are – or rather, were – counterweights: window up, weight down, and vice versa. You saw the ropes, but not the weights.

Anyway, a window slid up and a woman's head popped out. 'She's doing the hoovering, neighbour!'

It was the flat directly opposite our own, two floors up, and I remember thinking two things at once: gosh, someone's keeping a good eye on us, and okay, here we have a woman who spots someone vacuuming on the other side of the street – because we hadn't hung anything up at the windows yet, no curtains, no nets, no blinds – so, just like that, she slides up her window to give me her take on the situation.

Impulsively. No beating about the bush. Window up and mouth open. Straight out with that 'neighbour' too. It was impossible to make a distinction between nosiness and helpfulness. Although I'd been living in Amsterdam for ten years by then, I felt very The Hague at that moment, very reserved and very much the result of my mother's upbringing, with her fierce ideology that banned staring in at other people's windows. I couldn't get nets up quickly enough.

Nicholaas Matsier, *Close to Home* [*Dicht bij huis*] (1996)
translated from the Dutch by Laura Watkinson

❊ ❊ ❊

This irrisistible tirade by Jules Deelder humorously captures a Rotterdammer's resentment of Amsterdam and of people who think that city is the best thing since sliced cheese. (Or might it contain an element of 'Amsterdam envy'?)

Look, over there, across the road ... with the schnozzle. Fuck me! That cow's always harping on about Amsterdam ... "When I lived in Amsterdam this, when I lived in Amsterdam that ... " She can stick her Amsterdam where the sun don't shine and swivel on it. Not that I've got anything against Amsterdammers ... They're decent folk, with a good heart ... So good it should be cooked and hung down her back, low enough for the bleedin' dogs ... So it's not that. But that effing bitch ... Fuck me!

"When I was in Amsterdam the other week. AIDS-riddled friggin' freak! She can drop dead with her Amsterdam! Paradise on earth, from what she says! So what's she doing here in Rotterdam? Driving me up the wall? She should've stayed there instead of spoiling the view around here ... . You seen that mug of hers? One big blackhead! Can't believe they let that go out and about. She's an insult to the human race ... "When I lived in Amsterdam ... " In the Red Light District, I bet. She can choke on her Amsterdam! Imagine living next to one of them smelly canals, with those boats chugging past all day full of krauts and yanks gawping at you. Ugh. Gimme an early grave any day! What's the big deal about Amsterdam anyway? Capital of the Netherlands? Capital offence, you mean. Bunch of crooks! "Amsterdam's got it!" Yeah, great slogan, coz if they didn't have it they'd nick it! [...]

Still stuck in the seventeenth century, that lot. Bunch of losers. God they take themselves seriously! Whenever they fart the whole country has to put up with the stink. You only have to look at the papers. It's Amsterdam this, Amsterdam that. Amsterdam here, Amsterdam there. Amsterdam left, right and fuckin' centre ... [...]

Another example: the Concertgebouw was on the verge of collapse ... Good riddance, if you ask me! No such luck ... The whole bloody country was up in arms, because OUR national concert hall had to be saved. Cough up now please, thank you very much ... Cough up, my arse! We're pouring enough into that fuckin' city. The *whole* of Amsterdam is listed. Whatcha think it costs to save all them medieval piles? *Billions*! Fanfuckin'-tastic, but let them stump up their own cash.

Jules Deelder, *Deelder is Laughing* [*Deelder lacht*] (2007)
translated from the Dutch by Laura Vroomen

Amsterdam the Tolerant

From at least the seventeenth century, Amsterdam has been synonymous with tolerance and freedom – conditions necessary for the work of philosophers such as Spinoza and Leibniz, the focus of Matthew Stewart's The Courtier and the Heretic

Many aspects of life in Amsterdam astounded seventeenth-century travellers. Visitors gushed about the magnificent public buildings, the elegant private mansions on tree-lined canals, the fanatical neatness of the inhabitants, the low crime rate, the plentiful and well-endowed hospitals, the innovations in military methods, the scientific and technological marvels, such as the newfangled street lamps, the clocks, the telescopes and the microscopes, and, inevitably, the universal obsession with the painted image. Spinoza's first biographer and friend, Jean-Maximilian Lucas, writing in 1677, called Amsterdam "the most beautiful city in Europe."

But the feature of life that left the most vivid impression on visitors to Amsterdam – sometimes favourable, more often not – was the extraordinary freedom enjoyed by its people. The Dutch "loved nothing so much as their freedom," wrote a scandalized German traveller. Servants and their mistresses dress and behave so much alike, he added, that it is hard to tell them apart. Louis XIV, who saw freedom as a form of vulgarity, scoffed that Holland was "a nation of fishwives and tradesmen." Sir William Temple, the English ambassador in the 1670s, on the other hand, took a much brighter view:

> It is hardly to be imagined how all the violence and sharpness, which accompanies the differences of religion in other countreys, seems to be appeased or softened here, by the general freedom which all here enjoy ... Men live tighter like Citizens of the World, associated by the common ties of Humanity ... under the impartial protection of indifferent laws, with ... equal freedom of Speculation and Enquiry.

Leibniz himself could not but acknowledge this newfound spirit of Dutch freedom. "This *simulacrum* of liberty is one of the principal pillars of the Dutch State," he wrote, somewhat grudgingly, in 1671, five years before setting foot in the Republic. "Such is the manner by which the multitudes find contentment in their freedom of belief and speech," he added, "that the most miserable sailor, in the tavern where he drinks his beer, fancies himself a king, even though he must still bear the heaviest burden to earn his livelihood."

Matthew Stewart, *The Courtier and the Heretic* (2005)

✳ ✳ ✳

Geert Mak investigates the subject further – and treats us to an amusing anecdote about seventeenth-century children standing up for their rights.

"Among people of the seventeenth century, Amsterdam was famed as the stock exchange *par excellence*, the temple of trade," writes the French historian Henri Méchoulan in his book about the mentality of seventeenth-century Amsterdam. "But," he continues, "it has to be seen, in the first place, as the cradle of freedom," for although Genoa, Venice and Antwerp were also important trading cities of the day, they never managed to bring about a revolution in European consciousness. The new Amsterdam that had emerged after the peaceful revolution of 1578 was dominated by a formula for success which, until then, had been unknown; the pursuit of wealth in combination with a new conception of liberty. Money and freedom pushed aside, for the first time, the old medieval combination of "honour" and "heroism". With these vanished another idea, the belief that the greatest virtue lay in conquest, in war, and was embodied in the knight, the king, and his court. "The merchant, the new hero, vanquishes war every day by means of his trade, a fountain of power, of life, which can only flourish in an environment of freedom," Méchoulan writes. And the first freedom is undeniably that of "remaining oneself".

After the toppling of the last medieval regents, the city paradoxically grew into a realization of a medieval utopia: the safe, enclosed space in which the non-citizen could cast off the yoke of serfdom. "This church consecrated to God knows not enforced beliefs, nor torture, nor death," the Jewish immigrants, full of trust, wrote above the door of their Portuguese Synagogue. They called Amsterdam the Jerusalem of the West.

John Locke wrote his *Epistulae de Tolerantia* in Amsterdam, among other works. Baruch de Spinoza and René Descartes found the leisure and freedom here to conduct their researches, just as did the painter and inventor Jan van der Heijden and the composer Jan Pieterszoon Sweelinck. Jan Swammerdam laid the foundations for the science of biology and of entomology. [...]

After 1650, the power of the clergy within the city somewhat increased. Under the influence of economic depression, the Anglo-

Dutch Wars of 1652–3 and 1664–7, a terrible plague epidemic, and other things commonly perceived as God's wrath, Calvinism enjoyed a sort of renaissance. The struggle against immorality in general, and the stage in particular, was once more being vigorously fought, and it was during this period that Hendrickje Stoffels was arraigned before the Church Council and Vondel had big problems on account of his play, *Lucifer*. In 1655, the well-known surgeon Dr Tulp succeeded in pushing through a "luxury law" against excessive wedding celebrations, although this was not exceptionally draconian: the number of guests could not exceed 50 and festivities were not allowed to last longer than two days. In December 1663, Tulp and his camp went one step further: they prohibited the selling of the traditional Saint Nicholas gingerbread figures as "idolatry" and "papist perversion". The result was a small children's riot, and the ban was hastily lifted.

Geert Mak, *Amsterdam: A Brief Life of the City* (1999)
translated from the Dutch by Philipp Blom

✳ ✳ ✳

In his magnificent study of the Dutch 'Golden Age',
The Embarrassment of Riches, *Simon Schama considers*
what Amsterdam's legendary tolerance meant for its
Jewish population, many of whom had fled to the city
to escape persecution in other parts of Europe.

Traditionally, the response of the Dutch to Jews in their midst has been thought the *locus classicus* of benign pluralism: an exceptional case of tolerance in a Christian Europe that either ejected or confined them in humiliating and degrading circumstances. There is much to support this optimistic scenario. There was no Amsterdam ghetto, no yellow badge, horned hat or lock-up curfew behind gates and walls. The costume of the Sephardim from the Iberian world in particular was indistinguishable from that of gentile Amsterdammers and, most significantly, the demonological exaggeration of physical features disappears from the depiction of Jews in their artistic rendering by Rembrandt and Lievens. Instead, the Semitism of their physiognomy was actually mobilized to enhance the narrative immediacy of scripture painting, so that Rembrandt gives us not only a David but a St. Matthew and a Jesus with the features of his Jewish neighbours on the Breestraat.

This was a radical departure from iconographic convention. But no less telling was the sheer matter-of-factness by which Jews became absorbed into the standard genres of Dutch culture. By the time that Johan Leusden and Jan Luiken came to engrave their series on the rites and manners of the Jews, scenes of circumcision, the baking of Passover matzoth or the funerary *shiva* could be shown without any sinister overtones of arcane practice. Luiken's *Jewish Circumcision* is exactly akin to other scenes from ethnographic works that had become popular in the second half of the century, and was now wholly divorced both from demonology and from the use of Jewish custom as a counterreference for the Christian mysteries. […]

By 1690, however, this delicate cultural balancing act was threatened by the arrival of Ashkenazi Jews in much greater numbers. Of the 7,500 Jews in Amsterdam at that time, 5,000 were immigrants from Germany, Poland, Bohemia and Lithuania. These newcomers duly built their own synagogue opposite the Sephardic temple, and created their own autonomous education institutions, burial societies, dietary regulations and a Yiddish press. But their presence became much more conspicuously "alien" than that of the Sephardim. They settled thickly in streets like the Leprozenburgwal, the Nieuwe Kerkstraat and the Nieuwe Houtmarkt, which became known as the milieu of poor Jews, dressed strikingly differently from Dutch men and women and speaking a gabbling, incomprehensible tongue. And they turned to the menial "ghetto" trades disdained by the Sephardim like hawking, peddling, and old clothes dealing (much of it practiced without city licenses). There can be hardly any doubt that the Jewish fiddlers mentioned in *'t Amsterdamsch Hoerdom* as playing in the *musicos* were Ashkenazim of this generation of immigrants.

The influx of the Ashkenazim, then, in some ways re-marginalized the Jews within Dutch culture. Or rather it created, for a while, two sorts of Jews: those who were Jews first and Dutch second, and the smaller, older community of whom it might be fairly said the opposite was true.

Simon Schama, *The Embarrassment of Riches* (1987)

❊ ❊ ❊

Ian Buruma starts this extract with the tolerance of Jewish immigrants and goes on to consider subsequent waves of immigration and their consequences for the city.

Holland, and Amsterdam in particular, has a long history of taking in foreigners. [...]

Holland's reputation for hospitality is deserved, but immigration in the twentieth century is also a story of horror, opportunism, postcolonial obligations, and an odd combination of charity and indifference. Few Jewish refugees from Nazi Germany – Anne Frank was, for example, one who did not – survived the German occupation. Their fate was certainly not welcomed by most gentiles in Holland, but despite the bravery of many individuals, too little was done to help them. Altogether 71 percent of all Jews in the Netherlands ended up in death camps, the highest percentage in Europe outside Poland. Largely unmentioned until the 1960s, the shame of it poisons national debates to this day.

The end of empire in the Dutch East Indies, despite the problems with Moluccans, was less traumatic. The violence happened too far away. And those Eurasians and Indonesians who chose to move to the Netherlands in the 1940s and 1950s were relatively small in number, generally well educated, and easily absorbed. The same was true of the first wave of Surinamese from the former colony of Dutch Guiana. Arriving in the 1960s, when the Dutch economy boomed, these mostly middle-class men and women found work as nurses, civil servants, or teachers. The dirty work, in the boom years, was done by "guest workers" from Turkey and Morocco, single men cooped up in cheap hostels, prepared to do almost anything to provide for their families back home. These men were not expected to stay. One of them was Mohammed Bouyeri's father.

It was the second wave of Surinamese, arriving around 1972, that began to cause problems. […] The oil shock in 1973, when Arab oil producers punished the Netherlands with an embargo for its support of Israel in the Yom Kippur War, had created a crisis in the Dutch economy. There were no longer enough jobs for the guest workers from Turkey or Morocco, let alone more than two hundred thousand newcomers from a Caribbean backwater.

The result was widespread unemployment, dependence on the welfare state, petty crime, and a vicious circle of social discrimination and sporadic violence. There are still many Surinamese without an official job, perhaps as many as 30 per cent, but the Surinamese are no longer a "problem." They always speak Dutch, excel at soccer, and by and large have been moving steadily into the middle class. […]

The same is not true of the guest workers and their offspring. Like the Moluccans, these men were not regarded as immigrants. Their stay was supposed to have been temporary, to clean out oil tankers, work in steel factories, sweep the streets. When many of them elected to remain, the government took the benevolent view that in that case they should be joined by their wives and children. Slowly, almost without anyone's noticing, old working-class Dutch neighbourhoods lost their white populations and were transformed into "dish cities" linked to Morocco, Turkey, and the Middle East by satellite television and the Internet. […]

The Turks, backed by a variety of social and religious institutions, formed a relatively close-knit community of shop-keepers and professionals. Grocery stores in Amsterdam are often owned by Turks, and so are pizzerias. If Turks turn to crime, it is organized crime, sometimes linked to the old country – financial fraud, illegal immigration, hard drugs. There are links to political violence in Turkey, to do with militant nationalism or the Kurdish question, but not so much with revolutionary Islam. That appears to be more a Moroccan problem.

Moroccans in the Netherlands are mostly Berbers, not Arabs, from remote villages in the Rif mountains. Like Sicilian peasants, they are clannish people, widely distrusted by urban Moroccans, and often, especially the women, illiterate. Less organized, with the narrow horizons of village folk, and awkwardly wedged between the North African and European worlds, Moroccan immigrants lack the kinds of institutional support that give the Turkish immigrants a sense of belonging.

Those who manage, through intelligence, perseverance, and good fortune, to make their way in Dutch society, often do very well indeed. Those who don't, for one reason or another, drift easily into a seedy world without exit of gang violence and petty crime. Most vulnerable of all are those who find their ambitions blocked despite their attempts to fit in with the mainstream of Dutch life. Anything can trigger a mood of violent resentment and self-destruction: a job offer withdrawn, a grant not given, one too many doors shut in one's face. Such a man was Mohammed Bouyeri, who adopted a brand of Islamic extremism unknown to his father, a broken-backed former guest worker from the Rif mountains, and decided to join a war against the society from which he felt excluded. Unsure of where he belonged, he lost himself in a murderous cause.

During the last few decades, the guest workers and their children were joined by another group of newcomers, many of them scarred by political violence: Tamils from Sri Lanka, Syrians and Iranians, Somali escapees from civil war, Iraqis, Bosnians, Egyptians, Chinese, and many more. [...] When an Israeli cargo plane crashed into a poor suburb of Amsterdam in 1992, the number of victims was impossible to calculate, since the housing estates were filled with illegals.

Ian Buruma, *Murder in Amsterdam* (2006)

✳ ✳ ✳

The emergence of racist politics under the leadership of the subsequently murdered extreme right-wing politician Pim Fortuyn has somewhat changed the landscape of Amsterdam tolerance.

'The Netherlands is a country of apartheid,' said Fortuyn, and he had a point. In the past few years the country has ceased to boast so much about its tolerance, and in the process it has become less tolerant. When Fortuyn first popped up in the still-life that is Dutch politics, few people would admit to supporting him. By the time he was murdered six months later that stigma had vanished, and after his death it took some courage to say a word against him. The Netherlands is now a country with a large and respectable racist party.

Simon Kuper, *Ajax, The Dutch, The War* (2003)

✳ ✳ ✳

One aspect of Amsterdam's 'tolerance' known the world over is the city's red-light district. Rupert Thomson briefly introduces us to it, but with a hint that all is not as 'blithe' as it appears.

I walked out of Central Station, past the men loitering suspiciously near public telephones, past the tangled mass of bicycles in racks, and crossed that bleak, wide-open area beyond the trams, making for Zeedijk. I had always liked the red-light district during the day, especially when the sun was shining – some bleary, slept-in quality the streets had, the neon diluted, pale, and, every now and then, a girl on her way to work in full make-up and impossible high-heels – but it struck me, as I walked along, that I had been attracted to that world only because of its distance from my own. It had been a kind of romanticism, the naïve romanticism of the inexperienced, the uninformed.

Rupert Thomson, *The Book of Revelation* (1999)

✳ ✳ ✳

Living in the red-light district himself, Maarten 't Hart is able to give a fuller picture of the place and its people.

From the crack of dawn until the mid-morning coffee break – the best part of my day – the red-light district is the very picture of peace and quiet. There are hardly any cars. What you do see at this hour in many of the still-lit rooms are the bent backs of women in sleeveless aprons, performing their cleaning operations with grim determination. Everywhere there are vacuum cleaners droning, dustcloths flapping, and machines busily polishing the tiled floors. In many apartments the rooms in question are even hosed down, as though they're trying to wash away years of dirt. If you take a walk at six in the morning you imagine yourself to be in a past century, when maidservants still scrubbed the cobblestones every day. All the same, it seems like an inordinate amount of housework. Why do those rooms have to be cleaned so thoroughly? Do they have to erase every last trace?

After everything has been cleaned in the early hours, a strange, pure, peaceful atmosphere settles over the neighbour-hood. If you take a walk at this time you think you're in a deserted part of town full of forgotten canals. You could easily go home and write, "The place is quiet in the morning, which is the best time of day to work." As soon as you pick up a pen, however, you become aware of the screeching of countless gulls. At that hour it seems as though wanton female gulls are offering themselves in exchange for a crust of bread.

Around half past ten the first girls arrive, then the first men. One or two windows appear to be occupied already, but these early birds only receive regular customers at such hours. Only once did a scrawny girl, apparently wandering around by mistake at 9 a.m. in Bloedstraat – Blood Street – inform me in her heavy German accent: "I take it all off."

I've often noticed that the first men who arrive around mid-morning (many of them sporting moustaches) hang around the whole day. Most of these men – and how strange this is! – expend all their energy on a walk lasting from half past ten in the morning till late in the afternoon, without, it would seem, even once taking a break or going inside. I've been told there are even men who stroll past the windows, gaping, for fifteen solid hours, "spending the whole day doing nothing but window-shopping," as the girls say. You hear nothing but that curious, rhythmic, shuffling sound coming from inside, as though you were in Paris, listening to the sound of the subway rumbling past underground.

Most men apparently find their hungry journey past all those windows satisfying enough. They obviously don't need to go inside. At most they stop once in a while to ask the price. I've often overheard their whispered conversations. "How much?"

"Fifty guilders, sweetheart."

Then they'll walk to the next window and ask again – "How much?" – and be given the same answer. Sometimes such men ask the same question twenty times, only to receive the same answer twenty times. For some mysterious reason, however, some of the girls do it for half price, though there is nothing to distinguish these hookers – attractive or otherwise – from their more expensive colleagues. And the cut-rate price of only twenty-five guilders is apparently not even offered as bait to get a sybarite to set foot inside, only to hear, "Come on, hon, give me another twenty-five and I'll take off my top," because from the information that is often volunteered to me, I gather that such girls do in fact screw for half price. They also appear never to do it naked, but whether or not they take off their bra certainly doesn't justify a difference in price of twenty-five guilders. Why doesn't the Consumer's Guide take up this issue?

And so, simply because so many men limit themselves to window-shopping, their desire increases to the boiling point. The men saunter and stroll and once every hour and a half they seek relief in the urinal next to the Oude Kerk.

A real customer generally doesn't stroll. He appears with nervous, hasty steps from Warmoesstraat or Lange Niezel. He

148

wears a hat, or a baseball cap pulled down at an angle over his eyes. Not infrequently he wears sunglasses to shield his eyes from the blazing sun. Quick as lightning he hurries past the windows. He makes a choice, stumbles in his haste on the stairs leading to a red-lit basement room, and falls bang into the arms of an elderly lady in underwear. Of course there are also men who arrive at a calm, measured pace and go inside in an open and honest manner, and these are also the ones who accost you on the street or suddenly fall into step beside you and tell you about their experiences.

Maarten 't Hart, *Living in the Red-Light District*
[*Wonen op de wallen*] (1992)
translated from the Dutch by Diane Webb

✳ ✳ ✳

The essay on the red-light district – or 'Wallen' – by Annemarie de Wildt, curator of the Amsterdam Historical Museum, in the National Gallery, London, guide to the installation 'The Hoerengracht' by Ed and Nancy Kienholz, updates us on the area and the lives of the prostitutes who work there. (The installation, using life-sized constructions of prostitutes in their rooms, makes ingenious play with the name of the city's most famous canal, the Herengracht – Gentlemen's Canal– turning it into 'Hoerengracht' – Whores' Canal.)

Although Amsterdam's red light district is renowned throughout the world, the first sight of women sitting in windows still comes as a shock to most tourists. Scantily dressed, posing provocatively and behind them perhaps a glimpse of the bed on which the transaction is to take place, they tempt their customers with a glance, a smile, sometimes calling out or tapping on the window. Through a half-open door they negotiate their price (50 euros on average) and the nature of the services to be provided. This is basic commerce: sex for money.

However, this popular image of Amsterdam's red light district is outdated, as the area is rapidly changing. In 2007 the municipality introduced policies aimed at reducing the number of window prostitutes. To date, this support has enabled housing corporations to acquire around 110 of the 480 windows and workplaces, which they have in turn let, temporarily, to fashion and jewellery designers and artists. Compared to its character of only a few years back, the area is on the brink of becoming gentrified. [...]

How should a city deal with prostitution? Prohibit it entirely or regulate it, and thereby condone it? Around the time when *The Hoerengracht* was being made, prostitution was a major political issue in Amsterdam and the target of numerous pressure groups. Like most foreigners, the Keinholzes thought that prostitution was completely legal in the Netherlands. In fact, while it had been illegal to run a brothel since 1911, the Dutch authorities did not enforce the law in the 1970s and 1980s, just as they turned a blind eye to the illegal practice of soliciting. Many of the streetwalkers were heroin addicts. Drug dealers hung around the area; needles littered the streets. Fights broke out regularly, although the Hell's Angels gang maintained a certain order in the district, for a price.

It was difficult for the authorities to devise rules to contain the disruption caused by prostitution and drug dealing. The Dutch language actually has a word to describe activities that are officially prohibited yet unofficially tolerated: *gedogen*. Even in tolerant Holland, it proved impossible to regulate these activities: it was an area of commerce that did not officially exist. Municipal officials who mapped the area were not allowed to use the word 'brothel'; they described these in their reports as 'alternative businesses'.

In 1984 a group of women in the local council organised a conference on Prostitution and Municipal Policy. They argued for a system of licenses to enable some regulation of the work conditions and legal status of 'sex workers', as prostitutes had started calling themselves. It was time prostitution was recognised as a profession. In an unprecedented move, former prostitutes joined in the debate. As one of their number, Violet, commented, 'Prostitutes are women who have made a virtue of necessity, because they were able to take up the profession of whore.' A year later prostitutes even set up their own union: the Rode Draad (Red Thread).

Optimistic proposals were made in the 1980s suggesting that co-operative prostitution companies run by women might be a step up. One of the minor socialist parties on Amsterdam's local council issued a manifesto in 1983 entitled *Prostitutes out of Oppression*. Instead of focusing on maintaining public order, they were concerned with the welfare of the prostitutes themselves. [...]

It was not until 2000 that the 1911 ban on brothels was repealed. In the preceding years, Amsterdam had already begun to create regulations for the impending legislation. Civil servants had started to tackle the issues associated with the red light district and the two worlds had met: the twilight world of the Wallen and the glaring daylight of the town hall bureaucrats. [...]

From the 1980s and 1990s onwards, women from different ethnic groups started to become more visible in the Wallen. Dutch prostitutes were becoming increasingly more independent, and some brothel keepers preferred to take brutal advantage of immigrant sex workers who had poor language skills and few rights.

Some streets were populated with mainly Thai women. In other streets there were mostly Ghanaian. Oudekerksplein was where the Dominican women tended to work. South American transsexuals frequently worked in Amsterdam brothels; they came to Amsterdam for their sex change operation and to earn money they turned to prostitution. [...]

A major consequence of the legalisation of brothels in 2000 was that prostitutes required work and residence permits and proprietors were responsible for checking the status of their tenants. Some of the non-European prostitutes went into the escort business or moved into the deserted harbour areas or suburbs of south-east Amsterdam.

Annemarie de Wildt, *The Hoerengracht:*
Kienholz at the National Gallery London (2009)

✳ ✳ ✳

Dubravka Ugresic ponders the traffic in human flesh
coming from Eastern Europe.

One day, passing a group of American tourists that had gathered round an old Kalverstraat organ-grinder, and hearing them gush over him with the word 'cute', I was reminded of its equivalent, 'leuk', in Dutch and realized that leukness was the key to the problem. Leukness was an antiseptic, a disinfectant that removed all spots, all bumps, put everything on an equal footing, made everything acceptable. Near my house there was a gay bar called the Queen's Head with a display of ten male dolls, ten Kens, in the window. It was a leuk display. Whenever I passed it, I thought of the live Barbies – young women from Moldavia, Bulgaria, Ukraine, Belarus – the traffickers, traders in human flesh, bought up for export. I thought of the fresh East-European flesh setting off on the long journey west. If it didn't get bogged down in some Serbian or Bosnian backwoods, it would end up here. I thought of them and of the East European Kens who had come to this Disneyland to entertain the grown-up male children here, to give them alien flesh in which to insert their male members. How leuk it all was. And what is leuk is beyond good and evil; it is amoral not immoral; it is simply take it or leave it.

Dubravka Ugresic, *The Ministry of Pain* (2005)
translated from the Croatian by Michael Henry Heim

✱ ✱ ✱

After smoking a joint in a coffee shop, Jon, in Stan Shevez's The Devil's Playground, *takes a stroll through the red-light district.*

Soon his mood was distracted by the bright flickering neon and bustling streets of the red-light district. He stopped in a coffee shop – the first one he came to that wasn't shaking with dance music – found a seat, a small table by the window, watching everyone go by. He bought some grass and rolled a joint. Tourists walking the streets stared at him and he realized how he'd become a tourist attraction, safely pinned behind the glass front of the shop, the strange feeling of doing these things out in the open. He smoked the joint and listened to the second side of the first Springsteen album on the house system. To his left was a message-board. Handwritten pieces of paper pleading for jobs, accommodation, money, hung like discarded dreams. One of the pieces had a photo on it. A young man, goateed, with long hair and lost eyes. Jon squinted to read the text. 'Please come home, Carl,' it said and the shakiness of the handwriting, the slope and slack of the letters seemed to make it all the more poignant. 'Les has had a breakdown, Denise loves you. Daddy forgives. Please come back to us. We love you.'

There was something there, in the language of public facsimile, the syntax of cliché and nuclear family, that almost undid him. He turned away. What had happened to him that he could be so easily moved by such things? He stared back out of the window. By the second joint, the whole place seemed more comfortable, the paint had gradually subsided to a gentle throb and he felt himself sinking into the barstool. [...]

He walked around stunned, drawn by the procession of delights as he turned through the winding streets of the District, buzzing on weed and excitement. The closeness of the streets held him, their illogical design intrigued him, leading him further into its heart then looping around, always back to the same place.

He stopped in front of a sex shop, drawn by the bouquet of dildoes in the window, strange brutal things of all shapes, colours and permutations, that seemed more like instruments of torture than any kind of pleasure devices that he could imagine. Not so unusual for Jon who, while enjoying girls and fumbled moments as much as anyone, never really found that sex was the great big thing that mitigated all the horrors of life as everyone else seemed to think. Not to say he didn't enjoy it, he almost always did, it was just that it was nothing special, no fireworks, no moving earth, none of the above.

It was eleven o'clock and the streets of the District were packed and pulverized by strollers, drug dealers, husbands holding on tightly to their wives, sneaking surreptitious glances at the girls preening and pouting behind their windows, businessmen and drinking buddies on a lost weekend and cops walking their beat. Jon let himself flow with the mass of people, unaware of where he was going and not caring too much either, happy to be entertained for the time being by the sights and smells, the movable feast of flesh and neon that decorated the streets. There was a tightness to the roads in Amsterdam that was entirely lacking in London, a sense of clustered communality that he found strangely comforting.

He walked along a narrow alley, only about three-foot wide, with rows of windows on either side. He found himself sneaking glances, too embarrassed to catch the eyes of the women, avoiding the staccato beat of fingernails tapping on glass that tried to entice him. People walked slowly, surveying the girls, checking out their figures and wondering whether to lay their Euros down. Comparison shopping.

Stav Sherez, *The Devil's Playground* (2004)

✻ ✻ ✻

Just as famous as Amsterdam's sex industry is the city's tolerant attitude towards drugs. The narrator of Geoff Dyer's story, 'Hotel Oblivion', tries some during a weekend trip with friends.

Nearly everyone in our party liked the idea of dinner followed by a few joints in a bar, but only Amsterdam Dave was committed to making it a truly memorable weekend in the sense that he would remember nothing whatsoever about it. I was in the twilight, the long autumn of my psychedelic years, and this was to be my last hurrah – or one of them, at any rate. I had never met Amsterdam Dave before but I took to him from the moment he explained the philosophical basis of the weekend.

'It's all about moderation,' he said in the Greenhouse on Friday night, after a deliciously inauthentic Thai meal. 'Everything in moderation. Even moderation itself. From this it follows that you must, from time to time, have excess. And this is going to be one of those occasions.'

'I couldn't agree more,' I said, impressed by the rigour of his thinking. 'As I see it we are here to do the Dam. We want to have the Amsterdam experience.'

'Indeed we do,' said Amsterdam Dave. On Saturday morning, accordingly, we made our way to the Magic Mushroom Gallery on Spuistraat. Amsterdam Dave looked slightly the worse for wear; that is to say, he looked in better shape than he would for the rest of the weekend. This was partly because he had stayed on at a club called the Trance Buddha or Buddha Trance or something long after we had turned in, but mainly it was because Amsterdam Dave never looked better than slightly the worse for wear. I have seen him on several occasions since that weekend in Amsterdam and I have never seen him look anything like as good as he did then. His face had some colour in it. That colour was grey, admittedly, but at least it was a colour. Other times, only his eyes and the hair at his temples were grey; the last vestige of colour had been completely drained from the rest of his face. Even his lips were pale. But that October morning in Amsterdam he looked great, relatively speaking.

Dazed looked lovely too, unequivocally so. She was wearing a woolly hat that I had bought her as an advance Christmas present and this, combined with her wonky tortoiseshell glasses, gave her the appearance of an eccentric intellectual beauty, a nutty archaeologist, say, as played by a Hollywood actress who was in her thirties and trying not to rely solely on her looks, determined to show that she could do character. And me? Oh, doubtless I looked a complete joke. From the outside you would have thought I was the kind of person whose over-youthful wardrobe – skateboarding T-shirt, trainers, hooded sweatshirt – could not disguise the fact that he was forty-two, an intellectual with nothing but ink to his name; but, for much of that weekend, I felt myself to be at the height of my powers – or thereabouts. I concede that we may have looked an oddly matched trio as we sat down in a café to consume our newly purchased mushrooms but I was not expecting to get thrown out quite as soon as we did. Not thrown out exactly, but given a very stern talking-to by the barman. He didn't want us doing mushrooms in here, he said. This took a moment to sink in: we were being ejected from a bar in Amsterdam for taking drugs?

'That's like getting chucked out of a pub for drinking beer,' said Dazed.

I have achieved very little in my life – perhaps this is why I felt a faint glow of adolescent pride at our undesirable status. The barman had one of those old, fanatically grizzled druggie faces, and his dull eyes did not regard us at all sympathetically. I couldn't take issue with him because my gullet was clogged with gag-inducing mushrooms which I was trying to swill down with the remaining drops of water from Dazed's bottle of Evian, but evidently the three of us collectively registered sufficient surprise to generate some kind of explanation from the barman.

'I don't want you puking,' he said.

'Several things,' said Amsterdam Dave, who had succeeded in swallowing his mushrooms. 'First, at my age, I do not need lessons in how to behave. I am a very civic-minded person. Second, my friends and I have a combined age of almost a hundred and fifteen years and we have, I think it's fair to say, no intention of throwing up. Third, if we do feel like throwing up, we'll make sure we step either outside or into the toilet. Fourth, if we are going to throw up it's not going to happen for at least half an hour. In the meantime, perhaps you would be so good as to bring us three coffees.'

It was an extremely impressive speech and, for a moment, I thought the barman was going to oblige. Then, with no alteration of expression, he clicked his fingers, pointed to the door and uttered two words. The first was 'Asshole!' The second was 'Out!' [...]

At some point conditions began to deteriorate. The wind picked up. It began raining heavily, and then, once it had begun raining heavily, some kind of maritime gale kicked in. We wanted to get out of the wind-whipped rain, but in order to get out of the rain it was necessary to continue walking in it, at least for a while. We headed for the relative tranquillity of the Van Gogh Museum, where the paintings pitched and reeled in a blaze of yellow. Not that we saw anything of them. Conditions had deteriorated to the extent that everyone in Amsterdam had just one aim in mind: to get out of the rain, to get out of the rain and into the Van Gogh Museum. Everyone was wet and steaming and at any moment a soggy stampede seemed a distinct possibility. Occasionally, in the background, a sun burst over the writhing corn of Arles, a Roman-candle night – starry, starry – swirled into life. Blossom-tormented trees reared into view, pigment-coloured faces beamed brightly, but mainly there were just the drenched backs of museum-goers in their foul-weather gear, jostling for position.. [...]

Somehow we were all out on the streets again, walking through the UV haze of the hookers' windows in the red-light district that might better be termed the black-light district. A guy in an Arctic parka said something to me I did not quite catch, then I realized he was offering me drugs, specifically Viagra. I said I didn't want any.

'You look like you need it,' he said. It was an unkind remark but I pushed it to one side of my mind. Some of our party, including Matt and Alexandra, had already said goodnight and headed off to bed. Those of us who were left went into a bar and smoked some feverish skunk, and then there were just the three of us again, Dazed, Amsterdam Dave and I, and we were no longer in the bar but out on the streets, back, in a sense, where we started. Under the influence of this hydro-whatever-it-was grass, the mushrooms, which had not worked very powerfully during the afternoon, made an unexpected comeback, and all the accumulated confusion of the day burst in upon us and left us stranded in an alien city that bore only an occasional resemblance to the Amsterdam of maps and guidebooks.

We were completely deranged, unsure of our bearings, utterly unsuited to the task of finding our hotel. [...]

At various points I completely lost track of where in the world we had fetched up. It seemed to me that I was in six or seven cities at once. I was in Sydney, in the area known as King's Cross, which meant I was also in the area of London of that name and, at the same time, I was unable to get my bearings because what I saw persuaded me that I was in Paris and Copenhagen. I was everywhere at once.

'There is some place I have not yet been to,' I said in a blur of absolute lucidity, 'some place of which every other place has been no more than a premonition. But how will I know I'm there? If I can't answer that question then, for all I know, I could be there already.'

How easy it was to become confused in Amsterdam, on that autumn night in Amsterdam particularly.

'What we must do,' said Amsterdam Dave, 'is concentrate on finding our hotel.'

'Of course we should,' I said. 'Of course we should. But the phrase "Easier said than done" comes to mind.'

'Here's a canal,' said Dazed, as though that solved everything, as though we had not seen hundreds of canals – or this very same canal hundreds of times – in the course of what was starting to seem a long and ill-advised excursion.

Geoff Dyer, 'Hotel Oblivion' from
Yoga For People Who Can't Be Bothered To Do It (2003)

❉ ❉ ❉

In Tommy Wieringa's novel, Joe Speedboat, *a young Joe tries something a little stronger than he's used to ...*

One day in late autumn, Joe and his classmates went on an excursion to the Van Gogh Museum. During the ten minutes he stood there, the queue advanced only a few meters. Right in front of them was a busload of Japanese tourists, behind them a group of disgruntled day-trippers from Groningen who were doing their best to keep spirits high. Joe looked around. His feet were cold. Bag this, he thought suddenly, stepped out of line without a word and disappeared in the direction of Museum Square.

And there he stood, far from home and with no reason to go back. He took a deep breath, looked around and decided to stay in Amsterdam for a while and see how things worked out.

Around dinnertime he started thinking about a place to stay. He knew only one person in the whole city: P.J. Eilander. He

159

phoned P.J.'s mother, who gave him her daughter's address on Tolstraat, just above a coffeeshop. The coffeeshop was called Babylon, if she remembered rightly.

Joe took the tram. He experienced giddying happiness – no one knew where he was, life could go any which way, there were as many possibilities as combinations on a fruit machine and every direction he chose was the right one, because it was time for the machine to pay out.

P.J. wasn't home. Joe waited in Coffeeshop Babylon, sitting by the window where he might see her come by. Meanwhile, he had plenty of time to feast his eyes on the economics of soft drugs. In Lomark it had been sport for awhile to smoke a few quick joints and then cross the border into Germany – to come back with stories of a different planet. That was just for laughs, but smoking here was taken very seriously, it was bitter earnest. The users seemed to avoid daylight as much as possible, and applied themselves with cultish dedication to the rolling and routine firing-up of huge bombers. It was truly something to see. A native from the jungle who was dropped here and saw this for the first time would think he was observing an official religious rite.

- Hey, man, want a drag?

Joe looked up. A man with black curly hair beneath a red cap was holding out a trumpetlike joint.

- No thanks, Joe said. I'm waiting for someone.

Don't be an ass, man, that's what it's made for.

No, really, thank you.

You look like you could use a toke.

Joe accepted the joint.

My name's George, the man said. The Urban Indian. But you probably picked up on that.

Joe reappeared from behind the cloud.

My name's Joe Speedboat, he said in a squeaky voice.

Joe Speedboat! You're all right, man, you're all right!

Like tens of thousands of tourists, on his first day in

Amsterdam Joe got stoned ("Jesus, man, you know, if I could just build all the things I see ... "). It was completely dark outside when George the Urban Indian left, from outside the window he had shouted "Good luck, Joe Speedboat! Good luck, man!" and cycled away on his delivery bike. Joe remained behind in the blessed dreams of his first, second and third joints ("I was really dying for a strawberry yoghurt drink, so I ordered one. That stuff ran down into my stomach like a cold mountain stream. You never tasted yoghurt drink like that.").

It will never be clear what would have happened had P.J. not run out of cigarettes that evening. She had returned home at around seven, and now she went downstairs without a coat to buy a pack at the coffeeshop. The men at the pool table looked up; walking over to the counter with the jar of tobacco, rolling papers and lighters she said: "Could I have a pack of Marlboro, please?"

Any time for you, baby, anytime.

On her way out she saw, in the shadow of the rubber plant by the window, a familiar face. The boy, his eyes half-closed, was sitting at a table littered with empty bottles of strawberry yoghurt drink. P.J. went over to him.

- Hey, Joe, she said. You're Joe, aren't you?

His eyes opened a little further.

Hi.

It's me, P.J., we went to school together.

Oh. Hey. I. Know. You.

What are *you* doing here? No one from Lomark ...

That was how Joe made his arrival, floating in a basket of papyrus and encircled by feminine attention and lots of questions. Where he was staying? Nowhere? He could sleep in her bed. She always spent the night at her boyfriend's place, she'd be back in the morning. He must be hungry; she started talking about something she called the "munchies", triggered by the smoking of marijuana. But it would have been wiser for Joe not to have touched the pasta she prepared for him. He made it to the toilet just as the gusher of rosy-pink yoghurt drink, commingled with tagliatelle and tomato sauce, came rocketing up, spreading a sweet-and-sour dairy smell throughout her toilet and living room.

Oh. Shit. Oh. Sorry.

Jesus, Joe, what did you do? Did you smoke the little plastic bag along with it?

Tommy Wieringa *Joe Speedboat* (2008)
translated from the Dutch by Sam Garrett

❋ ❋ ❋

And a pot-smoking couple enjoy New Year's Eve in the city centre.

Though it was only a short distance to the Nieuw Markt, it took us twenty minutes, the crowd thickening as we drew closer. Once, somebody lit a firecracker that must have been at least fifteen feet long, and people scattered in all directions. I felt Juliette tighten her grip on my hand as we backed against a wall. We watched from a distance as the firecracker writhed and twisted and flung itself about, loud as a machine-gun in the narrow street, then the crowd flowed on, laughing, drinking, making jokes, and, all of a sudden, we were in the square ...

The atmosphere was jubilant, chaotic. Bonfires had been built on the cobblestones, using whatever came to hand: cardboard boxes, broken chairs, fruit crates – even a rowing-boat. We passed two men who were wearing giant, painted papier-mâché heads. We saw a girl on stilts stalking through pale, drifting clouds of smoke. Fireworks fizzed horizontally through the darkness, missing people by inches, and the air shook with constant explosions.

We sat down by the fountain and opened the champagne.

'I've got some pot,' Juliette said.

She took a joint out of her pocket, lit it and passed it to me. I drew the smoke into my lungs and held it there. [...]

162

Just then all the clocks began to strike. It was midnight, and we hadn't even realised. I laughed and took Juliette in my arms and when the last note sounded, a roar filled the square, as if a furnace door had been opened, or a great wind had descended, and we clung to each other, and we kissed for so long, my tongue touching hers, that when I opened my eyes I was dazzled by the eerie silver light that seemed to surround us. I stood back and looked at her and even though I was stoned by now, drunk too, I still had the same feeling of absolute certainty that I had had while I was looking into the mirror at my parents' house five days before.

At half-past twelve we left the square and walked back to my apartment in the Kinkerbuurt. The streets were covered with the remnants of firecrackers, scraps of dull-red paper that lay in heaps, like autumn leaves. We passed a young couple dancing slowly on a bridge. The girl was humming a tune I didn't recognise, her eyes closed. The boy's leather coat had the gleam of chrome.

Rupert Thomson, *The Book of Revelation* (1999)

✳ ✳ ✳

Amsterdam's drug culture all goes back to the sixties, of course – a period which also gave rise to the street actions of the 'Provo' movement ... which developed into the Squatters campaiging and subsequent riots, significantly changing the political scene in Amsterdam over twenty years or more. In an email letter to his granddaughter, Piet Reinewald gives a glimpse into the time he remembers well. It shows there were limits to the tolerance of Amsterdammers themselves and of the authorities.

Hi, Maria!

So, you're doing a history project on the Provos and Squatters. That makes me feel old: I am already 'history'! But your dad is right, I do remember it well and even got involved in demos, though I certainly wasn't a ring-leader. I was already a bit too old for that, and had a job and young family to consider, anyway. I'll answer your questions briefly and if you need to know more you can always give me a call. I'm also sending you photo-copies of some leaflets and magazine articles I've saved from the time that might give you a flavour of what went on. So, here we go …

The Provos (short for 'Provocation') started in the mid sixties but faded out by the seventies. But the Squatters' movement, big in the late seventies and eighties, grew out of it.   I t started with a street performer, Jasper Grootveld (an ex-window cleaner!) who did things like paint Ks (for Kanker [cancer]) on cigarette adverts around the city. (By the way, I hope you and your friends don't smoke). He was soon joined by philosophy student Roel van Duyn who really founded the Provos.

There were only ever a couple of dozen really active Provos, but they had lots of support from the general population (people like me and your gran) – so much that in the 1966 elections they even won a seat on the City Council. People liked their ideas and the mainly 'humorous' way they went about trying to achieve the changes they believed necessary for the good of the city's population. One of their suggestions was to ban cars from the city centre and supply lots of bicycles for the public to use. WHITE bicycles! (Something similar has recently been tried in Paris, with great success – though the bikes aren't white – which shows how the Provos were quite ahead of their time.)

Although the Provos officially disbanded in the late sixties, it led on to the Squatters movement, which provoked a lot more violence from the police. Young people who could not afford accommodation began to take over empty buildings and to object to so much space being given over to big business rather than housing projects. When the council claimed it couldn't afford to do so, then went on to spend vast sums on the coronation of Queen Beatrix on 30th April 1980 and on refurbishing her palace, there were lots of protests that turned quite violent, with some pretty heavy-handed responses from the police. Yes, I was there ... but no, I didn't get hit by a truncheon. And I didn't actually do anything violent like wrecking cars or setting fire to trams. I didn't think that was a good way to keep public sympathy. But I guess some young people were just so angry and got a bit carried away. Or maybe I was just a coward and didn't want to get injured or arrested. The Squatters always got evicted in the end, even though they had lots of public sympathy and support.

I suppose the last 'echo' of the movement was the campaign against the building of the 'Stopera' – which failed, of course, because it's standing there, big and a bit ugly. But we're getting used to it, aren't we?! And at least it's for the public, not for 'big business'.

Well, that's the basics. I can fill in more detials of you need them, but I think you'll find some useful extra material in the bundle I'm sending you. Hope you get a good mark for your project. (If not, you can blame me!)

Hope to see you soon.

Much love,

    Grandpa XX

> Piet Reinewald, email to his granddaughter
> translated from the Dutch by Jennifer Reinewald

'In Old Amsterdam ... '

The seventeenth century was truly Amsterdam's Golden Age. But behind the great art and nice houses and impressive white ruffs, what was daily life actually like for most people. Simon Schama provides a dose of reality by recreating the smells of the busy city in earlier times.

From a seagull's gliding altitude, the great city resembled: a half-moon; a rat-gnawed cheese; a cradle lying with its base to the southern meadows, the top open to the dark waters of the IJ; the tubby hull of a *noordvaarder* awaiting masts and sail, sheets and shrouds, so that it might be off about its business; a straw-filled bolster indented with the weight of heavy heads.

And somewhere amidst its more than hundred thousand souls there would have been a workaday painter turning out yet another *Allegory of the Five Senses*.

First, the Zuider Zee itself, sucked through the inlet of the IJ, washing against the slimy double row of palings separating the inner from the outer harbour, carrying with it a load of tangled wrack and weed, worthlessly small fish, and minute crustaceans generating a briny aroma of salt, rotting wood, bilgewater, and the tide-rinsed remains of countless gristly little creatures housed within the shells of periwinkles and barnacles. In the yards behind the first row of houses facing the docks there were better things to smell. Lengths of green timber were stood on end to season, some already bent to form a rib in a ship's hull. A man might walk down the alleys parallel to the harbour, inhale the sharp tang of fir (for masts) and oak and beech (for hulls), and for the moment think himself in a fresh-cut wood in Norway.

The illusion would not survive the taverns and brothels. Behind the seasoning yards, columns of heavy odour arose from the slops. The base of this olfactory architecture was supplied by layers of mussel shells; above them rose the sickly sweet ossuary of discarded parts of shrimp, crab, lobster, and prawn, the remains picked over by cats. Even this was better than the night-soil boats, moving slowly but profitably through the Amstel locks, heading out into the IJ toward the strawberry growers of Aalsmeer and the carrot growers of Beverwijk to the west and Hoorn to the north, who would pay a pretty penny for the manure. The *vuilnisvaarders*, the dung shippers, were, in their way, carefully specialised in their supplies, taking sheep shit to the tobacco growers around Amersfoort; horse shit to the horticulturalists, who would constitute from it the magically fertile soil, from which cabbages, cole seeds, and beans sprang with a copious regularity unseen anywhere else in Europe. If the playwright Bredero was to be believed, there were even some Amsterdammers prepared to buy urine for resale to the tanneries. In Holland, waste was a contradiction in terms. Even industrial residue like the soap-boilers' potash could be recycled as fertilizer. The rich cargo of the dung boats was supposed to travel by night, but those along the route still made sure to fasten their shutters before dark, anxious that the awesomely potent stench would find a way through vents and cracks.

The worst was the smell of death hanging over the Karthuizerkerkhof in the summer months of a plague year – 1624 or 1635 – when there were too many bodies to bury and not enough arms to dig graves and the little yard was full of black-garbed processions, formed up two by two, in absolute silence, waiting to go in and out of the enclosure, traffic jams of grief. When there was room, the linens of the dead were laid out to dry on the ground, decently saturated in vinegar to avoid adding to the contagion. No one who gagged easily would want to work there, or for that matter among the tanners or tallow renderers or the pig-gut packers, who stuffed tripe, liver, and lard along with a filling of groats into intestinal casings to make winter sausages.

Against the foulness, Amsterdam countermarshalled fragrance in quantities, intensity, and variety to please the most demanding nostrils. On spring mornings, a walker, selecting his route carefully and avoiding the sections between the Prinsengracht and the harbour that had been set aside for dye vats (the Bloemgracht) and soap-boiling (the St. Jacobskapelsteeg), might even deceive himself into supposing that the whole city had turned into a pomander. In the herb markets there were dittany, lavender, rosemary, and cicely plant packed into "sweetbags" to be hung about the wrist or the neck as a nosegay keeping contagion at bay, just as well since the cadavers of dead animals – dogs, cats, pigs, the occasional horse – rose without warning to the scummy surface of the canals. For wealthy men, the Turkish rosewater that scented their calf or kid gloves helped somewhat to mask the odour of putrefaction. And around the warehouses of the East India Company there hung invisible clouds of spicy vapour: cinnamon and cloves, nutmeg and mace. Morningtime the bakers' ovens near the Nes gave off the thick, yeasty scents of those same nails, powders, and studs, darkening and cracking to release their aroma into the breads, tarts, biscuits, and sweetmeats cooked for the tables of the high-hats and opulent ruffs.

Fastidious noses sniffed daintily from their tall flutes at the bouquet of green Moselle or dark Malmsey. Common noses, young and old, smooth and warty, were tickled alike by the malt ales served up in dull pewter pots or green glass *roemers* day and night. Come morning, slops and puddles which had taken on a smell all their own were banished by the astringent, cleansing soaking lye, the alkalized solution of vegetable ashes used to wash down the floors and walls of both modest and grand houses. But try as they might, even the most conscientious servants and the most fanatical *huisvrouw* found it difficult to expel entirely from their rooms the musty air of mildew that crept with the Amsterdam damp into the best-lined linen chests and the most thoroughly aired curtains and rush mats. Remedial or defensive measures might be taken. In fastidious houses, parcels of dried flowers and herbs, especially lavender, were set in bed linens before night-time. Elsewhere in the house, bookcases began to be custom-designed with glass fronts to prevent the invasion of the fungus that foxed and freckled fine paper even when the books were stored in the heaviest chests. Turkey-work rugs were kept on tables, not floors, for the same reason.

Against the dankness there were remedies to hand. In the spring and summer, fleshy damask or musk roses might be set on the buffet in ceramic pots, perhaps in the company of gilly-flowers and candy-smelling spotted lilies. In the wintertime (or, its devotees claimed, anytime), long pipes of tobacco "sauced" with spices or narcotics like black henbane seed, belladonna, or even the "Indian berries" which we know as coca produced fumes said to desiccate the aguey dampness. Come spring, as the days brightened and lengthened, an hour's saunter south along the banks of the river Amstel, past the fishing rods and trotting dogs and the white rumps of swimming boys, would bring the walker to pastures and shallow coppices. A little further and the air would be freshened by linden blossom and mown hay, and the occasional stand of poplars or sycamores could be discovered, edged with oxlips and harebells. If the excursionist was mounted and rode back at sunset toward the city gates and walls, he might find his horse sniffing and pricking his ears as Amsterdam's tower-punctured skyline came into view, as if already scenting the whiff of humanity sweating in its layers of serge and linen.

Simon Schama, *Rembrandt's Eyes* (1999)

❊ ❊ ❊

In order to understand why characteristics such as 'tolerance' have come to define Amsterdam, one needs to take a look at the city's earlier history. Here's Geert Mak ...

Amsterdam was never a truly medieval city. No king has ever held court here, the Church has never played a truly all-encompassing role, the social and political structures were never determined by the relations between ruler, vassal, and serf. From the very beginning it was a modern city, its citizens were independent and stuborn enough to take care of themselves.

At the same time, however, Amsterdam was a child of its time, with medieval houses, streets and squares in which, as the historian Johan Huizinga has described it in his timeless manner: "all of life's situations had outer forms more accentuated than they are today." "Everything people experienced had that degree of immediacy and absoluteness which joy and sorrow still have in the mind of children (...) There was less protection from catastrophe and illness, which struck more horrifically and more painfully. Illness was more obvious than health; the barren frost and the terrible dark were more substantial evils.

170

Honour and riches were enjoyed more fervently, since their power to hold at bay the terrors of poverty and exclusion was more apparent." [...]

From 1491 there was a cattle market in the Kalverstraat, a dairy market on the Dam, and vegetables, fruit, wood, and medicines were sold along the Damrak. Sea and river fish were offered for sale on the locks, sometimes even a seal or a porpoise. The annual free market was the climax of the year; there was even an elephant there in 1484.

Every year, too, the so-called "miracle procession" was held, a colourful display which drew the entire city out on to the streets. First came the members of the guilds carrying lit candles, each group with its own banners and pictures of its patron saint. This was followed, according to a description of the occasion, by a small group of "girls and young boys", who performed, among other works, the short play *St Joris and the Dragon*. More children followed: little angels with wings on their shoulders, and little devils carrying pitch-black sticks and smeared with soot, "with terrifying grins on their faces", as though they had just leapt from Hell. These always succeeded in making the smallest children among the spectators cry when they saw them coming. Behind them walked the archers in full accoutrements, with drums and banners; then the singing students of the Latin school in white surplices; the monks of the city monasteries in their black, grey, and brown habits, with crosses and images on their backs; then the clergy with their banners; a group of penitents going through the streets barefoot and almost naked because of this or that vow; and, at the end, underneath a magnificent baldachin carried by the four burgomasters, the priest, holding the monstrance with the holy Host inside. Meanwhile, the city band played "very finely and beautifully on pipes and shawms."

Traditionally the procession started by the Nieuwe Kerk, went round the city via the Kalverstaat, then back to the Nieuwe

Brug and thence to the IJ, where it halted to bless the ships and guarantee their safe passage. Then the route continued to the Oude Kerk, where the Holy Sacrament was exhibited for worship.

The patron saint of the Oude Kerk, Saint Nicolaas, the "water saint", was also very popular, as he protected the sailors and those living on the polders [land reclaimed from the water] from the dangers of the sea. Later he was to have something of a second career as a friend of children, riding his horse over the rooftops of Amsterdam on the eve of his name day, 6 December, and distributing presents by dropping them down chimneys.

Geert Mak, *Amsterdam: A Brief Life of the City* (1995)
translated from the Dutch by Philipp Blom

❊ ❊ ❊

Simon Schama uses the 1638 visit of Marie de Médicis – when she descended on the city for some serious shopping – as the trigger for his vivid picture of the many goods available in what Voltaire was to refer to in the following century as 'le magasin de l'univers'.

The real interest of Fokken's account is the richly detailed description given of the worldly pleasures to be sampled in Amsterdam. Along with the usual survey of public buildings and monuments, he lists streets and districts specializing in particular wares as though he were addressing himself to the prospective shopper. (And indeed a novelty of Marie de Médicis' visit in 1638 had been her descent on the Amsterdam shops, where, it was reported, she haggled like an expert with the shopkeepers.) On the Nieuwe Brug, Fokkens tells us, are to be found bookshops, stationers and nautical goods purveyors dealing in charts, maps, pilots, sextants and the like. In the same area may be found hardware and ironmonger shops, dye-shops and apothecaries with precious and arcane physics from Palestine, Greece and Egypt. On Bicker's Island in the IJ are ships' chandlers and salt-refining houses, on the Singel Canal the market where farmers bring their horticultural produce by barge and where the coastal packets from Flanders and Zeeland dock. In the Nes are the famed pastry shops and bakers; in the Kalverstraat print shops and haberdashers; in the Halsteeg cobblers and bootmakers. The Warmoesstraat, the ancient medieval heart of the city that connected the old dock and wharf area on the IJ with the Dam and the Rokin, was the center of fabrics and fine furnishings crammed with stores of all sizes. On two hundred houses, Fokkens notes, there are two hundred and thirty shop signs (the *uythangboord* had become so much a popular decorative art in Holland that whole books were devoted to anthologising them). In the cornucopia of the Warmoesstraat, the dedicated shopper could purchase Nuremberg porcelain, Italian majolica or Delft faience; Lyons silk, Spanish taffeta, or Haarlem linen bleached to the most dazzling whiteness. [...]

The cheerful vulgarity of Fokken's shoppers' tour is reinforced by his habit of noting, now and again, prices and values. It was evidently hard cash value, as much as aesthetic gorgeousness that excited him, and that he cited to impress his provincial readers and perhaps to advertise the going rates for the most desirable Amsterdam residences. The house of Wouter Geurtsen on the Rokin was so fine that it then rented for sixteen hundred guilders. Beyond, on the Prinsengracht, houses might commonly be let for twelve to fifteen hundred. But it was for the most fashionable of all addresses, the Herengracht, that Fokkens reserved his most breathless acclaim:

> Here you will see no houses with open shops; all the buildings stand tall ... some of them two, others three or four storeys high; sometimes their great cellars

filled with merchandise. Within, the houses are full of priceless ornaments so that they seem more like royal palaces than the houses of merchants, many of them with splendid marble and alabaster columns, floors inlaid with gold, and the rooms hung with valuable tapestries or gold- or silver-stamped leather worth many thousands of guilders ... You will also find in these houses valuable household furnishings like paintings and oriental ornaments and decorations so that the value of all these things is truly inestimable.

[...] Dutch taste and the legacy of much less pretentious late-medieval establishments conditioned a preference for interior, rather than exterior, display. Even when Amsterdam embarked on the construction of the radial canals, designed to create expensive residential units, the "royal measure" laid down by the *stadsfabriekmeester* and the city fathers only offered a frontage of thirty-odd feet as against a depth of a hundred and ninety. There were, of course, many ways for determined architects and their clients to evade or at least circumvent these constraints. Philips Vingboons specialized in creating a peculiar trapezoidal shape of house, like that of 1638, at Herengracht 138, where the left side of the central and rear rooms was broader than the front. By the time that the lot reached the garden it was almost a third as broad again as the façade. Families who were determined to impress with a façade of imposing proportions could collaborate on an early form of condominium, with two interior houses united by a single continuous façade, usually borrowed from Palladian stylebooks. [...]

Sometimes architects who were also masons and sculptors would be commissioned to create custom-ordered sculpture for exterior ornament, like the busts that de Keyser produced for Nicolas Soyhier's house on the Keizersgracht, or the cascade of decoration with which he adorned the Bartolotti house on the Herengracht.

The Bartolotti house is the most splendid example of the grand style of patrician building that survives from the early seventeenth century (1617–18).

Simon Schama, *The Embarrassment of Riches* (1987)

❊ ❊ ❊

Even the greatest civilisations have their underside. These eighteenth-century diary entries by Jacob Bicker Raije (1732–1772) capture some of the tragedy and desperation that existed alongside the beauty and achievements of the city.

1740

25 January. Mr Hendrik de Veer, the eldest son of Joost de Veer, passed away. He had been watching the ice breaker on the Amstel and was so taken by the cold that his bowels clogged up and he died the following day.

22 June. A woman drew a bucket of water from the Singel next to the Latin school. When she plunged the bucket deep into the water it returned all at once with a newborn baby in it, tossed into the Singel as it had come into the world with the cord still attached to its tiny body. It was a strapping lad.

1764

9 June. Justice has been done. A man has been hung and brought thereafter to the gallows-field. He had gone to war as a ship's hand under Captain Dabenis who chased him between decks for bad behaviour and had him severely punished on board. He then enlisted as a soldier, but when he was garrisoned at Zutphen he caused such a commotion there too that he was scourged, branded on his back with a gallows, and sent packing as a scoundrel. A few days later he made his way to Amsterdam. He arrived on a ship from Zutphen in the morning, only to rob a distiller or wine merchant on the Papenbrug between nine and ten the same evening, hitting the man with a tobacco box in his fist so hard that he passed out. He then took the man's money from his pocket, removed the buckles from his shoes and even took off his jacket, which he promptly donned himself. But when some people arrived and the man started to make a noise, he took to his heels. A butcher's apprentice caught up with him on the Ouderkerksplein, however, grabbed hold of him and brought him with the help of a number of bystanders to the Papenbrug.

The distiller, who had been taken into a nearby house and had come to himself after a bloodletting, identified him immediately as the man who had robbed him, which was also apparent from the jacket he was wearing and the buckles that were found on his person. When they stripped him naked to search for the buckles, they discovered the still unhealed mark of the gallows on his back. He thus bore his own death certificate. He should have been executed a fortnight earlier, but because of certain important revelations he shared with the government, which were carefully withheld from the public, the dispensation of justice was postponed for fourteen days.

Machiel Bosman, *Jacob Bicker Raije* (2009)
translated from the Dutch by Brian Doyle

❊ ❊ ❊

Of all the arts, painting is the one most often associated with Amsterdam. But the city has always enjoyed a thriving literary culture, too, especially in the nineteenth century when young poets such as Frans Erens was determined to infuse his friends with the literary spirit of Paris and the new ideas he had picked up there.

Ah, the chatter that went on in those rooms in De Pijp or in the cafés – Willensen, Mast, Krasnapolsky, De Poort van Cleve or the many small cafés in Amsterdam. How we talked. How I talked! How I argued, explicated, defended, interrupted! That's how it all began, the new ideas about literature and the arts;

176

things were brewing on all sides – with Breitner and others as well – sitting in the evenings in the cafés with the literati, jawing away, as it was called, even if it is an unattractive word. In Amsterdam, as in Paris, new ideas about art were born in the cafés. In Paris you had La Vachette, Le Voltaire, La Source, Le Chat Noir, and of course Le Procope, where portraits of some of the Encyclopedists, patrons from an earlier age, gazed upon later habitués from their frames on the wall. [...]

Now that I'm older, I don't find such things very important, but this thought is the beginning of discouragement, so I won't allow myself to give in to it. In those days enthusiasm was our master; *back then* was full of wonderful moments; it was a wonderful time, *back then*, not now. Now we look back at that time with a certain disdain. The thought of arguing and talking until late in the night is unimaginable to me now. But that isn't how we used to see it. We could not stop talking. We would walk each other home and upon reaching the door of one of our party, rather than going inside, he would turn around and walk the person home who had brought him to his door. We postulated on every street corner, the presence of a few late passersby unable to quench the stream of words, and along the row of dark houses our voices rang out in the night. I wonder if there are still literary cafés in Amsterdam!

Frans Erens, *Bygone Years* [*Vervlogen jaren*] (1938)
translated from the Dutch by Patricia Gosling

✽ ✽ ✽

On the whole, royalty in Amsterdam has tended to conduct itself in a less pompous manner than many other monarchies. But Gerrit Komrij recreates the Queen's visit to Dam Square as the nineteenth century turns into the twentieth, using the event to hint at the city's future.

A restive shuffling can be observed at the entrance to the Palace.

Prominent figures are arranged in rows, their wives at their sides, a conspicuous Vening Meinsz with his chain of office in front. The mayor looks for all the world like a child awaiting his reward. The master of ceremonies, and the ministers, commissioners, judges and lawyers are lined up behind him. I can see a choice selection of robes, birettas, three-cornered hats and sashes, powerful people to a man, people of prestige in the balance books of the banking houses.

Who's that? In the midst of all those stiff and self-conscious heads I see the bald cranium and side-burns of Nicolaas Bruyningh.

He's standing in the front row of the reception committee.

Mrs Bruyningh is at his side, wearing an enormous wide-brimmed hat. [...]

The choirs fall silent. A trumpet blast.

The queen appears, her short legs under a red velvet coat edged with white ermine. The cloud of peacock feathers has made way for a crown of diamonds.

At that very moment the sun breaks through.

She smiles at the waiting dignitaries. The reception committee jack-knifes respectfully. She then begins her walk beneath the vaulted veils, followed by heralds, chamberlains, equerries, admirals, grand officers and a slew of other honoured and decorated figures.

The entire square is now filled with the sound of carillons, pealing bells, psalmody and fanfares.

A cannon shot.

Four well-heeled squires bear the ermine train, all four dressed in white. Just as the queen passes the cordon, I recognise Junior among the squires. Frederik junior.

His parents were probably detained because of work.

A smile curls my lips. In my mind's eye I picture a future in which all the ideas and ideals of the present have been tossed into a pot, left to simmer in a brown broth. The present scurries past with the same astonishing speed as the onrushing future. The banners of war become wind vanes, modern experiments dogmas, and the passion for experimentation rigid resistance. The children of innocence become the minions of hell.

Not on your life. I shake the thought from my head. People shouldn't entertain such fantasies. Too absurd for words.

> Gerrit Komrij, *The Poltergeist* [*De klopgeest*] (2001)
> translated from the Dutch by Brian Doyle

✳ ✳ ✳

Only a few years after the Queen's visit described by Komrij, Europe was plunged into the horrors of the Great War. The Netherlands having remained neutral, Amsterdam became the 'place of choice' for many well-heeled refugees fleeing the political and social turmoil of the rest of Europe. A brief glimpse of the scene from German writer Gustav Meyrink, as created in his haunting and visionary novel The Green Face.

For months now Holland had been flooded with people of all nations. Since the war had ended, giving way to growing inner political conflicts, they had left their homes, some to seek permanent refuge in the Netherlands, others to stay there temporarily whilst they made up their minds about which corner of the earth for their future home.

The common forecast that the end of the European war would produce a stream of refugees from the poorer sections of the population of the worst-hit areas had proved completely mistaken. Even if all available ships to Brazil and other parts of the earth considered fertile were full to overflowing with steerage passengers, the outflow of those who earned their living by the sweat of their brow was infinitesimal compared to the number of wealthy people who were tired of seeing their fortunes squeezed by the pressure of higher and higher taxes:

179

the so-called materialists. They were joined by members of the intelligentsia, whose professions, since the enormous rises in the cost of living, no longer brought in enough to keep body and soul together. [...]

And so it came to pass that the great mass of European intellectuals were on the move, crowding the harbours of those countries that had been more or less spared by the war, gazing westwards, like Tom Thumb climbing a tall tree to spy out the fire from a hearth far away.

In Amsterdam and Rotterdam the old hotels were full to the very last attic, and every day new ones were being built; the streets of the more respectable districts resounded to a pot pourri of languages. [...]

In the better restaurants and chocolate houses people sat shoulder to shoulder reading overseas newspapers – the local ones were still wallowing in officially-prescribed enthusiasm for the current situation – but even the overseas ones contained nothing that did not boil down to the old adage, 'I know that I know nothing, and I'm not even sure of that'.

Gustav Meyrink, *The Green Face* (1916)
translated from the German by Mike Mitchell

World War II – The Occupied City

And then, of course, there was World War II.

The rise of fascism in Italy and of National Socialism in Germany had not passed unnoticed in Amsterdam. Already in 1933, shortly after Hitler's ascent to power, there was a demonstration by anti-fascist youths on the Rembrandtplein which was directed against the showing of *Morgenrood (Dawn)*, the first German film with an overtly Nazi message. There were other protests. At one, in the Rembrandt Theatre, slogans were chanted, stink bombs thrown, and white mice and doves of peace released. There were anti-fascist committees and exhibitions. In 1936, there was even one against the Olympic games in Berlin using the acronym DOOD (dead), short for "De Olympische Spelen Onder Dictatuum" (The

Olympic Games under Dictatorship). Even the heiress to the throne, Princess Juliana of the Netherlands, visited the Joodse Invalide (Jewish Hospital) shortly after her marriage to the German Prince Bernhard, so as to demonstrate her contempt for Nazi anti-semitism.

Jewish refugees from Germany, and later from Austria, had meanwhile begun to arrive in Amsterdam in their thousands, and many established themselves in the spacious new areas of Berlage's Amsterdam South, particularly in the area around the Beethovenstraat. There was a relatively large number of writers and artists among these exiles, and their presence reawakened the Amsterdammers, who were especially taken by their cabaret and literature. It was a repetition, in miniature, of the situation during the seventeenth and eighteen centuries, in that, for a brief period, the city became a kind of sanctuary. The Amsterdam publishers Allert de Lange and Querido began to publish émigré literature in the original language, and there was a special literary journal for emigrants in German, *Die Sammlung (The Collection)*.

Here and there, however, especially among the city's petty bourgeoisie and the upper middle classes, National Socialism also found favour. […] In the municipal elections of 1939 Amsterdam was the only city in the Netherlands in which the NSB fielded candidates. The party gained three seats. […]

So Amsterdam renewed its acquaintance with war, for the first time in almost four centuries. On Sunday 12 May a German plane dropped a bomb on the Blauwburgwal, on the corner of the Herengracht. The carnage was terrible, with 51 people killed. Otherwise the city was not severely damaged, apart from the harbours and Schiphol, which were heavily bombed. The tragedies were mostly human. Despite the wonderful weather, smoke could be seen issuing form some chimneys, as countless "dangerous" books and pamphlets were burned. In the Joodse Vluchtelingencomité (Jewish Refugee Council), volunteers had begun work incinerating dossiers in the central-heating furnace from 8 a.m. on 10 May.

Meanwhile, many thousands of Jews had fled to IJmuiden hoping to gain passage on a ship to England. While a panic-stricken crowd was moving along the North Sea Channel in cars and buses, and on bicycles, all laden with suitcases and bags, three stately ocean steamers, the *Johan de Witt*, the *Jan Pieterszoon Coen*, and the *Bodegraven*, steamed through the canal like a torment of Tantalus. The authorities, however, decided on Tuesday 14 May to close off the area around the IJmuiden harbour "out of concern for public order". The *Johan de Witt*, the last ship to leave, sailed according to schedule for the Dutch East Indies, taking on board at the last minute a handful of Jewish families by means of a rope ladder. Save for a few Jewish orphans, the gigantic passenger ship *Bodegraven* set a course for England almost empty. The refugees saw the *Coen* pass by, a ship that could easily have accommodated almost all of them, but she was scuttled in order to block German access to the IJmuiden piers.

Then the suicides began: Alderman Emanuel Boekman and his wife, the criminologist Professor Bonger, and about 150 others – Jews, known anti-fascists, stranded refugees, some of them alone, but also entire families. Walking through Amsterdam's Jewish cemeteries today one can still find them, the stones bearing the dates of 15 and 16 May 1940, some narrow, some much broader, so as to accommodate the names of an entire family, husband, wife and children.

On the 15 May 1940, German troops entered the city, via the Weesperzijde and the Berlagebrug, watched by thousands of Amsterdammers. [...]

Of the 80,000 Jews in Amsterdam, only 5,000 were alive at the time of the Liberation in 1945. In total, 98 deportation trains with more than 100,000 people were able to leave the Netherlands without a single incident. [...]

Dutch Railways arranged, without the slightest objection, special night trains to Westerbork and to the German border, for which the bill was paid punctually by the occupiers.

Geert Mak, *Amsterdam: A Brief Life of the City* (1995)
translated from the Dutch by Philipp Blom

✳ ✳ ✳

Bianca Stigter's The Occupied City *[De bezette stad] is an excellent study of the period. Here she records the early stages of the war.*

The war began in Amsterdam with noise. At three in the morning, Germans planes roared over the city on their way to bomb Schiphol. By dawn the smoke could be seen from Amsterdam. The evening edition of the *Algemeen Handelsblad* published a photo-reportage of the city's 'First Morning at War'. The captions read: 'Central station closed to anyone who cannot prove his identity'; 'All policemen to wear helmets'; 'British subjects report to consulate'; 'Home guard stop cars in search of suspicious elements'; 'Air-raid defence posters require our full attention now.'

But the city was scene to more that day. It witnessed not only the capture of 150 officially listed persons to be interned in the event of war, but also the detainment of thousands of National Socialists and Germans, including Jewish refugees. Most of them were held at the Markthallen in Jan van Galenstraat, although some National Socialists went into hiding. Opposite Markthallen, in the Hallentheater cinema, evacuees from Kattenburg (railway works) and from North Amsterdam (Fokker factories) were forced to enroll for new housing. Evacuated cows were herded onto football pitches in Watergraafsmeer. Schools, theatres and stock markets closed down. In Artis, the zoo- keepers killed their poisonous snakes. Alcohol was banned. National Socialist centres were kept under surveillance. Strategic buildings including the post office HQ on the Nieuwezijds Voorburgwal and the telephone exchange in the Spuistraat were held under guard. Volunteers offered their services to the department of military affairs stationed in the courtyard of the city hall. And on the evening of 10 May, for the first time blackouts were enforced.

The next day, panic and excitement were rife. On 11 May the first air-raid alarm was heard. The very same day two German bombs were dropped at the corner of the Herengracht and Blauwburgwal, causing more that forty deaths.

The city was in the grip of 'parachutist fever'. German soldiers were spotted everywhere, in uniform or in disguise. People were terrified that the 'fifth column' of Germans living in Holland would distribute poisoned chocolate, so the Dutch army, police force, air defence and home guard kept everyone including one another – under close surveillance. The Germans were rumoured to have occupied Amstel and Muiderpoort railway stations so an infantry company was summoned from Alkmaar to oust them. Only once the company had arrived at the police station in Leidseplein was there a phone call to say that it had been a false alarm. Germans were also spotted on the IJsselmeer, only they turned out to be a shipment of livestock.

'Amidst shouts and screams, a number of soldiers charged, on the basis of no authority but their own, onto the streets yelling and firing their guns, without knowing whom they were shooting, and sometimes, in the ensuing confusion, firing at one another as well,' read a subsequent report written by Captain Verschoor, billeted in North Amsterdam. Near Durgerdam, a marine captain shot N.A Rost van Tonningen dead in a fearful attempt to avert treason. Van Tonningen had been Amsterdam's commander of maritime operations and brother of a leading member of the Nationalist Socialist Movement.

A few commanders remained optimistic. The chief of police even informed his personnel on the morning of 14 May that Fortress Holland was 'completely intact and the army leadership fully in control.' The British army set fire to the oil tanks in Petroleumhaven in order to prevent them from falling into German hands. Smoke could be seen rising from rows of chimneys during those warm days in May; people were burning incriminating personal documents as well as books they thought would be banned. Some of the canals were white with paper. On 14 May the 39th German corps was ordered to advance through the Defence Line of Amsterdam. That same evening the Dutch army laid down their arms, after the Rotterdam blitz. Utrecht was rumoured to be next. 'Unlike the air raid, the enemy had not been seen, but by the end of 14 May we were all utterly exhausted,' reported Captain Verschoor

Many Amsterdam Jews tried to escape to England via IJmuiden. Others committed suicide, including City Councillor Emanuel Boekman. As one ambulance driver said: 'We've just been to Smaragdstraat for a case of asphyxiation. When I get there I find this family with a suicide note saying, "We went to IJmuiden but the boat had already left so we came back home."'

Bianca Stigter, *The Occupied City* [*De bezette stad*] (2001)
translated from the Dutch by Imogen Cohen

❉ ❉ ❉

A glimpse of the times from a child's point of view.

He doesn't take much notice of the war. His father and brothers can discuss it for hours, but he's not interested. His brothers even squabble about how it's going to turn out. They're following it secretly on English radio and apparently it's very exciting. Their faces are so animated they could be listening to a football match.

But it's only when the sirens wail on the other side of the Amstel that anything really happens. It's then that the streets fall silent and his father shuts up shop – given that there aren't any customers anyway – and he follows his older brother up to the attic to see whether there are any air battles going on above Amsterdam.

Up in the loft they can see for miles, almost as far as Theater Carré. Suddenly planes are zooming overhead. 'It's the English,' whispers his brother, 'on their way to Germany, to bomb them.' High in the sky the planes look tiny, as tiny as the sticklebacks in the Amstel. But suddenly he sees clouds of smoke pouring out of them. 'German anti-aircraft guns,' his brother mumbles. The clouds taper into long wisps.

'They're done,' says his brother. Just then he hears the sirens wail again. People have gone outside and are looking up from time to time. He races downstairs and out onto the pavement. He scours the street left and right for shards of shrapnel. The first piece he finds is still warm. It's heavier than he thought. It's a fine specimen with sharp edges.

Jan Fontijn, *Steak and Petrol* [*Biefstuk en benzine*] (2003)
translated from the Dutch by Imogen Cohen

✳ ✳ ✳

But the most famous 'young' perspective on the war is, of course, provided through the world-famous diary kept by Anne Frank.

FRIDAY, 9 OCTOBER 1942

Dearest Kitty,
Today I have nothing but dismal and depressing news to report. Our many Jewish friends and acquaintances are being taken away in droves. The Gestapo is treating them very roughly and transporting them in cattle-trucks to Westerbork, the big camp in Drenthe to which they're sending all the Jews. Miep

told us about someone who'd managed to escape from there. It must be terrible in Westerbork. The people get almost nothing to eat, much less to drink, as water is available only one hour a day, and there's only one lavatory and sink for several thousand people. Men and women sleep in the same room, and women and children often have their heads shaved. Escape is almost impossible; many people look Jewish, and they're branded by their shorn heads.

If it's that bad in Holland, what must it be like in those faraway and uncivilised places where the Germans are sending them? We assume that most of them are being murdered. The English radio says they're being gassed. Perhaps that's the quickest way to die.

I feel terrible. Miep's accounts of these horrors are so heartrending, and Miep is also very distraught. [...]

But that's not the end of my lamentations. Have you ever heard the term 'hostages'? That's the latest punishment for saboteurs. It's the most horrible thing you can imagine. Leading citizens – innocent people – are taken prisoner to await their execution. If the Gestapo can't find the saboteur, they simply grab five hostages and line them up against the wall. You read the announcements of their death in the paper, where they're referred to as 'fatal accidents'.

Fine specimens of humanity, those Germans, and to think I'm actually one of them! No, that's not true, Hitler took away our nationality long ago. And besides, there are no greater enemies on earth than the Germans and the Jews.

Yours, Anne

MONDAY, 19 JULY 1943

Dearest Kitty,

North Amsterdam was very heavily bombed on Sunday. There was apparently a great deal of destruction. Entire streets are in ruins, and it will take a while for them to dig out all the bodies. So far there have been two hundred dead and countless wounded; the hospitals are bursting at the seams. We've been told of children searching forlornly in the smouldering ruins for their dead parents. It still makes me shiver to think of the dull, distant drone that signified the approaching destruction.

WEDNESDAY, 23 FEBRUARY 1944

My dearest Kitty,

The weather's been wonderful since yesterday, and I've perked up quite a bit. My writing, the best thing I have, is coming along well. I go to the attic almost every morning to get the stale air out of my lungs. This morning when I went there, Peter was busy cleaning up. He finished quickly and came over to where I was sitting on my favourite spot on the floor. The two of us looked out at the blue sky, the bare chestnut tree glistening with dew, the seagulls and other birds glinting with silver as they swooped through the air, and we were so moved and entranced that we couldn't speak. [...] But I also looked out of the open window, letting my eyes roam over a large part of Amsterdam, over the rooftops and on to the horizon, a strip of blue so pale it was almost invisible.

'As long as this exists,' I thought, 'this sunshine and this cloudless sky, and as long as I can enjoy it, how can I be sad?'

Anne Frank, *The Diary of a Young Girl* (1947)
translated from the Dutch by Susan Massotty

✳ ✳ ✳

Acts of betrayal, acts of generosity: this next little incident suggests that life (and love) can somehow go on, even in the midst of terror.

An incident from World War II. Gerard Vermaat Jonker is studying violin and composition at the Utrecht Conservatory.

Sometimes he takes the train to visit his mother in Amsterdam. He gets out at Amstel Station, then walks to Sluisstraat, which is quite a way. The incident takes place on 18 September 1943. The Germans have occupied the Berlage Bridge for surveillance. Gerard is seventeen at the time and as handsome as an exotic prince. His mother comes from the Zeeland countryside; his father is a Jewish knife grinder. The Germans have not made the cordon watertight. Gerard slips through, but is seen. The situation is unclear. He walks slightly too hurriedly along Noorder Amstellaan, a soldier follows him but fails to catch him up. A woman leaning out of the window observes the situation. She beckons to Gerard, who dashes into the doorway. The soldier has lost the scent. Gerard and the woman drink a cup of tea and then make love. The child that is born is, according to the woman, fathered by Gerard Vermaat Jonker. The woman, incidentally, is the only one who knows this; Gerard is never told and the husband is also left in the dark.

> A.L.Snijders, *Mind You, I Don't Consider the Reader*
> [*Belangrijk is dat niet aan lezers denk*] (2006)
> translated from the Dutch by Rosalind Buck

❋ ❋ ❋

The end of the war was, inevitably, a messy business, with the occupiers trying to escape and the liberators entering the city and bringing their own problems ...

Abraham van Santen was in hiding for two years in an alley near Oudezijds Achterburgwal, behind white-painted windows. In April 1945, he went outside for the first time. "I was walking along Oudezijds Achterburgwal and there I saw a house with big windows and through the glass I could see drawings and sculptures. I had such an irrepressible desire to look at something beautiful!"

Not all the Germans gave themselves up easily after capitulation. On 7 May, drunken naval officers from the *Kriegmarine* opened fire on the celebrating crowd in Dam Square. Elsewhere in the city, too, it came to shootouts between the BS (Dutch National Forces) and the Germans. Members of the Nazi Party Security Service attempted to pass for ordinary soldiers. The gates of the prison in Weteringschans were opened. The BS immediately incarcerated new prisoners there. A list had been drawn up by the BS of twelve thousand suspects. They dragged 'Kraut whores' from their homes and shaved their heads in the street. Apparently, lists had been made during the war of women with German lovers. They painted swastikas on the women's heads in red paint. A big camp was set up in Levantkade for collaborators, where the conditions differed little from those that were the norm under the Germans. Two hundred members of the Security Police were arrested. Like the rest of the liberated Netherlands, Amsterdam was put under military rule.

The new mayor, ship owner Feike de Boer, had a proclamation posted: "We can breathe freely again and are no longer hounded and persecuted like wild animals"

People were celebrating everywhere. The big liberation parties were planned for the end of May, but that was soon changed to the end of June. There was still no electricity and many people were too weakened for partying, in any event.

The food parcels dropped by the allies from 30 April (Operation Manna) could not be distributed until 13 May. When the central kitchens started working again on 17 May they had even more customers than during the war. In the twenty-two starvation clinics that were opened on 19 May, people with starvation oedema could immediately get a couple of tins of condensed milk. The Dutch Popular Recovery organisation had to help more than half the families in Amsterdam. [...]

For the majority of the people the best part was the arrival of the liberators, the Canadians and English who drove into the city on 8 May. Some people tried to touch them. In no time, the tanks driving towards Dam Square via the Berlage Bridge, Van Baerlestraat and Leidseplein were swamped. "Women crying, men waving their hands like crazy. Welcome boys. Welcome."

The allies moved into the buildings that had been occupied by the Germans. More soldiers soon arrived. In June, Amsterdam became a leave centre for Canadian soldiers from Germany, who were not allowed to fraternise with the population there. In Amsterdam they were. "Every time automobiel tru street me denk [thinks] Bill. But no niks [nothin'] neffer [never]," a girl wrote after her soldier had left again. The Tourist Information Office published a booklet to help soldiers get around in the city. "The fact that Amsterdam has been chosen as a leave centre, is mainly due to the circumstances, that you got there in time to save it from becoming a rubbish heap" it says in the introduction. "Don't waste time learning Dutch. We have all done our best to brush up our English".

After the initial euphoria, there was a lot of criticism of all the girls with their Canadian boyfriends. Many of Amsterdam's residents were afraid of moral degeneracy. They had to set up youth centres for the neglected young people who had no longer been able to go to school and were now roaming the city 'while everyone was getting pissed and screwing'.

On 1 June, the first train carrying repatriated persons arrived in Amsterdam. The reception of those who had survived the concentration camps was far from warm. Not everyone got his old home back or his possessions. The Netherlands was more anti-Semitic after the war than before. The camp experience was compared with the starvation winter: things had been really bad in Amsterdam, as well.

In resistance circles, too, the ones who came back from the camps attracted little attention, in the beginning. Willy Wielek was involved in the CS6 resistance cell and spent six months in the prison on Amstelveenseweg. Long after the war, she wrote of the liberation, 'I can still see Eddy de Wind, in a Russian uniform with a belt around his waist, really flattering, yelling, "How can you lot celebrate, do you actually know what has happened, don't you know how many people are dead, have you all gone completely mad?" I said nothing, but I thought, "Yeah, okay, you don't have to get so hysterical, not just yet, let's celebrate first".'

In the summer of 1945 Amsterdam gradually returned to the kind of city people had been used to before the war. The trams and trains started running again, the central kitchen was shut down, more and more items were taken off ration. The Germans walked home, the Forces of the Interior were disbanded, the Canadians left (with 1,886 brides and 428 children), military rule was lifted, the purge was completed, most political prisoners were released. And so, the war passed into history.

Bianca Stigter, *The Occupied City* [*De bezette stad*] (2001)
translated from the Dutch by Rosalind Buck

✻ ✻ ✻

Two days after capitulation, on 7 May 1945, a great crowd was celebrating in Dam Square when the Germans opened fire on the revelling Amsterdammers from the Groote Club on the corner of Kalverstraat and Paleisstraat.

Dam Square was thronging with a multitude of party-goers, cheerfully decked out in orange and red, white and blue. A real Amsterdam street organ was playing. And a good thing, too; the crowd that had congregated from all over the city was becoming impatient in its long wait for the Canadian troops. Along Rokin, where our observation post was, from the Mint in the direction of Dam Square, the waiting masses began to surge. Unaware of what had happened behind the palace, the arrival of the Canadians was jubilantly announced. They proved only to be forerunners. First a passenger vehicle full of naval officers, probably English, as they were driving on the left. The passengers saluted the crowd with the V sign. A moment later, two other passenger vehicles followed, one of which was marked, in big white letters, PRESS WAR CORRESPONDENT. On the roof of the car sat a uniformed correspondent. Thirty metres before the car was due to arrive in Dam Square, heavy shooting broke out from the Groote Club and from the windows and roof of the SS building on the corner of Dam Square and Nieuwendijk. The war correspondent jumped from the car and sought cover behind the concrete shelter opposite the Rotterdamsche Bank on Rokin. The people fled panicking in all directions. Shooting continued. Members of the BS were present in small numbers and took up positions on the corners of Damrak and Rokin and Vijgendam. The BS showed no signs of confusion; on the contrary, in general they exhibited good self-control. They waited until the public was out of range and then opened fire on the buildings from which the SS and the German naval officers waylaid and claimed their last victims from their hide-out! Twenty dead and wounded were spread around the deserted street organ. In the meantime, the shooting became heavier. The public, at first shocked, started to become interested and pressed its way back towards Dam Square. Then, finally, it became clear that we had learned something in this war. A number of brave fellows from the public took the initiative to clear the street and, within ten minutes, at least Rokin had quite calmly been practically cleared and the inhabitants had been warned to keep their front doors open to provide cover if necessary. By now, the war correspondent had taken several pictures, as had many of the photographers and cameramen from the CBS film archive. The BS took possession of the access roads to Dam

Square in various places. Young people, girls and boys in civilian clothing, with delivery bikes and an improvised white flag rode fearlessly into Dam Square to recover the dead and wounded. The scouts joined them. Meanwhile, the shooting continued from both sides. [...]

Losses among the civilian population estimated by the various helpers thirty dead and dozens of wounded, many of them seriously.

'Germans shoot at celebrating crowd', *Het Parool* (1945)
translated from the Dutch by Rosalind Buck

✳ ✳ ✳

But a war is never simply 'over'. Even those who survived relatively unscathed physically are haunted by memories that can be triggered by the smallest thing – in this case, by the smell of pancakes or the sight of a glass of beer.

When I entered the pub with the morning papers, I found only the proprietor – a sombre toper who was voraciously swilling down beer as if trying to put out a fire. I limited myself to a cup of coffee – a rarity in this establishment – which he went grudgingly to fetch from the kitchen. As he pushed open the door marked 'Private', a pleasant aroma emerged to mingle with the stale smell of yesterday's drinking session.

A small grey man came in from outside and sniffed the air thoughtfully.

'Pancakes?' he asked when the publican returned with my coffee.

'Yes, my wife's frying them for my grandson; he's coming this afternoon,' was the reply. 'What'll you have?'

'Coffee,' said the man.

The publican opened the kitchen door again, and the smell became stronger.

'You know,' the man said to me 'there was a time when I cried because of a pancake.'

'When you were a child, no doubt,' I suggested.

'No, I was a grown-up,' he answered. 'It was 1943 – during the German occupation. My wife and I and four other Jews were hiding in the house of a very devout couple. Baptists, that's what they were. Religious fanatics. One day the man said to me "Do you realize that, by the power of prayer, I can move the tree in front of the house?" I said, "Don't do it. That tree looks just fine where it is." Strange people, those two. The six of us stayed with them for a year and a half, and every day they fed us sugar-beet mush until we choked on it. One evening a visitor came. A friend. We were all sitting in the living room. The woman got up and walked into the kitchen and began to fry pancakes. Oh, the smell! The wonderful smell! It almost made me faint. When the pancakes were ready the man whose faith could move trees said, "All hiders to bed." We didn't get a single pancake. Off we went meekly, shooed away. Then I lay on my bed and cried. Not because of the pancakes, but out of sheer rage – because of our terrible helplessness.'

The pubkeeper put a cup of coffee down in front of the man and tapped himself another large glass of beer.

'We're supposed to forget all that,' the man went on, 'but how can we forget? If I smell pancakes, I can't help thinking about that night I lay in bed sobbing with rage.'

He pointed at the glass from which our host was taking a huge swig.

'Beer,' said the man. 'I don't like beer. But one time in my life I said "God bless beer." You know why?'

He smiled rather bitterly.

'It was in 1942,' he said. 'My wife and I were hiding at another address then. In a little attic room full of junk. One night we heard a car stop outside. German police – the Grüne. We heard them come into the house. We heard them bellowing. My wife and I thought: this is the end. We stood crushed against the wall of that tiny room, beside the door. The door could only open a crack because a heavy piece of furniture was shoved close behind it. As we were standing there stock still, we heard footsteps coming up the stair towards the attic room. The handle turned and the door opened – as far as it could. A normal person would have been able to get through. But the Grüne was from Bavaria, I think, for he had an enormous beer-belly. Two or three times he tried to worm his belly inside. But he couldn't. So he closed the door, without having seen us. "God bless beer" I whispered then.'

He looked at me.

'Forget?' he said. 'If I smell or see beer, that moment comes back to me. And it always will.'

And to the publican, 'Come on, have another beer on me. It's a life saver.'

Simon Carmiggelt, *I'm just kidding:*
More of a Dutchman's Slight Adventures (1972)
translated from the Dutch by by Elizabeth Willems-Treeman

✲ ✲ ✲

In Ajax, the Dutch, the War, *Simon Kuper considers the fate of Amsterdam's Jews partly through the disturbing facts of the city's famous Ajax football at the time. The treatment of the Jewish population was a hard truth Amsterdammers had to come to terms with in the decades after the war.*

Imagine a city tour that starts at the Anne Frank house. Every day from 9 a.m. this building tells hundreds of tourists the following story: the Germans wanted to kill the Frank family, so the Dutch hid them, but in the end the Germans killed them after all. So sad are the Dutch about this that they have dedicated this large house in the centre of their capital city to Anne's memory.

Another version of the story is that the Franks were among the lucky few Dutch Jews able to find a hiding-place, but were betrayed by a Dutch person and seized from their hiding-place by a German and three Dutch policemen, one of whom was still working for the Amsterdam force in 1980. [...]

The Amsterdam tour proceeds eastwards along the city's beautiful canal streets, barely changed since the seventeenth century, until it reaches the old Jewish Quarter. Bits of it have gone, but the Amsterdammers have preserved an astounding amount. There are façades with Hebrew letters, and the great Portuguese synagogue (more a monument than a place of worship these days, as it is barely used except on high holidays). This city has welcomed Jews for hundreds of years and is sorry that it now has almost none left.

The goodness of Amsterdam is advertised by the whole Jewish Quarter, but it is embodied in the statue of the Dockworker on the square in front of the synagogue. The Dockworker honours the Amsterdam proletariat, which protested against the first German raids on the Jewish Quarter by staging a general strike in February 1941. Every February there is a march past the Dockworker. [...].

The last stop on our tour is the white stucco Hollandsche Schouwburg theatre on the pretty Plantage Middenlaan. The building where Amsterdam's Jews were rounded up is now no longer a theatre but a monument. On its façade a verse (helpfully printed in English as well as Dutch) informs tourists:

> at home in gathering isolation
> waiting at night in fear
> rounded up by soldiers
> caught in a trap ...

But the verse is a lie. Most Amsterdam Jews did not sit at home waiting for soldiers. Instead they were collected by Dutch policemen, who were coerced by the Germans with the harshest sanctions imaginable: they could lose their Whitsun leave. 'Concerning the Jewish Question, the Dutch police behave outstandingly and catch hundreds of Jews, day and night,' wrote Hanns Albin Rauter, the senior German police officer in Amsterdam, to Heinrich Himmler in September 1932. After the war Rauter's colleague Willy Lages would add: 'We would not have been able to arrest 10 per cent of the Jews without their help.' The rigour of the Dutch police, and of the Dutch state generally, was matched in western Europe not even by Vichy France. […]

As Renate Rubinstein phrased the country's new intellectual consensus: 'Even in Germany you had slightly more chance of surviving the destruction than in the Netherlands. We were not anti-Semitic, we were just cowardly.'

Simon Kuper, *Ajax, The Dutch, The War* (2003)

* * *

Martin Bril brings this section to a close with a picture of the 'two minutes silence' with which the dead of the war are remembered each year on the fourth of May.

Commemorating the dead is about sound, or better said, the absence of sound. There's nothing more to it. Two minutes silence and it's done.

Throng to Dam Square.

And there you stand, in your thousands, tightly packed, and even that's important – a warm, silent jumble, a multitude like no other: public at a pop concert, pressed commuters at the station, shoppers on a Saturday afternoon. No one elbows to the front in this crowd and there's not a single indecent word to be heard.

Melancholic bustle.

Strutting majesty.

Wreaths, men, uniforms.

The doleful trumpet.

For those who need at least something to listen to, there's the rattle of the flag at half-mast on top of De Bijenkorf, held in check by a couple of soldiers, a flock of gulls hovering over the garbage bins on the Damrak, and a child, far in the distance, crying, fleetingly.

The traffic lights are stuck at flashing amber and, if you're lucky, the street lights slip softly into gear halfway through the silence, the lamps dangling bashfully for a moment between the tram's overhead cables.

The gathering is inescapably reminiscent of attending church: the way people make their way to the Dam across the Rokin and the Damrak, arm in arm, talking under their breath, resolute, Dutch; their composure as they comply with the nature and logic of the ceremony, the spectacular force of habit: a mother hanging a sheet out to dry with clothes pegs between her teeth, or something similar. How she spreads her arms, a billowing sea of white in between, which she finally leaves hanging above the grass, taut and helpless.

It's civilisation imposing itself, or more precisely: history, a procession of the opposite, barbarism included, is the real reason we're here.

Reflection.

The past is the past, but not entirely, although memory gets shorter and shorter. That's basically what it amounts to.

In the meantime the magic minutes tick by, much too quickly of course. Hours would be better. Drawn for barely a moment into the bosom of the nation, then it falls apart again and you're alone wherever you are.

As the people scatter, slower than they assembled – still lost in thought, but you already sense it evaporating – a young girl glides into view, heading in the opposite direction, towards the monument. She has a serene smile on her face and a bunch of daffodils in her hand. One of the flowers dangles broken over the cellophane.

Martin Bril, *New Herring Day* [*De dag van de nieuwe haring*] (2005)
translated from the Dutch by Brian Doyle

That was then ... this is now

Visiting a city means learning to negotiate its transport systems. Sean Condon gives some potentially life-saving advice.

Amsterdam is not a city designed for automobiles. It's full of rivers, canals and dykes and it's been my direct and unhappy experiences that cars tend to sink when negotiating waterways (Edward Kennedy would agree with me, I'm sure), even if they *seem* frozen. Clearly, the city's transportation ethic was developed with floating in mind. Floating, cycling and perhaps riding horses, but nothing bigger than a Shetland pony. However, quite apart from the tininess, often one-wayness, frequent blockedness and always slippery cobblestonedness of its numerous *straats, wegs* and *laans* (all varieties of the basic road), there are many other reasons not to drive in Amsterdam. In order of dangerousness, they consist of the following:

Trams. Amsterdam's trams are enormous, twin-carriaged, artic-ulated behemoths which have right of way over everything and stop for just about nothing. The very basic braking system seems to consist of a concrete-block anchor and is only employed in the most dire of circumstances, such as for a group of old women in wheelchairs carrying boxes of kittens across the road. And even then, the look of undiluted hatred that kitten-carrying old ladies would receive from the tram driver would make them wish they were dead anyway. So always carry a box of kittens when strolling around Amsterdam and, if possible, try to be old. And a lady.

Bicycles. There are approximately two million *tweewielers* (two-wheelers) in this city, but it seems like more. A *lot* more. They're absolutely everywhere, silently bearing down on the idiot pedes-trian (me) who has wandered into the bicycle-only lanes in order to get a better view of an old, skinny building, or weaving in and out of traffic with a glare and a swear at whom- or whatever has caused the sudden stoppage (me again, this time by standing in the middle of a road staring up at another skinny building). In addi-tion to their plague-proportion numerousness, they are a danger to vehicles because cyclists despise cars and will do everything they can to irritate, confuse and imperil the lives of their drivers. This is because drivers hate cyclists and will do everything *they* can to irritate, confuse and imperil the lives of cyclists. The whole city is therefore full of cars and bikes screeching to head-on stops, or drivers and cyclists screaming at each other to sell their car/bike and buy a car/bike. (And Dutch not a particularly pleasant language in the first place, as many of the Dutch themselves will attest, is simply horrible when it's loud. It's dangerous and it's noisy.)

Cars. Despite all the water, bikes and tiny streets, Amsterdam is nevertheless full of cars. And other cars are a danger to cars. Especially the sorts of cars which are most practical in a city of canals, bicycles and alley-sized roads. They are, fittingly, small cars – with names like the Renault 'Twingo', the Nissan 'Micra' and the Toyota 'Sub-Atomic Particle'. The danger with small cars is that their drivers (especially the male drivers) tend to compensate for the puny size of the vehicle by driving them as fast as possible along the twenty or so metres of clear road available at any time in Amsterdam. I have been a passenger in a small car (a BMW 'Flea') driven by Keith and it was extremely frightening – although I was very glad not to be a cyclist at the time.

Another problem is that the Dutch have completely disavowed the use of the indicator when turning, overtaking, changing lanes and any other potentially fatal manoeuvres. Apparently they think it's too much trouble to move their hand a quarter of an inch to flick it on and avoid an accident; or they think that it's some sort of instrument to be employed in moments of auto-vehicular celebration. 'Oh look Piet, here comes Queen Beatrix. Quick, turn on one of those orange flashing lights.'

Canals. Every year more than fifty cars are pulled out of Amsterdam's canals.

Pedestrians. Every year more than one hundred pedestrians are pulled from the city's canals.

Taxis. Like in most major cities, taxi drivers think they own the roads. The difference here is that they do: the taxi companies in Amsterdam are run by the Dutch equivalent of the Mafia, who also have a very big 'interest' in road construction. They are allowed to drive on tram tracks but show even less respect for human (or kitten) life than trams. The only reason they stop is to pick up passengers – but even then they kill them with the fare as they are the most expensive taxis in Europe.

Sean Condon, *My 'Dam Life* (2003)

✳ ✳ ✳

If you MUST try cycling around Amsterdam, you would do well to read Renate Rubinstein on the subject first.

From the traffic point of view, the centre of Amsterdam is a mess. Not just as it always was, no, even worse than last week.

Yesterday, I chose the side streets, but whichever I took to avoid the other, there was always a hole right across, or in the length, always flashing lights and little red flags and municipal cranes and the half a metre of asphalt along the edge of the pit as a fairway through the exhaust fumes. Once the council starts breaking up and mending, it does so on a grand scale: all the alleyways at the same time and if any bridges need renovating they automatically do two successive ones together, so there is no longer any way out and car drivers, fucked, steer backwards in long columns towards the traffic jams in the main street.

Cycled south along Rokin this morning. Holes and barriers everywhere, bits of bent tram rail shoved to one side, double parked cars with – for the sake of convenience – the doors open on both sides. You have to steer round all that and still avoid getting into the tram rails or between the wheels, that's just the way it is and you simply have to hope that the traffic lights are with you and you can pace your breathing. After a number of nasty swerves, I swish, still unharmed but too late, between a truck and the pavement, up to the lights. In front of me is a bunch of cyclists, who make me impatient because I have to turn right, so they shouldn't stand there waiting so obediently while I can't get through. Turning right at a red light is a cyclist's privilege.

I manage it after all. A cyclist in front of me breaks away from the fold, I follow. Just then a policeman on a motorcycle shouts, "Come back, sir!" With the frustration of yesterday still in me, I furiously dismount as well: I do not want to participate in such a society. Looking round on the zebra crossing to see if there is a shop with a telephone where I can call and cancel the dentist, the policeman's order reaches me, too: "You come back, as well, madam".

Oh yes? Is that what he wants? Well, then he's asking for it. Strong in my fury, I go up and stand in front of him. "Come back? Officer, I'm not doing this any longer. I'm chucking it in. I'm going home. I'm not taking part in that traffic of yours! I've had enough! Holes in the road and trucks all over the place and then you want to kick up a fuss!" By this point, evidently a need for a kind of logic, in other words for blaming someone, started to stir within me and, delighted, I found the arguments. "I'm not riding my bike any more. I refuse to. You lot do nothing. You do nothing about the trucks. You're scared of them. But you do dare to have a go at cyclists! Well, I'm done with it. I'm off home."

Well that told him. The lights changed to green and the astonished policeman revved up and drove off in relief. He had been dealing with a madwoman, a crazy bitch who rides through a red light then threatens to go home, not to take part any longer, not to grace the traffic with her presence any more. As a punishment! As far as I'm concerned, she can go home, thought the policeman, as long as she stays there. She's capable of occupying her own house and we'll have to get her out of there. Let her do what she likes. Good riddance.

Of course I meant my threat; otherwise I wouldn't have come out with it. I really would have gone home and washed the hands of my reasonableness of town, country, lake and canal, for good. But when the lights turned green again, I just cycled on anyway, as normal, just like everybody.

Renate Rubinstein, *Everybody's Mad for Change*
[*Ieder woelt hier om verandering*] (1979)
translated from the Dutch by Rosalind Buck

✣ ✣ ✣

A vivid picture of travel on the city's trams, including a word of warning about where not to put your money … from Remco Campert.

One of the topics you could go on about indefinitely is the quality of public transport. I think the quality is okay, but then I still remember when everything used to be much worse. In my school satchel days every tram was a death trap. Most of the passengers on the inside suffocated (conductors only lasted about three trips) and the bunches of people hanging on the outside were brutally mowed off by lorries parked too close to the tram rails.

If you've ever seen an old engraving of a raft crammed with shipwrecked sailors surrounded by desperate wretches still floundering in the wild billows, wanting to get on as well, then you've got a pretty good comparison.

Now and again you succeeded in wriggling your way to the middle of the tram. The pretty girls you were hoping to be squeezed up against, naturally you were never squeezed up against them. Vile old men in faded coats that smelled of rain and never having been to the cleaners, little old grannies with grey curls through which you could see their skull or great big, bony women coming back from the market with gigantic shopping bags that stripped the skin from your legs, that's who you were squeezed up against. And you only managed to leave the tram three stops after you should have got off.

But these days! They come swishing by like luxurious limousines. You can often get a seat, but if not there's always plenty of room to stand. Personally, I like to sit in the seat designated for disabled people – they're nice and close to the exit and give a good view of life going on outside the tram. As I take my place in one of these seats I always rehearse a kind of apology: I'm just sitting here for a moment as there is nobody disabled handy, but of course I'll stand up as soon as one gets on. After all, I'm actually extremely polite.

Naturally, modern tram travel is not without its snags. Like modern writing, actually. People always think that you just write down any old thing, that you simply sit down and write whatever comes into your head.

Well, it's not like that at all! It's an extremely mysterious profession with one secret that is closely guarded by all confreres, namely that you simply sit down and write whatever comes into your head. But of course some sit slightly better than others and some heads are better equipped than others. A writer is someone who can walk perfectly well when he gets on the tram and sits in a disabled seat and has to be hauled off half lame at the end of the journey.

A lot of people stick their money in the slot where you have to put your ticket to get it stamped. Those are wonderful moments for the innocent bystander.

A couple of the categories I hate have survived the big change. The housewives with their big shopping bags are still operating, sometimes alone, often in well-organised gangs. And another disagreeable character seems to have nine lives. The man who, with the air of being closely related to the tram business, starts chatting with the driver, half leaning over him with his unattractive rump swathed in too baggy trousers obstructing access to the tram, and gives expert commentary, in that rather disapproving Dutch tone of men who are party to information for which outsiders are too stupid, on the driving habits of non-public transport.

As you may have noticed, I've missed out the bus and I didn't want to start on it either. I'm not fond of the bus. A kind of 1950s atmosphere hangs around the bus, of rain, wind and out-of-the-way neighbourhoods. You can't sit comfortably on the bus; the seats are too close together and too narrow. Evidently, a spartan faction of public transport management has been given free rein there.

> Remco Campert, *Where is Remco Campert?*
> [*Waar is Remco Campert?*] (1978)
> translated from the Dutch by Rosalind Buck

✳ ✳ ✳

Like public transport in most European towns and cities, the trams of Amsterdam fill up, in the evenings, with youngsters off to enjoy themselves. Here is an older man enjoying the sight of the city's teenagers in their outrageous clothes and parent-free excitement as they collect for a night out.

When his restaurant recitals were over for the evening, the suspect always took the tram to the Leidseplein. The mass transportation of teenagers from the satellites and the suburbs gathered pace. The tram would steam up, sweet from cosmetics and sweat. The doors opened at the Leidseplein and the creatures of the night dispersed into the surrounding cafés and discos. The rest of the passengers remained in the tram, like silent parents leaving their kids behind for a school outing. This was the tram stop where the youth distinguished itself from the adults and, for the meantime at least, he still belonged to the former group.

He loved the metamorphosis the city underwent around eleven at night. It was time to stack the daytime terrace tables of the city under canvas, like pieces of scenery after a show. As the shops rolled down their shutters, the public space was transformed into one big amorous meeting place. Night-time lowered the contact threshold and raised the interactive tempo. Meeting someone during the day usually implied a measured trajectory with many an awkward silence, half-hearted invitations, and more approving smiles than was good for a person.

The city at night was carnivalesque, in the sense that every high-spirited participant was both actor and audience at the same time. He himself played the role of wandering pianist in a dinner jacket. The man who had sat at the bar after a performance, melancholic, drinking whisky and thinking about his girlfriend who had left him and what the future might hold for the world in general and for him in particular. As member of the audience, he also let himself by charmed by new teenage girls, the jewels of the city at night. Patent leather boots and fishnet tights, long, bored, defiant faces and navels stuffed with diamonds. Tanned bellies, washboard firm, and jeans with slivers of string peering over the top. The curve of buttocks in loud, fanned-out, baggy skirts and the and the oval-shaped dimples you occasionally came across on the lower back, either side of the spine. And let's not forget the dimples between the collarbones where silver pendants not infrequently dangle, or the leather handbags on the floor surrounded by dancing huddles, or the wavy hair and the hairgrips, bands and clasps that kept it in shape.

Christian Weijts, *Art. 285B* (2006)
translated from the Dutch by Brian Doyle

* * *

Time for a more lyrical and meditative take on the modern city from Cees Nooteboom.

For what does a city consist of? Everything that has been said there, dreamed, destroyed, undertaken. The erected, the disappeared, the imagined that never came to be. The living and the dead. The wooden houses that were torn down or burned, the palaces that might have existed, the bridge across the IJ, which was drawn but never built, the houses still standing where generations have left their memories. But there is much more than that. A city is all the words that have been uttered there, as unceasing, never-ending muttering, whispering, singing, and shouting that has resounded through the centuries and been blown away again. This cannot have vanished without having belonged to the city. Even that which is never to be retrieved is part of the city because once, in this place, it was called out or uttered on a winter night or a summer morning. The open-field sermon, the verdict of the tribunal, the cry of the flogged, the bidding at an auction, the ordinance, the placard, the discourse, the pamphlet, the death announcement, the calling of the hours, the words of nuns, whores, kings, regents, painters, aldermen, hangmen, shippers, lansquenets, lock keepers, and builders, the persistent conversation along the canals in the living body of the city, which is the city. Whoever wishes can hear it. It survives in archives, poems, street names, and proverbs, in the words and tonalities of the language, the way faces in the paintings of Hals and Rembrandt survive in the faces we see, just as our words and faces among all those words and faces will disappear, remembered and not remembered, blown away, forgotten, yet still present, located in the word that names the city, Amsterdam.

A sailor dies of scurvy in Ambon in the seventeenth century and sees once more the city of his birth, now forever beyond his reach. What he sees at that moment before death still exists in the way I look at the Schreierstoren, the Tower of Tears, where the seamen took leave of their wives. The city is a book to be read; the walker is the reader. He can start on any page, walking back and forth in time and space. Yes, the book may have a beginning but by no means has an end. The words consist of gables, excavations, names, dates, images. One house is called the Pelican, and would speak to us of distant voyages. Another is called Spitsbergen and commemorates a particular wintering. A street is called Bokking-hargen, and without smelling anything you can recognize the odour of smoked fish. A gable shows a golden portal, but the door underneath is new, so the walker has to reconstruct in his mind the golden portal that once stood there. This city is not silent; she hands you the words – *Melkmeisjesbruggetje, Varkenssluis, Kalverstraat* – and the walker's imagination sees what history might have told him: that calves were sold in that street; further along, oxen; and in the last part, sheep. A small alley is dubbed Gebed zonder End, Prayer without End, by an Amsterdammer who thought there were too many nunneries in the inner city. Thus the prayer never ended there, and in that street name one still hears the Gregorian chants and the high, thin women's voices. Vijgendam, because the load of figs just rejected by the food testers was used for filling up canals. The walker stops at a building pit and sees how archaeologists strain the dirt, comb it out, dig for the past with gentle fingers in search of signs of ancestors. He is surprised that they lived there, down below. Does the earth keep growing thicker? He wonders whether he could have understood those other, earlier Amsterdammers. Later he sees these finds in a museum. The shoes are recognisable as shoes: he would be able to wear them just as they are. Shoes, bowls, hammers, money. [...]

It is grey today, misty. If he closes his eyes, the walker can hear the wind in the riggings of all those ships, caravels, frigates, galleons, brigantines, brigs; he can smell the spices, hear the foreign tongues of the many who have taken refuge in his city: Portuguese and

Spanish Jews, Huguenots, Flemish Calvinists, but also loners like Descartes who could meditate so well between the rolling tonnage on the quays; or a visitor like Diderot, who was astonished by *"cette liberté compagne de l'indépendance qui ne s'incline que devant les lois,"* "this freedom accompanied by independence that bows down only to the law." This walk never ends, and the walker reads the images as they present themselves in his mind's eye: the skaters of Avercamp's paintings along the canals, the medieval processions around the Miracle of Amsterdam, the new palaces of the slave traders, those same slave traders chanting their slow psalms in the austere churches, stripped of any decoration by the Iconoclasts, churches we know from the paintings of Saenredam. But also those others, the conventicles of persecuted Catholics hidden away in attics, the hanged girl drawn by Rembrandt, the poet Bredero drowned under the ice, the death of Hendrikje and the auction of Rembrandt antiques, the rebellion of the Anabaptists and their execution, the ostentation and the chilling greed, the weight of wealth, the cheering for one's own and others' kings, the military march of Spanish, French, and German occupiers. And so he lands in his own time: the persecution of the Jews when the city was forever maimed, the places where the heroes of the Resistance were tortured or shot, the entry of the Canadians at the Liberation, an ever-growing history, which this city has inhaled and kept, which survives in monuments and small, almost invisible memorials and in the memory of the living, the words of humiliation and defeat as much as the triumph of old and new victories, a morality, a remembrance.

Evening falls on the city. The lights in the windows of the canal houses make everything look smaller, like a living room. The gentle melancholy of port cities, because the air is always filled with homesickness. The walker I am walks past the Dam Palace that once, when first built, towered over everything. It still stands on more than thirteen thousand poles in the same swampy soil, the soil of Amestelle. Here, in 1948, as a boy, I saw the Old Queen abdicate after reigning for fifty years. Right in the heart of the city, where now lie broad streets and a late tram rides past, once lay the ships. I know where the original Exchange stood, and the later one, and the still later version; where the Waag was, the Public Weigh House, and the Fishmarket, where the condemned were broken on the wheel, and grain was bought and sold. Now I go past the canals where once walked the poets – Hooft, Vondel, Bredero, Hoornik, Slauerhoff – who wrote in my secret language, which no foreigner can read. I walk past the patricians' palaces that have now been turned into office buildings, past the mercantile houses of the lost empire, see somewhere on a gable the splendid sign of the Dutch East Indies Company. Through the dark, low streets of the Jordaan I walk past the houses of the nameless ones of times gone by, without whom that vanished world power could never have existed. Nothing has remained the same; everything is the same. This is my city, a token for the initiated. She will never fully reveal herself to the outsider who does not know her language and her history, because it is precisely language and names that are the keepers of secret moods, secret places, secret memories. Open city, closed city. One city for us, one city for the others. A city on the water, a city of people, devised and written by man and water. A city of all times, and a city in time. A city that exists twice, visible and invisible, of stone and wood and water and glass and also of something that cannot be named in words.

Cees Nooteboom, *The Philosopher Without Eyes*
[*De filosoof zonder ogen*] (1997)
translated from the Dutch by Manfred Wolf and
Virginie M. Kortekaas

✳ ✳ ✳

*What – and how – does modern Amsterdam cele-
brate? Sean Condon takes us through the uniquely
Dutch phenomenon of Queen's Day (30th April)*

when everything turns orange ... And then, of course,
there's Christmas, Amsterdam-style.

It was the day before the day before Queen's Day and all over the country the subjects of the House of Orange were getting 'orange fever'. Cafés, restaurants and bars were festooned with orange crepe paper, orange-framed pictures of Queen Beatrix and flashing orange lights. Multi-Vlaai, the Limburg-based cake manufacturers, had proclaimed this 'Oranje Week' and were selling special orange *vlaais* with apricot, carrot, peach and scallop toppings. Billboards featuring women wearing orange underwear were everywhere. Sales of orange juice soared. Oranjeboom beer was *the* alcohol of the moment. Orangina was liquid gold. My favourite knock-knock joke enjoyed a new lease of life *(Knock knock. Who's there? Orange. Orange who? Orange you glad you're in Amsterdam and it's nearly Queen's Day?)*

The main reason for all this was that orange is the national colour of the Netherlands, and that's fine by me – it's a nice colour. Not very serious or threatening, and fashion-wise it doesn't really go with anything but itself, but a very pleasant colour it is all the same. The secondary reason was that Beatrix is the Queen of the Netherlands and widespread orangeness is the way her birthday is celebrated. Another inescapable element of the lead up to Queen's Day were the chalk marks proclaiming *Bezet!* (busy or taken) covering every bit of sidewalk. Everywhere you went there were big squares from building front to curbside with something like '*Let op!! Anapol and Jan komen!!*' written on them. The more enthusiastically territorial *bezeters* added a skull and crossbones to their squares. The lazier just wrote 'B'. But beware interlopers of either space, because this is how people reserve places for their stalls. They have stalls because, apart from wearing, drinking, eating and thinking orange, the Dutch celebrate Queen's Day by selling stuff. The whole city turns into a giant flea market. Why a city which already has flea markets all over the place wants to become one giant one is almost beyond my simple powers of understanding, but my guess would be that it has something to do with the way the people of this country like to celebrate just about every other day of the year – by making some dough.

I was a little hung over on Queen's *Dag* and my condition was not at all helped by the fact that the colour orange was, as I've mentioned, everywhere, including on my actual self in the form of a very garish (but beautifully tailored) tangerine shirt. Add to this oompah bands strutting up and down the street bashing big bass drums and honking big brass *neder*phones, and you have a hangover cure that is swift and brutally effective.

In accordance with tradition, every bit of sidewalk was taken up by some sort of stall selling everything from shirts to Shinola to shoelaces. ('For all your shoelace needs,' I advised the two young-sters to put on a sign, since I was once again becoming an adman. 'C'mon, that's gold!!' They ignored me.) Everywhere Sally and I turned there were groups of kid choirs screaming out the national anthem, old people trying to shift the contents of their attics, bars and cafés with karaoke machines and beer taps set up out front; and above it all a very strong sense of conviviality that sometimes seemed to approach a sheer mass joy that was impossible not to be swept up in. The first time round, anyway.

December in Amsterdam is exhausting; there are so many official and unofficial excuses for drinking, dancing, eating and talking to excess. Officially the Dutch like to recognise several Christ-mas-like events, beginning with the night before Sinterklaas. For maximum confusion, Sinterklaas is the name of both the event – the feast of Saint Nicholas on December 5th – and the name of a Santa Claus-like figure who struts about the country around that time. By early December, Sinterklaas (the guy, rather than the event) has been in Holland for a couple of weeks, having arrived by boat 'from Spain' (the Dutch equivalent of the North Pole, but with better weather and food) back in the middle of November. When the bearded, mitre-clutching Sint arrives, he rides a white horse through the *stads* and *dorps* (cities and towns) accompanied by Moorish 'Black Petes' (the Dutch equivalent of elves but with heavily racist overtones) who distribute sweets to the good children and allegedly put the bad children into sacks and haul them back to Spain, thus providing the youngsters of Holland with material for a lifetime of horrific nightmares, terrified as they are of having to live in a land of sunshine, merriment and flavoured food. Due to the already-mentioned racist aspects of having a tall white man with a white beard on a white horse being attended to by a number of small black helpers, attempts have been made by the relevant Dutch authorities to turn the Black Petes into multi-coloured Rainbow Peters, thereby offending persons of red, yellow, blue, green and cerise descent. However, every year it's been tried, it fails and next time round Black Pete the Bag-Carrying Enforcer is back. But the problems don't stop there. Amsterdam has a substantial Muslim population and they have their own reasons for eschewing Sinterklaas, chiefly that he is seen as a Christian infidel and a dangerously Westernising influence on Muslim children. So who exactly is this troublesome fellow?

As older readers will recall, during the Middle Ages saints were an important part of life, being called upon to win wars, protect ships, locate lost items and assist with not getting the plague. Even school children had their own patron saint, Saint Nicholas of Myra (modern-day Turkey), about whom a number of (possibly unreliable) stories sprang up. One such tale concerns three young boys who sought shelter from a storm at an inn where the innkeeper and his wife cut the lads into small pieces and preserved them in a barrel of brine to be served as a meal for the next guest. The next guest, however, was Saint Nick, who, after a mouthful or two of pickled kid, realised what he was eating and promptly brought the youngsters back to life then delivered a stern lecture to the hotelier and stripped the inn of its Michelin star. Another story, this one less likely than the other to traumatise and nauseate, is about the three daughters of an impoverished nobleman. Being poor, the girls (who were probably good-looking, but nobody knows for sure) had no dowry and therefore no suitors and were about to turn to prostitution when Saint Nicholas, then a young priest, heard about their sorry circumstances and began showing up at night and tossing money into their bedroom through an open window. On the third night the girls' father collared Saint Nick and demanded to know what was going on. 'Throwing coins into your daughters' shoes,' Saint Nick told him (although I'm paraphrasing). The father demanded to know why. 'Because I think it could become a nifty tradition.' (Again, I'm paraphrasing.) Then he disappeared, the only trace of him a gingerbread man on the floor. (Here I am not so much paraphrasing as simply inventing.)

And so it did become a tradition; seventeenth-century Holland was a place brimming with people leaving secret gifts in shoes and suitors placing gingerbread men on doorsteps as signs of their intentions towards maidens. These days, on December 5th, people suffering hangovers from celebrating the night before still exchange small gifts hidden in footwear, as well as poems, specially written by Sinterklaas himself, mercilessly lampooning the recipient. It's also customary on this day to eat seasonal comestibles such as *specwaas* (a horribly sweet cinnamon gingerbread) and, for reasons I cannot fathom (or even invent), chocolate capital letters of the person's first name.

Sean Condon, *My 'Dam Life* (2003)

* * *

Any consideration of modern Amsterdam has to look further than the exquisite centre of the city. In this passage from Adrian Matthews' The Apothecary's House we accompany Ruth to the outer urban sprawl.

The train doors opened and the crowd surged off.

The sign over the platform read 'Zuid/WTC'.

She got up, yawned and followed the stairs and passageways to Line 50.

She was just in time for the connecting train.

RAI – Overamstel – Van der Madeweg ...

The old picture-postcard Amsterdam had been left trailing behind. A satellite metropolis took its place under the amber grids and necklaces of sodium lamps. It had mushroomed on an old polder of reclaimed land in the late sixties and seventies. Road bridges. Viaducts. Underpasses. And the first zones of slab blocks, honeycomb repositories for humanity, rectangular concrete boxes for the living, dropped haphazardly from the developers' cranes onto the featureless terrain.

This was the Bijlmer or Zuidoost, the city's south-eastern extension.

It was the most notorious failed housing project in the Netherlands, a monument to group-think, a place without rhyme or reason, where thousands of poor saps had been cast down to live out the rest of their days, not knowing quite what had hit them.

This was where Dutch society touched bottom.

Housing-wanted ads in the Amsterdam papers always ended with 'Geen ZO': No Zuidoost.

The train rumbled on: Duivendrecht-Strandvliet/ArenA ...

The floodlamps were burning white at ArenA, the new 50,000-seat Amsterdam stadium, home to the Ajax football club, and here investment had poured in unstintingly. A state-of-the-art development zone now extended its electronic tentacles: American-style clusters of high-rises and business parks, urban-fringe tech industries, designer plazas and atriums, the Pathé, the Heinken/Mojo concert venue, theme shopping in the malls and megastores of the Arena Boulevard and Villa ArenA, the Transferium commuter car park, and so it marched on. A brave new digitally specced world, magicked up from the architects' and planners' neo-platonic imaginations and graphic interfaces into glass, concrete, steel.

Ruth had cycled out this way one summer's day and was familiar with the principal landmarks: the KPN Telecom centre, the Sparklerweg zone, the glitzy BMW dealerships and the six towers of the Bijlmer 'can' or prison, which were only a little more forbidding than the district's infamous ten-storey deck-access housing units.

Yes, here it was, somewhere in the vicinity: the dear old Bijlmer. Behind the window dressing were some seven square kilometres of instant dysfunctional ghetto.

Just add a few thousand immigrants – preferably those who had never wanted to live there in the first place – stir, bring to the boil and serve.

She got off the train at the elevated station. A smell of chewing gum in the air from the Sportlife factory. She walked a few blocks, hurried through the muggers' paradise of a rundown shopping precinct and took the lift to the community centre offices on the top floor of the unpretentious block.

Adrian Mathews, *The Apothecary's House* (2005)

✳ ✳ ✳

After the actions of the Provos and the Squatters Riots (see the item in 'Amsterdam the Tolerant'), a programme of 'urban renewal' had done away with or renovated some of the worst of the city's housing. The process of 'gentrification', however, didn't quite banish all of the more exotic inhabitants from one such area, described here by F. Starik.

Half the houses here have been newly built, at the end of the 1980s, maintaining the same pattern of streets, in the place the squatters used to live in old, run down buildings dating from the beginning of the twentieth century. Whatever was worth saving has been properly renovated. An estate agent would say that the character of the neighbourhood has been preserved and still in keeping with the urban street plan. It's all very upmarket now. Hardly anyone is unemployed or on disability, or a wastrel, already broken back in their younger days, even though a whole lot of elderly are still ambling around on their walkers. Or sitting in an electric wheelchair. Nice to do your shopping from a motor-ized wheelchair. Most of the people here have managed to find work, something to do. It's rush hour in the supermarket from five o'clock to half past six. Men in suits, the women in flowered skirts and high heels. Children crying, tired and hungry from a long day at the childminder's. The new houses have attracted respectable tenants. From the looks of things prosperity has considerably increased. Folks here have it good.

The junkies are still around, the psychiatric cases, the home-less, the Spanish squatters. Although they're more of a pleasant exception now, rather than the norm, here to remind us how good we have it. There's an old hippie who squats on his haunches for days, vacantly staring into the middle distance, while blowing on a small copper flute, although not, apparently, with the intention of making music. There's the small fat man who crosses through the neighbourhood at a rapid clip. He's tireless. In the time it takes me to do my shopping I'll have run into him three times. When I return home on my bike late at night I see him going out. If I were to have a dog that needed walking early in the morning, I would certainly run into him then too. He ought to get a dog, or two dogs would be better, as such a creature would want a rest now and then from all that restless back and forth.

F. Starik, *The Outsider [De gastpeler]* (2009)
translated from the Dutch by Patricia Gosling

❋ ❋ ❋

Amsterdam's cafés still form an important part of the city's social fabric, especially in areas like the Jordaan. In this extract, we see Youri Egorov, a Russian virtuoso pianist, enjoying some time off in the city's cafés, but using his nimble fingers to good effect in a different context.

Marco often took Youri to the Café Weltschmerz on Wester-straat. To drink of course, but mostly so that Youp – he called him Youp, with an explosive 'p' at the end – could break his umpteenth record on the pinball machine. Youp's nimble fingers were legendary. In the heart of the Jordaan the café was the local hangout for a crowd of slovenly characters in too tight leather jackets. Perhaps not exactly the underworld, but petty dealers who trafficked in their trade at the bar. While Youri played, they positioned themselves around the pinball machine and rewarded him with a head-butt, a glass of gin or a large beer. His tech-nique was astonishing. Like a sheriff grabbing for his pistol he shot from the hips, using his right pinky to operate the lever and working the knobs by alternating his thumb, index, and middle fingers. He kept the ball in play forever, the machine never seemed to go into tilt mode. In the Weltschmerz he was known as the Virtuoso, without any of the regulars knowing that he actually was such a thing on the keyboard. [...]

Before heading back home, we would stop by another café, usually some hole in the wall. The gentrification of the Jordaan had only just begun; it was a gloomy neighbourhood, old in the sense of battered, neglected and down at heel. The only thing that wasn't worn down was the neighbourhood's reputation. On Queen's Day, Willy Alberti climbed on the billiard table at the Café De Oranjerie on the Binnen Oranjestraat and, accompanied by an accordion player, pretended to be a street performer, but he himself had lived outside the city for a long time, like most of the artists who waxed poetic about the Jordaan as a place where the sun smiled on everyone. Yet it was still a neighbourhood of spontaneous laughter – and spontaneous quarrels. There was lots of French and Spanish blood in the inhabitants and there existed amongst all the small shopkeepers a strong feeling of solidarity. The Yiddish sense of humour hadn't been lost. While waiting for the butcher or baker you could hear plenty of joking around and the green grocer would puff out his chest and belt out the sentimental songs of Tante Leen, the 'Voice of the Jordaan'. But just as often you heard grumbling. The houses were too small and damp, the stairs to the upper floors too narrow, the streets too dirty. Schools had to be closed because children were falling through the floors. Building façades were on the brink of collapse and tree trunks were propped at an angle against the shop fronts. Ten years later yuppies would move into completely renovated buildings; that's when, one after the other, the original residents of the Jordaan left the neighbourhood, leaving behind a dilapidated hovel.

Jan Brokken, *In the House of the Poet*
[*In het huis van de dichter*] (2008)
translated from the Dutch by Patricia Gosling

✳ ✳ ✳

Continuing with the Jordaan cafés, here are some observations from Cees Nooteboom.

My house sits between the Singel and the Herengracht [Lords' Canal], close to the Brouwersgracht [Brewers' Canal], and it is via the latter canal that I travel abroad: to Jordan, or as we've been saying for centuries, De Jordaan. To get there I first cross the Melkmeisjesbrugje [Little Milkmaids' Bridge], cross straight back over the bridge to the Herengracht and then continue along the other side of the Brouwersgracht to the Pastoorsbrug [Pastors' Bridge] and on to Papeneiland [Papist Island], one of the city's oldest cafés. I cross the Lekkere Sluis [Tasty Lock], where the Prinsengracht [Princes' Canal] flows out into the Brouwersgracht and which marks the boundary between the Jordaan and the rest of the world.

Opinions on this boundary are extremely divided. Some say the Jordaan proper ends at Rozengracht [Rose Canal]. Others allow it to continue on the other side of the canal down to the quiet Passeerdersgracht, which doesn't derive its name from passers-by but from an old word for leather workers ("passeerders"). But there are no more cafés here nor any small shops selling all kinds of things, which have come to define the Jordaan, a part of town that during the post-war years has seen ordinary, working-class people make way for gallery owners, students, small restaurants, antiquarian booksellers, ethnic shops and above all lots and lots of cafés, old "authentic" and hyped-up new ones – in short, a labyrinth of new and old, working class and chichi, in which purple neon lighting sits cheek by jowl with the grey twilight of a "brown café" where old men reminisce behind small glasses of jenever, but where a few hours later you could just as easily come in to find a small crowd singing Jordaan songs, tearjerkers that everybody knows the words to and that were immortalized by popular crooners, songs of heart-rending pain and passion, with titles such as "my cradle was a cardboard box" and lyrics detailing the misery that inevitably follows such an inconspicuous beginning, all sung in the inimitable local accent.

Once upon a time, during the Golden Age, this area was home to the common people, artisans, and formed the heart of a cosmopolitan city that had developed into one of the world's great centres of power. But during its decline in the nineteenth century the people became the proletariat, while poverty and sometimes hunger were rife. And yet the neighbourhood retained an at times almost provocative sense of identity, completely different from other parts of the city; it was a family of sorts, a tribe with its own customs, sayings and above all laws. Marrying outside the neighbourhood was frowned upon, solidarity was strong and people lived literally on top of one another and knew everything about each other.

The Jordaan café is the not always neutral territory where both parties meet, or where they gather without really meeting each other. It depends on the café, on the time of day, and often also on the common sense of the outsiders – because everybody starts as an outsider. Entering such a café for the first time can be a precarious undertaking. Cafés in the Jordaan are living rooms. Enter at a certain time of day and you really feel as though you're entering a living room, an intimate setting where people have known each other for a very long time, an invisible barrier that you need to overcome, a world of aunts and uncles who are familiar with each other's habits, quirks, political persuasions and stories.

This is a world in which you have to earn your place, if that's what you want. Of course this isn't an issue for the one-time visitor, who is served and enjoys the atmosphere or feels excluded, depending on the situation. But those who live here need more time. We are not talking about an initiation rite here, but about a kind of novitiate, a period of slow, mutual habituation during which you shouldn't make a wrong move and certainly harbour no illusions that you can ever become a true Jordaaner, because either you are or you aren't.

Cees Nooteboom, *Café Papeneiland*
translated from the Dutch by Laura Vroomen

❊ ❊ ❊

Finally, we accompany Sean Condon to the Café Papeneiland on a bright, cold November day. As he waits for his coffee and cognac, he watches the world go by, leaving us with some images of everyday life in a quieter corner of this unique, sometimes puzzling, always interesting city where modern attitudes dwell in ancient houses, and the special light of a water city plays over everything: Amsterdam.

November 11th, 1998

At the moment Amsterdam is quite beautiful. And when I say 'at the moment', I mean right at this very moment – 3.28 p.m. – because at any moment it could change from cold, crisp and eye-wateringly clear and bright, to dark, cloudy and nose-runningly icy. So I've decided to go for a short walk and have a coffee and a cognac in a small, woody, *gezellig* bar called Café 't Pape-neiland at the intersection of two canals, Brouwersgracht and Prinsengracht. It's a wonderful place with a low, exposed-beam ceiling, a tiny staircase leading up to a tiny toilet, wood-framed windows and a panel of antique Delft porcelain allegedly discov-ered in the basement during renovations fifteen years ago. The bar has been here since 1641 and comfortably holds no more than thirty people. The ornate, twin-spouted beer tap is about one hundred and fifty years old and has a garish but charming woodland scene featuring two typically majestic deer painted on it. The whole place is heated by a single man-sized upright stove. Covering every wall are dozens of dusty framed etchings, paint-ings and photographs of the bar, seen from every possible angle. It's fabulous and exactly the right place to go when you're feeling as low-down and blue as I do, right now; worrying about the usual matters – where to live, how to live, what to do with my life. That sort of thing and whether or not Dutch director Paul Verhoeven will ever be able to repeat the artistic triumph of *The Soldier of Orange* and the box-office success of *Basic Instinct*.

The barman, a guy around sixty with a face like a wry and maudlin dog, greets me with a nod, which I return before asking in fractured Dutch for a *koffie verkeerd*, which trans-lates as 'coffee the wrong way', and seemed wrong because it has *melk* (milk) in it. After I order a cognac, the barman spur-tles another sentence at me, and thinking that he is asking if I want anything else, and pretending to be Dutch but unusually short in stature, I say *'Nee, dank je wel,'* ('No thanks') and shake my head, feeling semi-bilingual and semi-proud over this brief transaction.

'I'm sorry,' the barman says, 'but I asked what sort of cognac you'd prefer – Courvoisier, Rémy or Martell?' He speaks English perfectly.

'Ummm ... Rémy Martin,' I reply, not leaning too heavily on the French accent. He nods, not patronisingly or anything, just a run-of-the-mill barman's nod. But I need to regain some dignity first, so I change my coffee order to an espresso and I think I see him smile.

The trees are leafless, grabbing at the low sky with thin fingers; there are birds' nests in the tops. Boat and bicycle traffic is heavy, but obviously doesn't cause the road rage that automobile traffic does. This languid corner of the city – far away from the tourist shopping street Kalverstraat and the red-light area on the other side of Dam Square – feels a bit like a school at the end of term: empty, yet full of wistful memories. I see a paperboy on his bike straining up the small cobblestone bridge, *De Telegraaf* in sacks bulging over his back wheels. Riding a bike here, the icy wind on your scrunched-up face, makes you look as though you've been crying. The bright, gold sun hitting the facades of a row of chocolate-bricked five-storey houses. Coats, earmuffs, scarves, gloves and hats, and a Smart car zipping across the bridge. A tiny crimson, three-wheeled delivery van with a big plastic peanut on top. A mother pedalling a bicycle with a sleeping child folded across the handlebars.

Sean Condon, *My 'Dam Life* (2003)

Selective Index

* after name indicates writer whose work is excerpted in this book

Acknowledgements

Oxygen Books would like to thank the many people who have supported *city-pick AMSTERDAM* with their enthusiasm, professional help and generosity. We would like to mention in particular Maria Vlaar and Mireille Berman of the Foundation for the Production and Translation of Dutch Literature, Jasper Henderson for his help in selecting the extracts translated from Dutch, Laura Vrooman, Michele Hutchison, Eduardo Reyes, Mikka Haugaard, Catherine Trippett, Rohini Janda, Wendy Sanford, Jacqueline Smit, Judith Uyterlinde and, above all, our Amsterdam-based co-editor, Victor Schiferli, whose knowledge and enthusiasm have contributed so much to this anthology.

Martin Asscher, $H_2Olland$. First published in 2009 by Augustus, Amsterdam. Copyright © Maarten Asscher, 2009. Excerpt used by permission of the publisher. Translation copyright © Laura Vroomen 2010.

Paul Auster, *The Invention of Solitude*. Published by Faber and Faber. Copyright © Paul Auster 1982. Reprinted by permissions of Faber and Faber Ltd.

Abdelkader Benali, *Laat het morgen mooi weer zijn*. First published in 2005 by De Arbeiderspers, Amsterdam. Copyright © Abdelkader Benali, 2005. Excerpt used by permission of the publisher and The Susijn Agency Ltd. Translation copyright © Susan Massotty.

Machiel Bosman, *De polsslag van de stad. De Amsterdamse stadskroniek van Jacob Bicker Raije 1737-1772*. First published in 2009 by Uitgeverij Athenaeum-Polak & Van Gennep. Excerpt used by permission of the publisher. Translation copyright © Brian Doyle 2010.

Martin Bril, *De dag van de nieuwe haring*. First published in 2005 by Prometheus, Amsterdam. Copyright © Erven Martin Bril, 2005. Excerpt used by permission of the publisher. Translation copyright © Brian Doyle 2010.

Martin Bril, *Etalagebenen. Amsterdamse miniaturen*. First published in 1998 by Prometheus, Amsterdam. Copyright © Erven Martin Bril, 1998. Excerpt used by permission of the publisher. Translation copyright © Michele Hutchison 2010.

Martin Bril, *Stadsogen*. First published in 1999 by Prometheus, Amsterdam. Copyright © Erven Martin Bril, 2005. Excerpt used by permission of the publisher. Translation copyright © Michele Hutchison 2010.

Jan Brokken, *In het huis van de dichter*. First published in 2008 by Uitgeverij Atlas, Amsterdam. Copyright © Jan Brokken, 2008. Excerpt used by permission of the publisher. Translation copyright © Patricia Gosling 2010.

Ian Buruma, *Murder in Amsterdam: The Death of Theo van Gogh and the Limits of Tolerance*. Published by Atlantic Books, 2006. Copyright © Ian Buruma 2006. Reprinted by permission of Atlantic Books.

Remco Campert, *Het leven is vurrukkulluk*. First published in 1961 by De Bezige Bij, Amsterdam. Copyright © Remco Campert, 1961. Excerpt used by permission of the publisher. Translation copyright © Michele Hutchison 2010.

Remco Campert, *Waar is Remco Campert?* First published in 1978 by De Bezige Bij, Amsterdam. Copyright © Remco Campert, 1978. Excerpt used by permission of the publisher. Translation copyright © Rosalind Buck 2010.

Albert Camus, *The Fall*: published by Penguin Books, 1963. First published in France 1956 as *La Chute*. First published in Great Britain by Hamish Hamilton 1957. Translation copyright © Justin O'Brien 1957. Reprinted by permission of Penguin Books.

Simon Carmiggelt, *I'm Just Kidding: More of a Dutchman's Slight Adventures*. Published by De Arbeiderspers, 1972. Reprinted by permission of the publisher. Translation copyright © Elizabeth Willems-Treeman.

Sean Condon, *My 'Dam Life: Three Years in Holland*. Published by Lonely Planet Publications, 2003. Copyright © Sean Condon 2003. Reprinted by permission of the author.

Alain de Botton, *The Art of Travel*. Published by Hamish Hamilton, 2002. Copyright © Alain de Botton 2002. Reprinted by permission of Penguin Books Ltd.

Jules Deelder, *Deelder lacht*. Published by De Bezige Bij, 2007. Copyright © Jules Deelder 2007. Excerpt used by permission of the author and publisher. Translation copyright © Laura Vroomen 2010.

Peter de Graaf, 'Nog één keer Ramses' aanwezigheid'. Newspaper article in Het Parool, published December 2, 2009. Copyright © 2009, Het Parool, Amsterdam. Used by permission of Het Parool. Translation copyright © Patricia Gosling 2010.

Annemarie de Wildt, *The Hoerengracht: Keinholz at the National Gallery, London*. Copyright © The National Gallery Company

Acknowledgements

Limited, London, 2009. Reprinted by permission of the author and The National Gallery Company Limited, London.

Jan Donkers, *Zo dicht bij Amsterdam*. Published in 2007 by Uitgeverij Atlas, Amsterdam (extended and revised edition). Copyright © Jan Donkers, 2007. Excerpt used by permission of the publisher. Translation copyright © Michele Hutchison 2010.

Geoff Dyer, 'Hotel Oblivion' in *Yoga for people who can't be bothered to do it*. Published by the Little, Brown Book Group, 2003. Copyright © Geoff Dyer 2003. Reprinted by permisison of Little, Brown Book Group.

Frans Erens, *Vervlogen jaren*. Edited by Harry G. M. Prick, published by De Arbeiderspers, 1989. Original posthumous edition, 1938. Excerpt used by permission of the publisher. Translation copyright © Patricia Gosling 2010.

Chris Ewan, *The Good Thief's Guide to Amsterdam*. Published by Pocket Books. Copyright © by Christ Ewan 2007. Reproduced by permission of of Sheil Land Associates on behalf of Long Barn Books.

John Ezard, Obituary of Miep Gies, *The Guardian*. Copyright © Guardian News & Media Ltd 2010.

Jan Fontijn, *Biefstuk en benzine*. First published in 2003 by Uitgeverij G.A. van Oorschot, Amsterdam. Copyright © Jan Fontijn, 2003. Excerpt used by permission of the publisher. Translation copyright © Imogen Cohen 2010.

Anne Frank, *The Diary of Anne Frank*. First published in Holland in 1947 by Contact Amsterdam. Most recent edition published by Penguin Books, 2007. Translation copyright © Susan Massotty. Reprinted by permission of Penguin Books Ltd.

Nicholas Freeling, *Love in Amsterdam*. First published by Victor Gollanz 1962; Penguin Books, 1965. Copyright © Nicholas Freeling 1962. Reprinted by permission of Orion Books Ltd.

Sam Garrett, 'Cutting the Techno-Onion'. Copyright © Sam Garrett 2001. Reprinted by permission of the author.

James Gavin, *Deep in a dream: the long night of Chet Baker*. First published in Great Britain by Chatto and Windus, 2002. Published by Vintage, 2003. Copyright © James Gavin 2002. Reprinted by permission of The Random House Group Ltd.

Kees 't Hart, *De revue*. First published in 1999 by Uitgeverij Querido, Amsterdam. Copyright © Uitgeverij Querido, 1999. Excerpt used by permission of the publisher. Translation copyright © Brian Doyle 2010.

Maarten 't Hart, 'Wonen op de wallen'. Short story taken from the collection *Alle verhalen*, first published in 1982 by De Arbeiderspers, Amsterdam. Copyright © Maarten 't Hart, 1982. Excerpt used by permission of the publisher. Translation copyright © Diane Webb. This translation first appeared in *Amsterdam: A Traveller's Literary Companion*, published by Whereabouts Press, San Francisco, 2001.

Stefan Hertmans, *Steden*. First published in 1998 by Uitgeverij Meulenhoff/Kritak, Amsterdam/Louvain. Edition used: fourth edition, De Bezige Bij, 2007. Copyright © Stefan Hertmans, 2007. Excerpt used by permission of the publisher. Translation copyright © Laura Vroomen 2010.

'Het Parool' article, 'Germans shoot at celebrating crowd' (1945). Excerpt used by permission of 'Het Parool'. Translation copyright © Rosalind Buck 2010.

Arthur Japin, *In Lucia's Eyes*. First published in Dutch by De Arbeiderspers, 2003; published by Chatto and Windus, 2005; Vintage, 2006. Copyright © Arthur Japin 2003; translation © David Colmer 2005. Reprinted by permission of the Random House Group Ltd.

Gerrit Komrij, *De klopgeest*. First published in 2001 by Uitgeverij De Bezige Bij, Amsterdam. Copyright © Gerrit Komrij, 2001. Excerpt used by permission of the publisher. Translation copyright © Brian Doyle 2010.

Simon Kuper, *Ajax, The Dutch, The War*. Published by Orion, 2003. Copyright © 2003 Simon Kuper. Reprinted by permission of Orion Books Ltd.

Simona Luff, *Diary*. Copyright © Simona Luff 2006. Reprinted by permission of the author.

Geert Mak, *Amsterdam: A Brief Life of the City*. First published in Dutch by Uitgeverij Atlas, 1995. First published in Great Britain by The Harvill Press 1999; revised 2001. Copyright © Geert Mak, 1994. English translation copyright © Philipp Blom, 1999. Reprinted by permission of the Random House Group Ltd.

Richard Mason, 'Amsterdam'. Copyright © 2009 by Richard Mason. Originally published in Het Parool (June 2009). Reprinted by permission of the author and the author's agent, Anderson Literary Management, LLC.

Adrian Mathews, *The Apothecary's House*. Published by Macmillan, 2005. Copyright © Adrian Mathews 2005. Reprinted by permission of Pan Macmillan Ltd.

Nicolaas Matsier, *Dicht bij huis. Voorvallen, voorvallen, stemmingen.*

First published in 1997 by Uitgeverij De Bezige Bij, Amsterdam. Copyright © Nicolaas Matsier, 1997. Excerpt used by permission of the publisher. Translation copyright © Laura Watkinson 2010.

Sylvie Matton, *Rembrandt's Whore*. Published by Canongate Books Ltd 2001. Copyright © Sylvie Matton, 1997. Translation copyright © Tamsin Black, 2001. Reprinted by permission of Canongate Books Ltd.

Ian McEwan, *Amsterdam*. Published by Jonathan Cape 1998. Copyright © Ian McEwan 1998. Reprinted by kind permission of the Random House Book Group Ltd.

Victor Meijer, *Miskend talent*. First published in 2008 by Uitgeverij De Harmonie, Amsterdam. Copyright © Uitgeverij De Harmonie, 2008. Excerpt used by permission of the publisher. Translation copyright © Michele Hutchison 2010.

Doeschka Meijsing, *Over de liefde*. First published in 2008 by Uitgeverij Querido, Amsterdam. Copyright © Doeschka Meijsing, 1999. Excerpt used by permission of the publisher. Translation copyright © Jeanette K. Ringold.

Gustav Meyrink, *The Green Face*. First published in Germany 1916. First published by Dedalus 1992; new edition 2004. Translated by Mike Mitchell. Translation copyright © Dedalus 1992. Reprinted by permission of Dedalus Ltd.

Sarah Emily Miano, *Van Rijn*. Published by Picador 2006. Copyright © Sarah Emily Miano 2006. Reprinted by permission of Pan Macmillan Ltd.

Deborah Moggach, *Tulip Fever*. Published by Vintage 2000. Copyright © Deborah Moggach 1999. Reprinted by permission of the Random House Group Ltd.

César Antonio Molina, *Waiting for Years Past* © César Antonio Molina, 2007. © Ediciones Destino, S. A., 2007. Translation copyright © Kit Maude 2009.

Montesquieu, Charles de *Voyages*. Translation © Oxygen Books Ltd 2010.

Marcel Möring, *In Babylon*. First published in Holland in 1997 by J. M. Meulenhoff. First published in Great Britain by Flamingo 1999. Copyright © Marcel Möring 1997. Translation © Stacey Knecht 1999. Reprinted by permission of HarperCollins Publishers Ltd.

Multatuli, *Max Havelaar*. First published in Dutch, 1860. Copyright © 1982 edited by E. M. Beekman and published by the University of Massachusetts Press. Reprinted by permission of the University of Massachusetts Press.

Nescio, *Natuurdagboek*. First published in 1997 as volume of the Collected Works edited by Lieneke Frerichs by Uitgeverij G.A. van Oorschot, Amsterdam. Copyright © Erven Nescio, 1997. Excerpt used by permission of the publisher. Translation copyright © Laura Vroomen 2010.

Cees Nooteboom, *Café Papeneiland*. First published in 2004 by Stichting De Heeren Keyser, Amsterdam. Copyright © Cees Nooteboom, 2004. Excerpt used by permission of the author. Translation copyright © Laura Vroomen 2010.

Cees Nooteboom, Amsterdam. Taken from the essay collection *De filosoof zonder ogen: Europese reizen*, first published in 1997 by Uitgeverij De Arbeiderspers, Amsterdam. Copyright © Cees Nooteboom, 1997. Excerpt used by permission of the author. Translation copyright © Manfred Wolf and Virginie Kortekaas 2001. This translation first appeared in *Amsterdam: A Traveller's Literary Companion*, published by Whereabouts Press, San Francisco, 2001.

Thomas Olde Heuvelt, 'Harlequin on Dam Square'. Copyright © Thomas Olde Heuvelt 2010. Excerpt used by permission of the author. Translation copyright © Laura Vroomen.

Sue Rann, *Looking for Mr Nobody*. Published by No Exit Press, 2003. Copyright © Sue Rann 2003. Reprinted by kind permission of No Exit Press (www.noexit.co.uk).

Renate Rubinstein, *Ieder woelt hier om verandering*. First published in 1979 by Uitgeverij Meulenhoff, Amsterdam. Copyright © Erven Renate Rubinstein, 1979. Used by permission of Rubinstein Media, Amsterdam. Translation copyright © Rosalind Buck 2010.

Piet Reinwald, email to his granddaughter. Reprinted by permission of Piet and Jennifer Reinwald.

Simon Schama, *Rembrandt's Eyes*. First published in Great Britain by Allen Lane The Penguin Press 1999. Copyright © Simon Schama 1999. Reprinted by permission of Penguin Books Ltd.

Simon Schama, *The Embarrassment of Riches*. First published in Great Britain by William Collins Sons and Co Ltd 1987. First published in paperback by Fontana Press 1988. Copyright © Simon Schama 1987. Reprinted by kind permission of HarperCollins Publishers Ltd.

David Sedaris, *Dress Your Family in Corduroy and Denim*. First published in Great Britain by Abacus, 2004. Copyright © 2004 by David Sedaris. Reprinted by permission of Abner Stein Ltd on behalf of the author.

Stav Sherez, *The Devil's Playground*. Published by Michael Joseph 2004. Penguin Books 2005. Copyright © Stave Sherez 2004. Reprinted by permission of Penguin Books Ltd.

A. L. Snijders, *Belangrijk is dat niet aan lezers denk*. First published by in 2006 by AFDh. Copyright © A. L. Snijders 2006. Excerpt used by kind permission of the publisher. Translation copyright © Rosalind Buck 2010.

Maarten Spanjer, *Maarten maakt vrienden: Ontmoetingen*. First published in 2006 by Uitgeverij Thomas Rap, Amsterdam. Copyright © 2006 Maarten Spanjer. Used by permission of the author. Translation copyright © Laura Vroomen 2010.

F. Starik, *De gastpeler*. First published in 2009 by Uitgeverij Nieuw Amsterdam, Amsterdam. Copyright © 2009 F. Starik. Excerpt used by permission of the publisher. Translation copyright © Patricia Gosling 2010.

Matthew Stewart, *The Courtier and the Heretic*. Published by Yale University Press 2005. Copyright © 2005 Matthew Stewart. Reprinted by permission of Yale University Press.

Bianca Stigter, *De bezette stad. Plattegrond van Amsterdam 1940-1945*. First published in 2005 by Athenaeum-Polak & Van Gennep, 2005. Copyright © 2005 Bianca Stigter. Excerpts used by permission of the publisher. First excerpt, translation copyright © Imogen Cohen 2010. Second excerpt, copyright © Rosalind Buck 2010.

Rupert Thomson, *The Book of Revelation* published by Bloomsbury 1999. Copyright © 1999 by Rupert Thomson. Reprinted by permission of Bloomsbury Publishing Plc.

Salil Tripathi 'Visiting the Anne Frank House'. Taken from an article that first appeared on www.livemint.com , May 2008. Reprinted by permission of the author.

Dubravka Ugresic, *The Ministry of Pain*. First published in Croatian by Fabrika Knjiga. Published in English by Saqi Books. Copyright © Dubravka Ugresic 2005. Translation copyright © Michael Henry Hein. Reprinted by kind permission of Saqi Books.

H. M. van den Brink, *On the Water*. Published by Faber and Faber, 2001. First published in the Netherlands in 1998 by J. M. Meulenhoff, 1998. Copyright © H. M. van den Brink, 1998. Translation copyright © Paul Vincent, 2001. Reprinted by permission of Faber and Faber Ltd.

Acknowledgements

Janneke van der Horst, 'Rats and Herons' ['Ratten en reigers']. First published in *Het Parool* (18 April 2009). Copyright © Janneke van der Horst, 2009. Used by permission of the author. Translation copyright © Patricia Gosling 2010.

Marcel van Gestel, *De demon van Amsterdam*. First published in 1947 by Uitgeverij Phoenix, Amsterdam. Copyright unknown. Translation copyright © Laura Vroomen 2010.

Geert van Istendael, *Mijn Nederland*. First published in 2005 by Uitgeverij Atlas, Amsterdam. Copyright © Geert van Istendael, 2005. Used by permission of the publisher. First extract, translation copyright © Laura Vroomen. Second extract, translation copyright © 2005 Translation Summer School.

Dirk van Weelden, *De wereld van 609*. First published in 2008 by Augustus, Amsterdam. Copyright © Dirk van Weelden, 2008. Excerpt used by permission of the publisher. Translation copyright © Michele Hutchison 2010.

Voltaire, *Correspondance*. Translation copyright © Oxygen Books Ltd.

Christian Weijts, *Art. 285B*. First published in 2006 by Uitgeverij De Arbeiderspers, Amsterdam. Copyright © Christiaan Weijts, 2006. Excerpt used by permission of the publisher. Translation copyright © Brian Doyle 2009.

Kelvin Whalley, 'Cycling Amsterdam', 2009. Reprinted by permission of the author.

Tommy Wieringa, *Joe Speedboat*. First published in Dutch by De Bezige Bij 2005. Published in English by Portobello Books 2009. Copyright © Tommy Wieringa 2005. Translation copyright © Sam Garrett 2009. Reprinted by permission of Portobello Books.

Colin Wiggins, *The Hoerengracht: Keinholz at the National Gallery, London*. Copyright © The National Gallery Company Limited, London, 2009. Reprinted by permission of the author and The National Gallery Company Limited, London.

Every effort has been made to trace and contact copyright holders before publication. If notified, the publisher will rectify any errors or omissions at the earliest opportunity.

An exciting and unique travel series featuring the best-ever writing on European and World cities

Praise for *city-lit PARIS*

'An essential guidebook ... It maps the Paris of the imagination beautifully'

Kate Muir, author of *Left Bank*

'It's terrific ... all the best writing on this complex city in one place'
Professor Andrew Hussey, author of *Paris: The Secret History*

'A great and eclectic set of writings ... an original book on Paris'
Sylvia Whitman, Shakespeare & Co, Paris

'Whether you're a newcomer to Paris or a die-hard aficionado, this gem of a book will make you think of the city in a completely new way'

Living France

'The ideal book for people who don't want to leave their minds at the airport'

Celia Brayfield, author of *Deep France*

'The *city-lit PARIS* guide is essential reading for anyone remotely interested in Paris, or planning a visit'
Mike Gerrard, best-selling travel guide writer

'This innovative guide takes us from Marcel Proust on that perfect erotic moment to Gertrude Stein on the origins of the croissant to Agnès Catherine Poirier on the lure of the Paris café'

Paris Voice

£8.99 ISBN 978–0–9559700–0–9

Praise for *city-lit LONDON*

'This treasure trove of a book ... a unique way to explore the ever-changing landscape of a city, through the voices of those that know it intimately'

Rachel Lichtenstein, author of *On Brick Lane*

'For those visitors to London who seek to do more than bag Big Ben and Buckingham Palace, this is the ideal guide, a collection of writings that expose not only the city's secret places but its very soul ... I can't imagine a more perfect travelling companion than this wonderful anthology'

Clare Clark, author of *The Great Stink*

'Brings London to life past and present in a way no conventional guide book could ever achieve'

Tarquin Hall, author of *Salaam Brick Lane*

'The latest offering in this impressive little series concentrates on the spirit of London as seen through the eyes of an eclectic selection of writers. Part of the joy of this collection is that the writers span several centuries, which means that multiple faces of London are revealed. It's an exciting selection, with unexpected gems from novelists, travel writers, journalists and bloggers. Keith Waterhouse, for example, writes with gentle pathos about the double life of a transvestite in Soho; Vita Sackville-West wryly observes a coronation in Westminster Abbey; Virginia Woolf promenades down Oxford Street; and Dostoyevsky strolls down the Haymarket'

Clover Stroud, *The Sunday Telegraph*

'For some time now, small publisher Oxygen has been producing the excellent city-lit series, which uses descriptions of a city penned by writers, both living and dead to illuminate the metropolis in question. The most recent is London, compiled by Heather Reyes. This includes Jan Morris arriving at Heathrow, Monica Ali on Brick Lane, Virginia Woolf shopping in Oxford Street, Barbara Cartland at a West End Ball, Dostoyevsky strolling down Haymarket and Will Self inside the head of a cab driver'

Giles Foden, *Condé Nast Traveller*

'We can't declare it with absolute certainty, but it's a fair bet that Dame Barbara Cartland and Diamond Geezer have never before snuggled up between the same covers. *City-lit: LONDON* places these strange bedfellows alongside Will Self, Virginia Woolf, Alan Bennett and sixty others in a frenzied orgy of London writing. You'll love it'

Londonist

'The second volume in this enticing new series includes extracts from the work of 60 wonderfully diverse writers, including Will Self, Monica Ali, Alan Bennett, Dostoyevsky, and yes, Barbara Cartland (writing about a West End ball)'

Editor's Pick, *The Bookseller*

£8.99 ISBN: 978–0–9559700–5–4

Praise for *city-lit BERLIN*

'A gem ... an elegant, enjoyable and essential book'
Rosie Goldsmith, BBC Radio 4

'This wonderful anthology explores what it is really like to be a Berliner by bringing together extracts about the city from a range of genres, including some specially translated. This was the city of Einstein, Brecht, George Grosz, and Marlene Dietrich. It was 'the New York of the old world', a melting pot of new ideas and lifestyles ... This collection is timely: on 9 November 20 years ago, Berliners tore down the hated wall'

The Guardian

'*city-Lit Berlin* gathers more than a hundred extracts from writers on aspects of Berlin's conflicted heritage ... the editors have trawled widely to try to capture the modern city's rule-bound yet permissive tone, as well as its persistent state of cultural and architectural renewal. The result is an eclectic pillow-book ... a stimulating intellectual tour of the idea of the city that would complement any guidebook's more practical orientation'

Financial Times

'A new kind of literary travel guide where the reader can find snatches of literature relevant to Berlin'

BBC Radio 4 *Excess Baggage*

'A fascinating cornucopia of Berlin writing by authors such as John Simpson, Ian McEwan and Anna Funder; artists such as David Bowie and Marlene Dietrich, and writers such as Jeffrey Eugenides, Philip Kerr and Thomas Pynchon. The beauty of this clever series is the breadth and reach of its contributors, be they artists, musicians, musos or writers – in turn, each lays claim to the city.

Many were inspired by the Wall coming down, the inventive vibe, or simply the cheap rents – all took ease in the bohemian exuberance the city offered up. This collection of writing gives a flavour to a city that has long nurtured its artists, giving them space to create, whether for one week or a lifetime'

Caroline Eden, *Real Travel Magazine*

Praise for city-lit BERLIN

'Although there are plenty of old favourites such as Christopher Isherwood, Alfred Döblin and Len Deighton, the emphasis of the book is on unexpected vantage points and new, less familiar voices. So there is no dutiful trot through the city's history "from earliest times to the present day", but instead themed sections which try to get under the skin of the city.'

George Miller, *Podularity*

'Another in this sterling series of city-writings compilations, this one follows the pattern of short excerpts gathered into chapters, that this time vary from the arbitrarily-themed to the perfect. The simplest one is also the most gripping: it's called 'The past is another country', but don't let that put you off. Its well-chosen pieces take you through Berlin's history from the early 19th Century to today, and make for an almost perfect, and very moving, slice through history. (It's interesting to note that even in the 1920s Berlin was a place renowned for building over its history.) The book choices are as eclectic as you could wish for, taking in most of the authors listed above – including the obvious choices like Isherwood, Kerr, Le Carré and Deighton – and some stuff new to me. Top of the list of latter include Ian Walker's *Zoo Station* and Beatrice Colin's *The Luminous Life of Lilly Aphrodite*. Further interest is added by co-editor Katy Derbyshire's translations of bits from works not otherwise available in English. This manages to be not just a fine and fascinating introduction to the literature, but to rise above its expected status as a dipping thing to become a mighty fine cover-to-cover read in itself'

Jeff Cotton, *Fictional Cities*

'A welcome contrast to the many formulaic travel guides in print and online, *city-Lit Berlin* reveals the city as seen through the eyes of 60 writers of all description – from novelists such as Christopher Isherwood and Ian McEwan to local bloggers like Simon Cole, reporters (Kate Adie), historians (Peter Gay) and untranslated German writers, including Inka Parei, whose novel *Die Schateenboxerin* (The Shadow-Boxing Woman) captures the volatility of Berlin in the Nineties, just a few years after the Wall collapsed. We keep David Bowie company as he cycles around the city, and contemplate Marlene Dietrich's grave in a volume that has greatly enriched the field of travel books.'

Ralph Fields, *Nash Magazine*

£8.99 ISBN 978-0-9559700-4-7

Praise for *city-pick DUBLIN*

'For a population that barely reaches one million, Dublin has produced a staggering four Nobel prize winners. This new addition to the city-pick series is a reminder of Dublin's rich literary history, as well as an introduction to its contemporary forms. Drinking, music and rebellion loom large in these short pieces from Irish legends of letters such as Brendan Behan, Samuel Beckett and Sean O'Casey, which sit comfortably alongside extracts from modern writers such as Roddy Doyle and Colm Toibin. Cumulatively they build an elegant, incisive and always entertaining guide to the city's multitude of literary lives.'

Lonely Planet Magazine

'city-pick Dublin is the latest triumph of distillation. There's everything here from David Norris' defence of the significance of Joyce's *Ulysses* to Iris Murdoch's fictional treatment of The Easter Rising. You'll read about walking and drinking, being poor and being poetic, new wealth and newcomers, old timers and returning natives. In her introduction to *city-pick Dublin*, Orna Ross says that going by "great writers per head of population" Dublin is "the clear winner" in any "survey of literary destinations." As this is the city of Wilde, Shaw, Yeats, Beckett, Heaney, Swift et many a brilliant al how could anyone disagree?'

Garan Holcombe, Book fo the Month, *The Good Web Guide*

'A book you can't miss'

The Lady

'Bite-sized beauties ... You won't find pub recommendations or directions to art galleries in this little guide, but you will get a taste of Dublin's most important natural resource: stories.'

The Dubliner

'Vastly different from the usual travel guide, the city pick series offers first hand writing from a city's brightest wordsmiths and the Dublin edition brings the best out of its home grown talent. With over one hundred extracts from over fifty different writers including Roddy Doyle, Samuel Beckett and Chris Binchy there will be plenty of inspiration for exploring the famous streets of the Irish capital.'

Travelbite

243

Praise for city-pick DUBLIN

'A unique travel guide, shows a different side to Dublin by bringing to life its rich and diverse history of literature. city-pick Dublin, published by Oxygen Books, has brought together 50 writers and more than 100 extracts to bring famous Dubliners to life. Respected author and journalist Orna Ross, who writes the foreword, describes Dublin as one of the most literary rich cities in the world ... The timing for this book couldn't be better as Dublin celebrates becoming a UNESCO World City of Literature in 2010, which will showcase the diverse and experimental talent from this small city.'

The Irish Post

'The next in this excellent *city-pick* series, with some 100 plus extracts from a diverse collection of writers ... more than 50 of the very best writers on Dublin including William Trevor, Flann O'Brien, Joseph O'Connor, Brendan Behan, Anne Enright, Roddy Doyle and Maeve Binchy.

The Bookseller

'From Sean O'Casey to Anne Enright – the best ever writing on Dublin has been specially published in a new book entitled *city-pick Dublin*'

RTE

£8.99 ISBN 978–0–9559700–1–6

Coming soon – Venice, Istanbul, Mumbai, St Petersburg and many more. From Oxygen Books, a new publisher of surprising books about all kinds of journeys.

www.oxygenbooks.co.uk